PRAISE FOR
AFRIKAN WISDOM

"This unique and timely collection is a deep dive into the intersections of Black Liberation and spiritual freedom from a perspective sorely missing from the vast body of Buddhist writings. It is the inspired vision of its editor, Valerie Mason-John (Vimalasara), who begins their intro with a quote from Fred Hampton, the Black Panther revolutionary, and goes on to make poignant connections between the breath too often denied to Black people (I Can't Breathe) to the foundational breath of meditation. This compelling book is a must-read for all those seeking social, cultural, and spiritual liberation."

—PRATIBHA PARMAR, filmmaker and
professor

"What does it mean for Black folks to be free? In this uncommon collection of essays, Valerie Mason John (Vimalasara) has gathered together a fascinating, multifaceted selection of perspectives that explore the intersection of spirituality, liberation, and Blackness. This is one of those rare books that offers a holistic experience of illumination, as it unpacks the multifold path of Black Diasporic freedom in depth—through writing that ignites our mind while enriching our spirit."

—ANDREA THOMPSON, author and educator

"*Afrikan Wisdom* is such an important offering to and for African Diasporic people as we come to understand our traditional relationship to mindfulness and Buddhadharma. This book will help us continue dreaming and living into more liberated futures."

—LAMA ROD OWENS, author of
Love and Rage

"A celebration and a cry, a rich treasure chest and a brilliant contribution to the awakening of all."

—JACK KORNFIELD, author of *A Path With Heart*

"This is an important undertaking; a wealth of insights and resources that reminds us that contemplative practice must find unique expression within each culture and identity. To be truly liberatory in modern lives, ancient wisdom must also meet head-on the most pressing challenges of our times. This collection is a vital part of that work, and a gift to us all."

—JAMIE BRISTOW, author and clerk of the UK All-Party Parliamentary Group on Mindfulness

"This fascinating volume examines the topic of Black Liberation from a wide range of perspectives. Since it arose from a recent and historic gathering of Buddhist teachers and scholars of African descent, most of the contributions have a Buddhist slant but there are also essays from Christian, Muslim, and Rastafarian viewpoints. It is rich with eye-opening history and with different authors' takes on such challenging issues as nonviolence, the balance between mediation and external activism, the whiteness of American Buddhism, spiritual bypassing, and how to deal mindfully with systemic racism. This is an important book that comes at a time when the influence of racism in the US has rarely been more overtly supported and new voices on Black Liberation more needed."

—RICHARD SCHWARTZ, PhD, developer of the Internal Family Systems psychotherapy and adjunct faculty, Department of Psychiatry, Harvard Medical School

"Detailed liturgies for Buddhists of color appear amid the rich theorizing and individual reflections. These bite-size and profound essays are a powerful introduction to the overlooked possibilities of Black Buddhism."

—PUBLISHERS WEEKLY

AFRIKAN WISDOM

AFRIKAN WISDOM

New Voices Talk Black Liberation,
Buddhism, and Beyond

EDITED BY
VALERIE MASON-JOHN
(VIMALASARA)

FOREWORD BY PROFESSOR JAN WILLIS, PhD

North Atlantic Books
Berkeley, California

Published by
North Atlantic Books
Berkeley, California

Cover art and design by Jess Morphew
Book design by Happenstance Type-O-Rama

Printed in Canada

Afrikan Wisdom: New Voices Talk Black Liberation, Buddhism, and Beyond is sponsored and published by North Atlantic Books, an educational nonprofit based in Berkeley, California, that collaborates with partners to develop cross-cultural perspectives, nurture holistic views of art, science, the humanities, and healing, and seed personal and global transformation by publishing work on the relationship of body, spirit, and nature.

North Atlantic Books' publications are distributed to the US trade and internationally by Penguin Random House Publishers Services. For further information, visit our website at www.northatlanticbooks.com.

The Editor will donate all royalties from the book after expenses have been accrued to a Black African organization working for the liberation of African descent people in the Diaspora.

All materials can be used for your own rituals or teachings as long as you credit the author of the chapter and the book.

Library of Congress Cataloging-in-Publication Data
Names: Mason-John, Valerie, editor.
Title: Afrikan wisdom : new voices talk Black liberation, Buddhism, and
  beyond / edited by Valerie Mason-John (Vimalasara).
Description: Berkeley : North Atlantic Books, 2021. | Includes
  bibliographical references and index. | Summary: "A collection of
  spiritual essays written by Black thought leaders and teachers that
  discuss what it means to be Black in the world today"— Provided by
  publisher.
Identifiers: LCCN 2021002718 (print) | LCCN 2021002719 (ebook) | ISBN
  9781623175627 (trade paperback) | ISBN 9781623175634 (ebook)
Subjects: LCSH: African American philosophy. | African Americans—Politics
  and government—Philosophy. | Buddhism and humanism. | Buddhism and
  social problems.
Classification: LCC B944.A37 A378 2021 (print) | LCC B944.A37 (ebook) |
  DDC 200.89/96073—dc23
LC record available at https://lccn.loc.gov/2021002718
LC ebook record available at https://lccn.loc.gov/2021002719

1 2 3 4 5 6 7 8 9 MARQUIS 26 25 24 23 22 21

CONTENTS

PART THREE: Social Justice: The Revival of an Old Religion

PART FOUR: Decolonizing Mindfulness

PART FIVE: The Personal Is Political

PROLOGUE

The Negro National Anthem

by James Weldon Johnson, 1899

Lift ev'ry voice and sing
'Til earth and heaven ring
Ring with the harmonies of Liberty
Let our rejoicing rise
High as the list'ning skies
Let it resound loud as the rolling sea
Sing a song full of the faith that the dark past has taught us
Sing a song full of the hope that the present has brought us
Facing the rising sun of our new day begun
Let us march on 'til victory is won
Stony the road we trod
Bitter the chastening rod
Felt in the days when hope unborn had died
Yet with a steady beat
Have not our weary feet
Come to the place for which our fathers sighed?
We have come over a way that with tears has been watered
We have come, treading our path through the blood of the
    slaughtered
Out from the gloomy past
'Til now we stand at last

Where the white gleam of our bright star is cast
God of our weary years
God of our silent tears
Thou who has brought us thus far on the way
Thou who has by Thy might
Led us into the light
Keep us forever in the path, we pray
Lest our feet stray from the places, our God, where
    we met Thee
Lest, our hearts drunk with the wine of the world,
    we forget Thee
Shadowed beneath Thy hand
May we forever stand
True to our God
True to our native land

FOREWORD

by Professor Jan Willis, PhD

A BOOK LIKE THIS ONE deserves a bit of historical context. In the past two decades, there has been a small, but quite salient, explosion of publications dedicated to the Black experience with Buddhism. These publications have addressed a wide range of concerns and assumed diverse formats. For example, some of these publications have been memoirs. My own *Dreaming Me: Black, Baptist, and Buddhist* came out in 2001 but had been foreshadowed by a *Time* magazine article in December 2000 that called me one of *Time*'s "spiritual innovators for the new millennium" and "a philosopher with a bold agenda." My story was about being born in the Jim Crow South and coming to study and teach Tibetan Buddhism in the Northeast. Before my memoir, another quite different story had been published by Jarvis Jay Masters, a young Black man incarcerated since an early age on death row at San Quentin. His story, *Finding Freedom: How Death Row Broke and Opened My Heart* (1997), described how he had managed, against all odds, to find freedom while living inside one of this nation's most brutal prisons. In a similar vein, a documentary film by Jenny Phillips called *The Dhamma Brothers*—which chronicled a ten-day silent Vipassana retreat at Donaldson Correctional Facility outside

Birmingham, Alabama—debuted in 2007. The point is that all these works are, ultimately, about our universal search for healing and liberation.

Some of the publications of the past two decades have presented individual Buddhist teachings presented by Black Buddhist teachers, such as angel Kyodo williams's *being black* (2000) and Zenju Earthlyn Manuel's *The Way of Tenderness* (2015) and *Sanctuary* (2018); and Gaylon Ferguson's *Natural Wakefulness* (2010) and *Natural Bravery* (2016). Some of the works have been essays that seek to analyze the Black and Buddhist experience, like a number of those written by Charles Johnson, some of which are found in his *Taming the Ox* (2014), and my own "Buddhism and Race: An African American Baptist-Buddhist Perspective" (1996) and "Yes, We're Buddhists Too!" (2011).

Still other works creatively employ Buddhist practice techniques as pathways to Black freedom, like Ruth King's *Mindful of Race* (2018); and some provide an analysis of how systemic racism arises, as an aid to its cure. For example, see Larry Ward's recent *America's Racial Karma: An Invitation to Heal* (2020).

Other publications have sought to present in one space a variety of voices and views coming from Black Buddhists. Hilda Baldoquin's *Dharma, Color, and Culture* (2004) was an early example of such an anthology. More recently, just in 2020, there has appeared Pamela Yetunde and Cheryl Giles's edited anthology, *Black and Buddhist: What Buddhism Can Teach Us about Race, Resilience, Transformation, and Freedom.*

And today, there are a very few publications—like the one you are presently holding in your hands—that have gone a step further, by broadening both the "coverage area," so to speak, *and* the meanings of "freedom" and "liberation." In this volume, *Afrikan Wisdom: New Voices Talk Black Liberation, Buddhism, and Beyond,* Valerie Mason-John (also known by their Buddhist name, Vimalasara) has brought together and introduced a new

collection of Black voices, drawn from Buddhist as well as other
spiritual and liberative traditions, such as Rasta and Kemetic
Yoga and ancient African "Ancestralization," in one place. Yet,
again, all these new voices are joined in a singular and shared
exploration and enterprise, namely, getting healed, getting liberated, getting free. And so, as we BAD (Black African Descent)
people continue to seek liberation, we are expanding. We are
growing. And we are walking this path together.

In the following pages you will find Black voices, BIPOC
(Black, Indigenous, and People of Color) voices, and ADP (African Descent People, or African Diaspora People) voices—from
the United States, Canada, and the United Kingdom—that represent a variety of life experiences, spiritual practice experiences,
and freedom struggle experiences. Most of the authors here have
been influenced by Buddhism, but some have not, rather locat-
ing their spiritual home traditions in Rasta life, or Kwanzaa, or
Islam. Some present analyses of systemic racism and how their
respective Buddhist or other spiritual home traditions respond
to, counter, or otherwise help to heal the scourge of racism and
racial oppression. Some of the essays present actual re-creations
and reimaginations of Buddhist rituals in Black cultural form.

Other voices here focus more explicitly on freedom, liberation,
and social justice, tackling what both "ultimate" and "relative"
freedom might consist of and feel like. And so, there are presented here not only ideas about how and why certain Buddhist
constructs can be applied to help us move toward sane health and
healing; there are also suggestions about how our own ancient,
Indigenous roots already provide everything we need.

This book provides a feast of innovation and creativity. It
is divided into five parts, namely, Reappropriating the Buddha,
Black Liberation, Social Justice: The Revival of an Old Religion, Decolonizing Mindfulness, and The Personal Is Political;
but, like all complex living things, themes and approaches and

expressions here often "bleed" into one another. One finds here
re-visioned and Buddhist-themed rituals, like the exquisite tapestry woven by Justin Miles in his "Sadhana of Awakened Melanin: Devotional Practices to Help Transform Self and Other"
and by Rev. Seiho Morris's "A Twelve-Step Approach Exploring
Cultural Bias, Racism, and Otherism." There are shout-outs here
to Malcolm X (in a piece about his high regard in Canada by
George Elliott Clarke) and to the Rev. Dr. Martin Luther King
Jr. in the piece by Larry Ward. We learn about the meanings of
liberation afforded by the Rastafari life from the essay here by
Elisha Precilla and of those offered by the concept of "African-
ity" as told by Mama Yaa, the "Garveyite" and African elder
priestess, in an interview with her conducted by Vimalasara.
We hear about the steady, and balancing, ethical guidelines of
Kwanzaa from Dr. Afua Cooper.

In Audrey Charlton's essay, we hear directly from men incarcerated at Donaldson prison and about how Buddhist dharma
has given them a sense of freedom even while they live in such
brutal confines. There is a powerful essay here on the Black Lives
Matter movement by Cicely Belle Blain. And, in "Purification
and Protests: The Murder of Black Bodies in America," Alex
Kakuyo gives us a sometimes humorous, but ultimately chilling,
comparison between strict meditation retreats and the bloodletting that is currently happening in our streets. Some essays
speak about how applying Buddhist principles can help us raise
our children with more health and balance, such as the essay
here by Allyson Pimentel. Other pieces argue that Buddhism and
Yoga were, originally, Black/African traditions; see the pieces
here by Shaka Khalphani and Yirser Ra Hotep. There are mas-
terful pieces here—on "Ancestralization" by Cosmore Marriott,
on Black Liberation Theology by Andrea Murray-Lichtman and
Ashton Murray, and on Ubuntu and ancient African models of
reconciliation by Elizabeth Nyirambonigaba Mpyisi. There is,

indeed, much food for thought offered here, and much to be pondered.

As you will note, this book begins with the full text of James Weldon Johnson's "The Negro National Anthem." It ends with the beautiful prayer and dedication called "The Blessing" by Zenju Earthlyn Manuel for Black folks' safety, sanity, and wholeness. Vimalasara sent out a call for new Black voices and, here, thirty-four writers from across the United States, Canada, and the United Kingdom have answered with more, varied, and wide-ranging responses to being Black/BIPOC/ADP and BAD folks journeying together on a spiritual, nonviolent path to peace, joy, wholeness, justice, and liberation. These writers' efforts have prepared a feast for us. Now we should do what Buddhist texts suggest we do as the way of gaining true insight, namely, read and study, ponder and digest, and with meditation, allow our innate wisdom to dawn. You, dear reader, are now invited to enjoy the feast.

> —JAN WILLIS, PhD, is professor emerita of Religion at Wesleyan University in Middletown, Connecticut. Willis has published numerous articles, essays, and books on various topics in Buddhism: Buddhist meditation, saints' lives, women and Buddhism, and Buddhism and race. Her memoir, *Dreaming Me: Black, Baptist, and Buddhist,* appeared in 2001 and has seen several reprints. Her latest work (2020) is *Dharma Matters: Women, Race, and Tantra: Collected Essays by Jan Willis.*

INTRODUCTION

by Valerie Mason-John (Vimalasara)

*We're gonna have to do more than talk. We're gonna have to
do more than listen. We're gonna have to do more than learn.
We're gonna have to start practicing and that's very hard.*

*We're gonna have to start getting out there with the people
and that's difficult. Sometimes we think we're better than the
people so it's gonna take a lot of hard work.*

—FRED HAMPTON

KONDA MASON, NOLIWE ALEXANDER, angel Kyodo wil-
liams, and Myokei Caine-Barrett set the wheel of these teachings
in motion by reclaiming the "Fierce Urgency of Now." In 2019
at Spirit Rock Meditation Center in California, they brought
together more than seventy African descent Buddhist teachers,
scholars, and guests to connect at "The Gathering II: Buddhist
Sangha of Black African Descent."

Alice Walker welcomed us on our first day of gathering; and
five days later, the doors were opened to more than 300 African
descent people who were practitioners, curious about meditation and/or Buddhism, and, as angel said, some of us were just
Buddhish! The closing keynote ended with Angela Davis and Jan
Willis in conversation about their activist and spiritual lives.

I left the gathering inspired and with a call to action. "How can new voices be published?" I knew, after feeling the effect of what I had experienced at the gathering, that a publisher would open its doors. I was bowled over by Justin Miles's Sadhana [Liturgy] of Awakened Melanin, and with Seiho Morris's Twelve Steps exploring cultural bias. So I initially thought, what about a collection of works exploring Black Liberation through Buddhism?

However, this would have been a denial of the African experience, because Black Liberation has been expressed through the centuries in many guises since the day colonizers kidnapped us, chained us, flogged us, and shaped us into human cargo for the New World. Many African people of the Diaspora have trodden the paths of Christianity, Baptists, Jehovah's Witnesses, Seventh-day Adventists, Islam, Rastafarianism, Kwanzaa, Ubuntu, social activism, and much more. These differing paths inevitably influenced our expression of spirituality, Yoga, Buddhism, and other religions in the West. The gate had been opened, so I invited writers from faiths other than Buddhism to contribute as well.

This anthology brings an unlikely selection of people together to explore Black Liberation through the written word. Academics, activists, religious and spiritual practitioners, and first-time writers talk about liberation through their personal, lived, and political experiences.

Liberation in a spiritual context can mean enlightenment, awakened mind, acceptance of our mortality, freedom from the prison of one's own mind, and a heartmind filled with loving-kindness, compassion, sympathetic joy, and equanimity for all beings. This can be a big ask of Black people who do not have the same freedom to walk on the streets as their peers, of Black parents who are having to teach their children that they don't have the same civil liberties as their white counterparts.

The concept of enlightenment has also been popularized by the "Western Enlightenment" thinkers who pushed eugenics and created the culture that branded Black people as the most inferior of all of humanity, the lowest of the lowest. Colonizers believed that the Indigenous, First Nations people "could be educated," if stolen from their lands, forcibly taken from their families, and the Indian beaten out of them if placed in residential schools or reserves, and that there was no hope for African people. The nineteenth-century scientist Samuel Morton argued that Caucasian skulls were the largest, followed by Mongolian, Malay, Native American, and finally, African skulls the smallest. Based on these misconstrued facts, it was claimed intelligence was innate, and African peoples, considered the most inferior of all races, were deemed to be only slaves. So, although slavery may have been abolished in law, the rationalization of it still exists in many of our institutions today. We are still considered inferior on both a conscious and an unconscious level. Some of us even have internalized racism, which has been indoctrinated into us by all the subliminal messages in society.

The eugenics theory is still prevalent: Michelle Obama, First Lady from 2009 to 2017, was often likened to a gorilla, with offensive pictures trolling the internet. The English language is peppered with the word "black" likened to ugly, dirty, and impure; and "white" likened to purity, beauty, and cleanliness. In the UK, Black farmers have had the police called on them several times, because someone has believed they'd stolen their farmland. We are stopped at airport borders, in shops, or while driving brand new cars and questioned.

Therefore, the topic of enlightenment has a controversial place within the Black Liberation movement. We cannot transpose the same meaning into a Black context without acknowledging our historical and current struggles in today's society.

Black Liberation is said to have originated from African American seminarians and scholars. When we refer to the Maafa, African Holocaust, Holocaust of Enslavement, we are reminded that the atrocities and genocide inflicted upon the African continent is still continuing against our people. We are disproportionately incarcerated in prisons and mental health institutions and disproportionately killed by the police in the United States, Canada, Europe, and the UK.

When I think of Black Liberation, I think of liberating African people in the Diaspora from the systemic racism that still incarcerates us. It's time for us to say, "Get your knee off our neck!" We have been living with the pandemic of racism for centuries. In 2015 the United Nations announced the International Decade of People of African Descent, and in the same year Sheku Bayoh died after being restrained by the British police. Five years later in 2020 the world witnessed the public lynching of George Floyd, Jacob Blake, the slaying of Breonna Taylor, and others in the United States. And in Canada the murder of D'Andre Campbell and the mysterious death of Regis Korchinski-Paquet while police were conducting a wellness check. These are the ones that made the media. There are many others who have died at the hands of the police and did not make the news. When a white youth, Kyle Rittenhouse, on August 25 walked around with a semi-automatic rifle in the town of Kenosha, the police did not perceive him to be a threat, and even threw water to him. This is an explicit example of whose life is more valued today.

As a person who lives the Buddhist path, I have found myself thinking about my own liberation, and the places it has taken me to. From astral walking as a child, I could escape my body, to listening to Billy Graham saying, "Knock, knock, someone is knocking at your door, and all you have to do is open the door and let the Lord into your heart." In that moment I experienced freedom, I was filled with love and faith. I got up from my seat aged ten, and went into the tent to be blessed by Billy Graham.

It was my first experience of the spirit moving through me. I had been transported to another world. I went forth from my peers who were cracking jokes. I wanted to be saved. I didn't know what from, but I knew I wanted to be free. That lasted all of two weeks. I was back in my Anglican church, where I had been raised by white missionaries who gave up their lives to look after the poor little orphans.

Aged thirteen I had found Rastafarianism, and I escaped into shabeens. Aged nineteen I went to Israel, worked on a kibbutz, and gave up Christianity at the wailing wall in Jerusalem. If there was one God, why was every denomination arguing about who owned a piece of oblong stone in the main part of the church? Why did the People of Color have the poorest part of the church? I was angry with God: why had he not come to my rescue when I needed him? Why had he made me suffer so much? Why were Black people still suffering? I had no answers, and social activism soon became my religion.

I came home, stood on picket lines, protested in riots, found respite on the rave scene. I began writing about Aboriginal deaths in custody in Australia and about other oppressed peoples. I was desperately looking for liberation. The Aboriginal people of Australia who lived traditionally in Yirrkala Arnhem Land taught me mindfulness. I didn't know it then, because it didn't have a name. People were just still, just mindful, and spent days just "being and doing" by just sitting. It wasn't separate. My life for three months became pure awareness and compassion.

The elders asked: Where was I Indigenous too? I had no idea; I had been robbed of my African identity. Descending from Creoles in Freetown, Sierra Leone, means my ancestors were enslaved, but who knows from whence my ancestors were kidnapped. I was stateless, didn't know my tribe, traditional ways, or any African wisdom. I could not appropriate the DreamTime, and I knew I had to go home to find my liberation. I had experienced a taste of freedom, and now I had to return to England to do my work, with the gift of a new name, given to me by the elders: Buminjah, fruit of the tree.

It was a rocky journey, and meditation was my raft. Nobody taught me meditation. I had first accessed this place while in solitary confinement in children's prison aged fifteen to seventeen and a half. I accessed meditation again on the dance floors of nightclubs in London. Drug and alcohol free. It pointed me in the direction of liberation, Buddhism, and beyond. I got lost for a while and thought substances would bring me happiness. They didn't; they brought me depression, self-hatred, and resentment.

Meditation is our birthright. It belongs to every culture, every human being. I once heard angel Kyodo williams say, "We come into the world with a breath of inspiration and we leave the world with a breath of expiration." What are we doing in the bardo? In between birth and death? Breathing, and yet breathing has become almost a political act for Black Indigenous People of Color. Over the years we have heard factual stories of police who have murdered BIPOC while begging for their breath during the final moments of their life. COVID-19, a respiratory condition that has taken millions of lives, has impacted the BIPOC communities disproportionately. Meditation is breath, and breath is meditation. Every spiritual tradition and religious tradition has a form of meditation, be it prayer, chanting, or just sitting. And it is all about becoming one with the breath, which can be seen as the divine; coming home to the body of breath.

Those of us living in the African Diaspora have had the breath strangled out of us so much so that some of us have written off things like Yoga, meditation, mindfulness, or Buddhism as a middle-class white pursuit or hobby—practices that are in conflict with our Christian, Baptist, Catholic, Muslim, or other religions and faiths. However, all of these practices have origins in Africa. When the colonizers came, they did their best to destroy our culture, our ways, our religions. To the extent, that I remember being in school aged twelve, looking at a map of Africa, and scratching my head because I could not find Egypt.

It had been erased from the map of Africa. The Nubians, the ancient Africans, the Moors who came from all over Africa, the many tribes, had everything that can give us freedom. And much of our wisdom is still available to us, if we don't fall prey to the misinformation that tells us the continent of Africa is way behind in its civilization.

There are some of us challenging the systemic racism, the white supremacy in countries like the United States, Canada, and England. There are some of us reclaiming our traditions. And both are urgently needed. It's part of the same coin.

Afrikan Wisdom: New Voices Talk Black Liberation, Buddhism, and Beyond needs to be part of a volume of voices speaking to this subject. We must not forget Black Liberation: social justice movements have a long tradition, perhaps beginning with the first slave revolts, to the Underground Railroad, to the Black Panthers, and the Black Power left-wing movement in the United States, 1970s to 1981. More recently, Black Lives Matter was founded in July 2013 by Alicia Garza, Patrisse Cullors, and Opal Tometi. And then there were the uprisings around the world in 2020, where the destruction of part of the mythos became a reality. More than 200 statues that glorified those who engaged in trading enslaved people, enslavers, and the Confederacy were either toppled or taken down by the city or by the owner.

My own liberation is not enough. May I be the fruit of the tree for my community, and live out this teaching given to me by Aboriginal elders. And may I continue to live out the name my spiritual teacher gave me, Vimalasara, they whose essence is stainless and pure. And with these gifts I dedicate my life to the uplift of African peoples. May I and the contributing authors in this book leave a legacy of wisdom that predates us. While some of us may liberate from the prison of our minds, many will be victims of the manifold institutions that exude systemic racism. Reparations are not enough. The US, Canadian, UK, and

European governments, the police force, the banks, the education system, the newspapers, the export and import industries,
and other institutions that were originally founded by white colonizers and slavers must be dismantled and built up again with
different beliefs, attitudes, and values.

This book is just a glimpse of what is possible through the
lens of nonviolence. It is a privilege to get to a place of wanting
to change the world through nonviolence. These authors have a
part to play in the struggle for our freedom and liberation. Just
as householders had an important role to play in the days of the
Buddha, supporting monks and nuns, those of us who lead Buddhist, church, or mosque communities, or mindfulness or Yoga
workshops, have a role to play. We offer a place of refuge, filled
with compassion and equanimity. By changing the self, we have
the potential to change others.

Angulimala, which means the garlanded one, is a legendary
Buddhist story. In brief, he'd murdered ninety-nine people and
he wore all ninety-nine fingers on a necklace around his neck. He
was looking to kill one more person, so he could pay the fee to
his teacher whose mind had been poisoned by students jealous
of Angulimala. While out searching for his hundredth person, he
came across a man. With the intention to kill him, Angulimala
tried to follow but found he could not keep up with this person
despite the fact that this man was walking serenely, slowly, and
calmly. In his frustration he yelled, "Stop!" The person replied,
"I have already stopped. I have stopped killing and harming, and
it is time for you to stop too." Angulimala was so impacted by
the words of the Buddha, that he followed him back to the monastery and never killed again. Yes, people were still angry, even
threw rocks at him, when he begged for food. But, in stopping,
Angulimala found freedom from his tortured mind.

Do we have to wait for the police to stop killing us? Wait for
the institutions to completely dismantle? No! Just as the Buddha

took action, spoke up, and didn't wait for Angulimala to stop killing people, movements like the civil rights movement and Black Lives Matter need to be part of the collective voice that demands: stop killing our Black community, stop marginalizing our Black community. Without these movements, where would we be today? We have spent years in conference rooms asking for diversity, equity, and inclusivity. And very little has happened. There is a place for wrathful energy in both the spiritual and political worlds. And the time has come when many people have said enough is enough, you won't listen. And now you must listen to us, if it takes uprisings, and protesting in the streets.

Some of us have gone back to Africa: Sankofa—The Village Re-Membered. We have gone back home and fetched what was left behind when we were rounded up, shackled, enslaved, and shipped to foreign lands. Others of us have stayed in the Diaspora and found ways to live in this world that does not yet favor the Black person. And our freedom fighters like Malcolm X, Martin Luther King Jr., Harriet Tubman, Rosa Parks, Marie-Joseph Angélique, Viola Desmond, Chloe Cooley, Mary Seacole, Claudia Jones, Ignatius Sancho, Olaudah Equiano, Samuel Coleridge-Taylor, the Black Loyalists, the Maroons, and many more paved the way so I could live and be a free person in a land where my ancestors were sold into slavery.

It is now my turn to stand on their shoulders and continue to challenge the status quo and the systemic racism that still exists and impacts the safe movement of African descent people.

Everything now, we must assume, is in our hands; we have no right to assume otherwise. If we—and now I mean the relatively conscious whites and the relatively conscious blacks, who must, like lovers, insist on, or create, the consciousness of the others—do not falter in our duty now, we may be able, handful that we are, to end the racial nightmare, and achieve our country, and change the history of the world. If we do

not now dare everything, the fulfillment of that prophecy, re-
created from the Bible in song by a slave, is upon us: God gave
Noah the rainbow sign; no more water, the fire next time!

—JAMES BALDWIN

Freedom is a constant struggle.

—ANGELA DAVIS

PART ONE

Reappropriating the Buddha

THE BLACK BUDDHA

by Shaka Khalphani

"THERE WERE NO PEOPLE on earth except the Africans until 55,000 years ago," says Dr. Ivan Van Sertima. Egypt existed much earlier than most traditional Egyptologists are prepared to admit. The new archaeological evidence related to the Great Sphinx monument on the Giza Plateau and ancient writings by Manetho, one of the last high priests of ancient Egypt, show that ancient Egyptian history begins earlier than 10,000 BCE and may date back to as early as 30,000–50,000 BCE, cites Muata Ashby.

When Black people left Africa, India was the first place they settled. Ancestral South Indians inhabited much of the subcontinent 20,000 to 30,000 years ago. The proof is the Andaman and Nicobar islands. With the second-largest Black population in the world, and a significant percentage of those people having African heritage, some scholars say India to this day has the largest Black population of any country in the world. However, despite thousands of years of killing and miscegenation, some of the original Blacks have survived in pockets around India and nearby islands. Another African group, the Siddis, an ethnic group inhabiting India and Pakistan, were brought to the Indian subcontinent, beginning in the seventh century, as a result of the transatlantic slave trade by Arab and Portuguese slave traders. Now, we must connect the dots to arrive at the truth.

The first thing we must do is to determine where India is and its physical proximity to the African continent, especially to Egypt and Kemet, since these two great African nations were the most academic empires in the world. Muata Ashby deals with this subject matter in his book *The Ancient Egyptian Buddha*. He explains that the Ethiopian Kush or Cush refers to the Kingdom of Nubia, which according to the ancient writings of classical Greek historians is the source of both ancient Egyptian civilization as well as Indian civilization. The Greek historian Herodotus (c. 484–c. 425 BCE) wrote about his experience as he traveled throughout the Indian continent: "All the Indian tribes I mentioned . . . their skins are all the same color, much like the Ethiopians." And upon his return to Greece, people gathered around and asked, "Tell us about the land of the Blacks called Ethiopia." And Herodotus said, "There are two great Ethiopian nations, one in Sindh (India) and the other in Egypt."[1]

Some modern-day Hindus continue to believe Egypt is their ancestral home. Some Hindus claim the Nile to be one of their sacred rivers; they also regard as sacred the mountains of the moon (in Uganda-Congo) and Mount Meru (in Tanzania). Both in India and in the Indianized kingdoms, Southern Mount Meru was regarded as the mythical dwelling place of the gods. Each of these statements reflect millennia-old relationships between the Blacks of Africa and South Asia. The Ethiopian *Kebra Nagast* regarded Western India as a portion of the Ethiopian Empire.

Murugan, the god of mountains, the son of the mother goddess, is a prominent and typical deity of Dravidian India.

It is interesting to note that at least twenty-five tribes in East Africa worship Murungu as supreme god; and like the Dravidian god Murugan, the African Murungu resides in sacred mountains.[2]

> And at a time even beyond this there was a black-skinned people in India, who were Black, just as Black as you and I, called Dravidians. They inhabited the subcontinent of India even before the present people that you see living there today, and they had a high state of culture. The present people of India even looked upon them as gods; most of their statues, if you'll notice, have pronounced African features. You go right to India today—in their religion, which is called Buddhism, they give all their Buddhas the image of a Black man, with his lips and his nose, and even show his hair all curled up on his head; they didn't curl it up, he was born that way. And these people lived in that area before the present people of India lived there.[3]

> It is certain that the black Buddha of India was imaged in the negroid type. In the black negro god, whether called Buddha or Sut-Nahsi, we have a datum. They carry in their colour the proof of their origin. The people who first fashioned and worshipped the divine image in the negroid mould of humanity must according to all knowledge of human nature, have been negroes themselves. For the blackness is not merely mystical, the features and the hair of Buddha belong to the black race, and Nahsi is the negro name.[4]

One of the world's most prolific and philosophical religious leaders was the great sage called the Buddha.

> The religion of Buddha, of India, is well-known to have been very ancient. In the most ancient temples scattered throughout Asia, where his worship is yet continued, he is found black as jet, with the flat face, thick lips, and curly hair of the Negro.

Several statues of him may be met with in the museum of the East-India Company.[5]

At different stages of his development he was also referred to as Shakyamuni, Siddhartha, and Siddhartha Gautama. The Buddha's origin is traced back to India. Yet his philosophical doctrines spread throughout Southeast Asia, Tibet, China, and Japan. India had an Indigenous Black population that found its way into the subcontinent about 50,000 years ago from Ethiopia, ultimately establishing a great empire known as the Indus Valley civilization.

"There were two Ethiopias, one to the East of the Red Sea, the other to the West of it; and that a very great nation of blacks from India did rule over almost all Asia in a very remote era, in fact beyond the reach of history or any of our records," says Godfrey Higgins (1772–1833), British archaeologist, author, and historian.[6] In 1500 BCE this great empire was invaded by a tribe of barbarians from the north of India, igniting a series of wars upon the Indian subcontinent that lasted nearly a thousand years. The Rig Veda, the most ancient of India's works, describes this confrontation. The conclusion of these classic battles ushered in India's first historical golden age, the age in which the Buddha was born.

> The religion of this Negro God is found, by the ruins of his temples and other circumstances, to have been spread over an immense extent of country, even to the remotest parts of Britain, and to have been professed by devotees inconceivably numerous. I very much doubt whether Christianity at this day* is professed by more persons than yet profess the religion of Buddha.[7]

---

*Higgins wrote this in 1874.

SAMBHU/SAMBO

All of the religions of Asia can be traced to Africa and the African people of Asia.

"'When nothing else was, Sambhu was: that is the Self-Existent (svayambhu): and . . . he was before all.'"[8] The land of the descendants of Sambhu/Sambo was called Sambhujadesia. There were also other pronunciations for Sambhujadesia. Sambon was another name used to refer to the descendants of Sambhu/Sambo. Sambhu/Sambo was also referred to as Adi-Buddha. The term Adi-Buddha is used to define the primordial Buddha; it is also used in Tantric Buddhism. The Indonesian Supreme Sangha defines the term as the God Almighty.

> The first system of Adi-Buddha was set up in Nepal by a theistic school called Aisvarika, but was never generally adopted in Nepal or Tibet, and had practically no followers in China and Japan. The Nepalese school supposed an Adi-Buddha infinite, omniscient, self-existing, without beginning and without end, the source and originator of all things, who by virtue of five sorts of wisdom (jnana) and by the exercise of five meditations (dhyana) evolved five Dhyani-Buddhas or Celestial Jinas called Anupapadaka, or "without parents."
>
> When all was perfect void (maha-Sunyata) the mystic syllable aum became manifest, from which at his own will the Adi-Buddha was produced. At the creation of the world he revealed himself in the form of a flame that issued from a lotusflower, and in Nepal the Adi-Buddha is always represented by this symbol.
>
> All things, according to [Brian] Hodgson, were thought to be types of the Adi-Buddha, and yet he had no type. In other words, he was believed to be in the form of all things and yet to be formless, to be the "one eternally existing essence from which all things are mere emanations" (Monier Williams).[9]

THE BLACK UNTOUCHABLES OF INDIA

We already know that the original inhabitants of India were dark-skinned and closely resembled the Africans in physical features, according to V. T. Rajshekar.[10] They founded the Indus Valley civilization, which, according to historians, was one of the world's first and most glorious. However, according to Godfrey Higgins, and the massive work he produced, the *Anacalypsis,* published posthumously in 1836, he was able to show an initial and all-pervasive Black presence and influence upon early Asia's major civilizations. His numerous references to the Black Buddhas of India, the Black God Krishna, and the Black Memnon, along with many others, establish Higgins as basic reading material for students searching out the story of the Black presence in Asian antiquity. Higgins was convinced, along with many others, that humanity itself, of which the Black race was the first representative, owed its origins to Asia and specifically to India, rather than Africa. The ugly face of racism can also, unfortunately, be found in Higgins's work, for while he vociferously argued that the Black man was the original man, he was equally emphatic in his insistence that although first, he had subsequently become obsolete and utterly incapable of competing with newer and more evolved races. This is what Higgins writes:

> Now I suppose that man was originally a Negro, and that he improved as years advanced and he travelled Westwards, gradually changing, from the jet black of India, through all the intermediate shades of Syria, Italy, France, to the fair white and red of the maid of Holland and Britain. On the burning sands and under the scorching sun of Africa, he would probably stand still, if he did not retrograde. But the latter is most likely to have happened; and, accordingly, we find him an unimproved Negro, mean in understanding, black in colour.[11]

So, what happened to the Indus Valley civilization? Aryan tribes invaded India, destroying the Indus Valley civilization and employed a cunning, deceptive religious ideology to enslave the Indigenous people. Sounds familiar! Those who fled to India's forests and hills later came to be called "tribals." As these native Indians were gradually overcome, captured, and enslaved, they were kept outside village limits and "untouchability" was enforced upon them. These people became "untouchables."

The native people of India (currently known as "untouchables," "tribals," and "backward castes") were not Hindus. They were animists, nature worshippers. Since India's Dalits were once autonomous tribal groups, each group was known by its own tribal name. The Aryans created "caste" out of these tribal divisions by hierarchically arranging them in ascending degrees of reverence and descending degrees of contempt. So, the Black untouchables have hundreds of tribal names. Aryans based their whole philosophy on color (*varna*). The fourfold caste system is based on skin color. The natives are dark-skinned and the Aryans light. So, we can say that the untouchables and tribals are India's "Blacks," and that India's Black population is much larger than the entire population of Europe. It is also the world's largest Black population living outside of Africa.

The native "Blacks" are not confined to any one particular area. They are spread all over India. Some of the tribals in Central India closely resemble the African Blacks in their physical features. The Black untouchables of Tamil Nadu, on the southern end of India, perhaps more than any other group retain their original physical features, including dark skins and broad noses. Their language, Tamil, the oldest language of India, was once the language of the whole country. The whole of Bangladesh, a Muslim country today, was once a Dalit stronghold. Pakistan also has a large Dalit population.

The British, who, as we know, formerly ruled India, for the first time made a census of all these castes and put them under "Scheduled Castes"—the name given them in India's Constitution. But this is an English name that the Black untouchables can't understand. M. K. Gandhi gave them a new name: "Harijan," meaning "children of god." However, the people rebelled against this name, and the suggestion of Panchama, which meant fifth caste. But the leaders of the untouchables of Bombay formed the Dalit Panthers—named after the Black Panthers of the United States—and named themselves as Dalit. Dalit became the acceptable word, which meant crushed, downtrodden. Many of today's Dalits have gone back to their roots by reclaiming themselves as Buddhist.

The history of India is full of uprisings by the Dalits, Shudras, and other natives of India against the Aryan invaders. The Buddha, a great tribal chieftain with an Afro hairstyle, 2,500 years ago was the first to lead India's Black untouchables' war against Aryan oppressors. Buddhism, India's first virulent anti-Brahmin philosophy, achieved big successes, and the lower-caste people and women became its first adherents. Not only did Buddhism become popular all over India, but it spread to Thailand, China, Japan, and many other countries. The revered leader Dr. Babasaheb Ambedkar embraced Buddhism and called upon his people to follow him in his conversion. Millions of Dalits all over India followed him. On October 14, 1956, he led the largest ever conversion done on one single day, bringing the third wave of Buddhism back to India and freeing his people from the inequities of the caste system.

Remember when I said that Buddhism had spread to Britain? Well, listen to what Godfrey Higgins says concerning this matter:

> It [is] evident that Buddhism extended almost to every part of the old world; but we must remember that the British Taranis, and the Gothic Woden, were both names of Buddha. In my

Celtic Druids I have shown that the worship of Buddha is everywhere to be found—in Wales, Scotland, and Ireland. Hu, the great God of the Welsh, is called Buddwas; and they call their God Budd [one of the names of the Buddha], the God of victory, the king who rises in light and ascends the sky. . . . This is confirmed by Mr. Ward, the missionary, who tells us, that Buddha is the Deity of Wisdom, as was the Minerva of Greece. When devotees pray for wisdom to their king, they say, May Buddha give thee wisdom.

. . . The etymology of the word Buddha seems to be unknown to the Hindoos, which favours the idea of a date previous to any of the present known languages. In the Pali, of Ceylon, it means universal knowledge or holiness. . . . In Sanscrit we have, Sanskrit Root, *Budh,* to know, to be aware; *Budhyati,* he knows, is aware; *Bodhayāmi,* I inform, I teach.[12]

Another name was the Genie, "The Intelligent One."

RESOURCES

Thanks to the writers and scholars who provided valuable research through their books and lectures on this subject matter: Runoko Rashidi and Ivan Van Sertima and their book *African Presence in Early Asia. The Gods of Northern Buddhism: Their History and Iconography* written by Alice Getty. Muata Ashby's book *The Ancient Egyptian Buddha.* Malcolm X's speech "On Afro-American History." And *Anacalypsis, An Attempt to Draw aside the Veil of Saitic Isis; or, an Inquiry into the Origin of Languages, Nations, and Religions,* written by Godfrey Higgins, published posthumously in 1836.

NOTES

1 Diodorus (Greek historian, c. 90–c. 30 BCE).
2 U. P. Upadhyaya, "Dravidian and Negro-African," *International Journal of Dravidian Linguistics* 5, no. 1 (January 1976): 39.

3 Malcolm X, "Malcolm X on Afro-American History," *History Is a Weapon,* www.historyisaweapon.com/defcon1/malconafamhist.html.

4 Gerald Massey, *A Book of the Beginnings,* vol. 1 (London, 1881).

5 Godfrey Higgins, *Anacalypsis,* vol. 1 (London, 1874), 40.

6 Ibid., 52.

7 Ibid., 40–41.

8 Alice Getty, *The Gods of Northern Buddhism* (Oxford, 1914), quoting from the Guna Karanda Vyuha.

9 Ibid.

10 Ivan Van Sertima and Runoko Rashidi, eds., *African Presence in Early Asia* (1988). This statement opens the chapter on the Untouchables of India.

11 Higgins, *Anacalypsis,* 396.

12 Ibid., 198–199.

BLACK AFRICAN
DESCENDANT BUDDHAS

by Marisela Gomez

In order to save our planet earth, we must have a collective awakening. Individual awakening is not enough. That is why one Buddha is not enough.

—THICH NHAT HANH

THE PLUM VILLAGE COMMUNITY of Engaged Buddhism (PVCEB) tradition of Vietnamese Zen Buddhism emerged during the Vietnam War. Before and during the war, Venerable Thich Nhat Hanh was a young monk involved in challenging the conservative Buddhist hierarchy of the country to respond to the needs of society. In 1964, he co-founded this community of engaged Buddhist practitioners emphasizing mindfulness in everyday life, then called the United Buddhist Church.[1] At that time during the Vietnam War, its main tenet was to engage with society in the many challenges of injustices they were facing, particularly of poverty and war.[2] This practice of mindfulness engaged with daily life—in the mundane things— walking, brushing our teeth, answering the phone. This every- day, moment-to-moment mindfulness would lead to concentra- tion and insight into who we are and how to participate in the world from clarity and calm. During the war, Venerable Thich Nhat Hanh was exiled from Vietnam after touring the United States calling for peace and refusing to take sides with either the communist or anti-communist regimes. Exiled in France, he, along with Sister Chan Khong, eventually co-founded a monastery in southern France along with lay practitioners in 1982. Over time, this tradition became known as the Plum Vil- lage tradition and more recently the Plum Village Community of Engaged Buddhism.

Over the years, Venerable Thich Nhat Hanh was often asked by his lay and monastic students who would be his successor. He would respond that it would be the sangha—the commu- nity of practitioners. He emphasized that having a sangha was key to being able to maintain our practice consistently. The sangha would be a place to take refuge and support our prac- tice, which is often challenged in the world where we engage daily with nonpractitioners. In the past five to ten years, Vener- able Hanh continued teaching that we would need more than one Buddha to assure our society wakes up, that we would need a sangha of Buddhas, and that the next Buddha would be the sangha.[3] It is from this teaching that the following ques- tions emerge: What does that mean for us as practitioners of Black African descent? What would that mean if we as Black African sanghas were the new Buddhas? How could that be expressed in everyday life?

A PATH OF AWAKENING FOR
AFRICAN DESCENDANT PEOPLE

As African descendant people, an additional suffering, beyond those inherent as a human being, comes from being marginalized via continued racism, both in the West and beyond. The cause and effect of this suffering in our daily lives does not relent in a society that continues to elevate a superiority complex of whiteness. Buddhism's Four Noble Truths attempt to show us that suffering exists and that there is a path away from suffering, stress, or ill-being. Some ask why Buddhism is "obsessed" with suffering. Perhaps it's not so much an obsession as an affirmation of a truth so that we hasten to take up a path leading away from suffering, toward realizing awakening. For African descendant people, this persistent and particular path of suffering through racism urges us toward a search for a path away from this suffering in particular. In general, the Buddhist path of practice that teaches that mindfulness, concentration, and insight can lead to the end of suffering should be attractive to us, as it starts with acknowledging suffering exists. And yet we can find few teachers who acknowledge the suffering of racism as a suffering. Too many Buddhist teachers choose to leave the "social" frameworks outside their practices and teach students to focus on their personal transformation only. For many African descendant people and Black, Indigenous, and People of Color (BIPOC) in general, this is not sufficient and does not acknowledge our daily lived experiences, even within practice spaces. Because while we can transform the wounds of racism inside ourselves, the social structures persist. We therefore must acknowledge and engage with teachings to address these structures and enablers and the harms they cause, inside and outside of our practice centers.

The past ten years or more have seen a small movement— led primarily by African descendant people, BIPOC, and those in solidarity—of teachers and practitioners engaging with the socially constructed norms and frameworks that result in marginalization for different groups; i.e., BIPOC, queer, female identified, non-English speaking, low income, non-US/UK/European born. Using these constructs as a dharma door for teachings has invited in those directly and indirectly impacted by these oppressions. These teachers and practitioners have naturally become sanghas; for example, our sangha of Black African descent formally gathering in 2009 and twice since, in 2018 and 2019.

AFRICAN DESCENDANT TRANSFORMATION IN MAJORITY WHITE SANGHAS

The need for a collective awakening emerging through a community of awakened practitioners gathering in retreats and meeting locally weekly and monthly can be interpreted as the social awakening necessary to save our planet. For Black African descendant people, it is urgent for us to recognize that when we gather in white majority sanghas where we are uncomfortable, do not feel welcomed as all of who we are, and feel tokenized, our path to awakening may be slow and we may not be able to take refuge in our sangha. For some, this may be sufficient if we feel that we are transforming our individual suffering. For others, assimilation may also be at work with all its complexity.

If as individuals we still feel separated from our white sisters and brothers in these sanghas and choose to ignore the tension there, this will not lead us toward generating the power that comes from collective awakening. Ignoring the social separation as we cling to short moments of bliss in meditation will limit continued awakening. Unless the teaching of the dharma in these sanghas incorporates racial equity directly through the intentional practice of the wisdom of nondiscrimination, then all sangha members will need to seek this understanding outside the sangha; for example, by participating in racial equity trainings. Over time, this shared understanding will diminish the separation and tensions present in majority white sanghas with little understanding of racial equity.

Across the different traditions of Buddhism, PVCEB in the United States was one of the first to explore retreats for BIPOC, in 2004.[4] It was initiated by African descendant practitioners and led by Thich Nhat Hanh at Deer Park Monastery in Escondido, California. Without African descendant leadership, these retreats temporarily ended. In time, it required other African descendant and BIPOC practitioners present at the practice centers to organize BIPOC-only retreats. Currently, BIPOC-only retreats are no longer offered in the PVCEB monasteries in the United States, not because there are no BIPOC practitioners willing to organize them, or because there is no demand for these safe sangha spaces, but because our collective understanding of why retreats for BIPOC are needed is still unclear. Many maintain that in practice settings we must go beyond the dualism of Black and white and other social categories (male/female, queer/heterosexual, etc.) and practice in a "post-racial" and ultimate dimension—spiritually bypassing these mundane expressions of racial (in all its permutations: structural, cultural, institutional, interpersonal, personal) traumas occurring in the white majority Western-convert practice settings. For example, this comment was made by a practitioner after reading an announcement on Facebook for a BIPOC retreat in 2013:

> I'm confused; what is meant by people of color, are you meaning like black, yellow, white as in "racial"? It saddens me to see in this age that people still hang on to these concepts, even sadder to see a Buddhist community adhering to such an archaic way of thinking. THERE ARE NO PEOPLE OF COLOR, THERE ARE ONLY PEOPLE. [emphasis not mine]

But these sentiments of color-blind race ideology and the outcomes from such sentiments are not unique to our tradition of PVCEB. This is the process for most of the sanghas in the West where clinging to the majority white perceptions of what is dharma, spiritual, and Buddhism continues to be honored. Understanding the interbeing nature of inner and social transformation is still lacking in most Buddhist circles, of all traditions. Understanding why the refuge of racial/ethnic affinity retreats and sanghas is required for understanding, healing, and awakening for respective groups is part of the road of loving each other where we exist. Cultivating sanghas that offer safety for African descendant people, that do not dismiss or attempt to erase our historical and current lived experience, is urgent for our awakening to flourish. Such sanghas nourish our ability to look deeply and transform these sufferings instead of pretending that they do not exist or feeling shamed that we have such traumas to heal. In sanghas that dismiss our lived experiences of racial trauma, we are reprimanded for acknowledging the truth of our racial traumas, and are expected to "get over it," smile, and view everyone as "good" practitioners because they dismissed our full selves. It is difficult to transform our suffering when we are not able to acknowledge it exists. This is the First Noble Truth of Buddhism, acknowledging that a suffering exists, so we can identify the cause and realize its cessation through the Noble Eightfold Path. This is exactly what we as African descendant people seek.

AFRICAN DESCENDANT TRANSFORMATION IN MAJORITY BLACK AND BIPOC SANGHAS

For African descendant people, we can more easily experience moments of awakening as we release our old perceptions and meet the moment with openness and clarity—in spaces where we can drop the barriers erected in majority white spaces.

Our birthright as African descendant people is to find ways to stay sane and safe in a world of white supremacy. Swimming in whiteness is sometimes used to describe the pervasive atmosphere that we breathe in, day in and day out, the undertow that is daily navigated. In communities where there are a majority of people who look like us, we begin to put down some of these protective barriers, and breathe in an energy of acceptance and understanding. Without the pull of racial superiority upon our minds and bodies, we no longer assume the role of inferiority or face the outcomes when we don't. There is a resting that occurs, a release. In these spaces, a collective healing is more likely to occur because a major path of separation is removed and reconnection resumes its natural course. Because our collective and generational trauma of living in a racist society is acknowledged, healing is possible: the First Noble Truth.

Because we have this collective history, we know each other and are responsible for practicing deeply into love with each other. This knowing requires that we take the time to understand each other beyond our shared experiences; the places we feel we still don't belong to each other. In this sacred space of knowing, we are compelled to show up and be fully present, to listen deeply and practice loving speech, to honor the ancestors and the suffering we each carry of them in us, and to acknowledge that connected trauma and connected healing as we heal back into the past, in the present, and forward into the future. We are invited then to truly see each other, beyond the confines of the socially fabricated caricatures that have been pressed into our consciousness, hearts, minds, and bodies. To honor the sacred space, we must co-create our path of love back to each other by acknowledging our suffering and by trusting in the power and wisdom of this collective knowing to hold and heal. This is what happened at our gathering in October 2019 at Spirit Rock Meditation Center in Woodacre, California. We listened to each other's pain, we cried, we danced, and we sang. We lit incense, we touched the earth, we bowed, we prayed, and we testified. And we breathed, and in doing this with the power of sangha we brought the ancestors forward and healed their pain in us, healed our pain in this lifetime, and set the stage for healing for our descendants. We can expect no less from a sangha of Black African descendant people, and we must expect this depth of expression each and every time we gather, for a minute or for a month. These collective steps will build this road of truth toward our liberation and Buddhahood.

As we heal the trauma of racism in Black African descendant spaces, we begin to create the spaciousness that allows us to step back into mixed spaces with greater ease and understanding. From these spaces of clarity and connection, we can more easily engage with the challenges in white majority spaces in a way that leads to collective transformation—sanghas of Buddhas of all creeds and cultures.

THE SANGHA OF BLACK AFRICAN DESCENDANT PEOPLES AS THE NEXT BUDDHA

The tradition of PVCEB established the sangha as a priority of practice. From its beginnings in Vietnam, engaging in the world, even in the hostile environments of the Vietnam War, PVCEB maintained mindfulness as its center. The School for Youth and Social Service set up pilot villages, rebuilt bombed villages, and set up refugee camps and schools. Today PVCEB has an initiative called the ARISE sangha (Awakening through Race, Intersectionality, and Social Equity) whose focus is to engage within our mahasangha so as to bring collective awakening around racial equity as a path of practice.[5] This is all engaged

Buddhism. Similarly, our Black African descendant sanghas must be engaged in the world, willing to adapt to the needs of our people. Vietnamese Buddhism in general is just that:

> Vietnamese Buddhism is not merely a religious belief that limits itself, everywhere and at all times, to its mission as a faith. On the contrary, everywhere it spreads, Buddhism adapts itself to the customs, cultural climate and human elements of the land, influencing the local population's way of life.[6]

Our Black African descendant sanghas will be a collective of Buddhist practitioners from many different traditions who will go out and reach people in our many different cultural adaptations. Because of the continuous suffering of racial inequity, and the structures that propagate these injustices and traumas upon our mind and body in all aspects of daily life, there is much to engage with. This is sangha-building. But the sangha is not only "Buddhist." The sangha is in any space where we collect to address the suffering of our African ancestors in ourselves. In social justice organizations, this means we lead with love and not from anger; we practice breathing and grounding together before, during, and after meetings. In classrooms, workplaces, and play spaces, we collect our heart and practice respect, kind speech, and deep listening. In all these spaces, we remember we know each other and we take the time to remember how to understand and love ourselves and each other, even when our actions are contrary to love. We recognize when we are tired, and we take time to rest and offer the spaciousness for this to happen. These different forms of communities of practice, "sanghas," when inclusive of people practicing the dharma easily in every moment, become a sangha of Buddhas. African descendant people then practicing with collective intention and insight will naturally become Buddhas.

NOTES

1 Nhat Hanh, Thich, and Elsberg, Robert, eds. 2001. *Thich Nhat Hanh: Essential Writings* (Maryknoll, NY: Orbis Books), 7.
2 Nhat Hanh, Thich. 1966. *Fragrant Palm Leaves: Journals 1962–1966* (New York: Riverhead Books), 183–197.
3 Nhat Hanh, Thich, and Fourfold Sangha of Plum Village. 2010. *One Buddha Is Not Enough: A Story of Collective Awakening* (Berkeley, CA: Parallax Press), 213–214.
4 Nhat Hanh, Thich. 2005. *Together We Are One: Honoring Our Diversity, Celebrating Our Connection* (Berkeley, CA: Parallax Press).
5 Awakening through Race, Intersectionality, and Social Equity. http://arisesangha.org/newsletter092019/.
6 Nhat Hanh, Thich. 1967. *Vietnam: The Lotus in the Sea of Fire* (New York: The Fellowship of Reconciliation; Guildford and London: Billing and Sons Limited), 54.

PARENTING BLACK CHILDREN IN A JOYFUL AND SORROWFUL WORLD

The Buddha's Teaching of the Heavenly Abodes

by Allyson Pimentel

RAISING BLACK CHILDREN IN THIS society demands much and bestows much. It is an opportunity to experience the 10,000 joys and 10,000 sorrows described in the Buddhist teachings, and to mine them for the riches they offer. Parenting is a call to love, to protect, to give, to nurture, to teach, to grow alongside our children. Within a dominant culture that has historically conspired to diminish, harm, exploit, and abandon Black children, our parental labors of love are that much more challenging—and hold that much more opportunity for finding freedom.

As parents in the dharma, we can aspire—and be inspired—to walk the path of enlightenment with our kids. On this journey, we sometimes walk alongside them; sometimes we lead the way; other times we are led. Through our mindfulness practice, each challenge we face in parenting can become a "dharma door," a wisdom portal through which a path leading to freedom is found. Indeed, we can choose to turn the doorways to our very homes into portals to enlightenment. The light we embody can illuminate and penetrate our families, our communities, and the world beyond.

The dharma doors we walk through can lead us directly into what is known in Buddhism as the "heavenly abodes." These abodes, or dwellings, are resting places in our minds and hearts, a state of being where we can find refuge, safety, and peace. We can turn our hearts and homes into heavenly abodes by committing to the cultivation of the four *brahma viharas,* the Buddhist virtues of *upekkha* (equanimity), *metta* (loving-kindness), *karuna* (compassion), and *mudita* (joy in the joy of others).

Diasporic Black parents are parenting in a complex time. We are from the Caribbean, from the continent, from the South, from Harlem, Brooklyn, Baldwin Hills, Crenshaw, and beyond. Our families are varied, multifaceted, rich in culture and wisdom, rising up out of a historical legacy of slavery, displacement, and discrimination, and rooted in the cultural splendor of our African ancestry. We are raising children, stepchildren, grandchildren, cis kids, trans kids, nieces and nephews. Our kids are brilliant, challenging, special, gifted, compliant, defiant, unique. We co-parent with spouses, parents, exes, and friends. Our homes may be multigenerational or singly-parented, displaying unique and layered patterns of kinship and care.

The parents of Black children may not be Black themselves, by way of interracial unions or adoption. However, each and every one of us is parenting in a cultural climate of instability, violence, fear, and vast inequity. We are parenting in a time and place where bigotry is sanctioned by our most powerful political leaders, and hate crimes are on the rise. We are parenting in an age of technology that is changing our capacity for attention, connection, and eye contact.

Last year, a first-grade Black boy I know threatened to pull the fire alarm in his classroom. The young teaching assistant told him that if he dared to do it, the police would be called and he would be arrested. What kind of bias—unconscious or not—motivated a teacher to threaten a six-year-old with arrest? What kind of associations between Black boys and the criminal justice system were activated and reified in that moment? What effect did this have on the boy, and on the diverse group of children in the classroom who witnessed this exchange?

Dharma wisdom can support us as we navigate the complexities of parenting Black children in a wider world that is often hostile to them and to us. It is a teaching that can lead us to enlightenment, the ongoing process of becoming a beacon of light to ourselves, our children, and our communities. Enlightenment also enables us to "lighten up," to cast off the extra burdens, the second arrows, to become less weighted down by our fears and reactivity and to find new ways of skillfully engaging with our children and the world. The dharma enables us to hold and be held, fortifies us so that we are able to bear even the unbearable. The dharma supports us by reminding us that the world is also full of love and the possibility of light even in the darkest of times.

UPEKKHA: EQUANIMITY

Of the four heavenly abodes, equanimity is the unceasing spring from which all the others flow and are fed. Equanimity is like a stone dropped into the center of churning waters, solid, whole, intact amid the roiling waves. The Pali word for equanimity, *upekkha,* is variously translated as "to see with patience," "neutrality of mind," or "to look over." Equanimity enables us to be with the challenges of parenting from a core of stability, patience, and perspective. It enables us to stand in the middle of it all—the playdates, the heartbreaks, the injuries—physical and moral—in a centered way, with a mind that is steady, unconfused, and poised.

We may be able to imagine finding equanimity in the face of the daily pleasures and pains of family life—a broken bone, a broken heart. But we might ask how a parent could practice equanimity in the face of the kind of horrors that parents of Black boys face and have faced for generations. Tamir Rice is one such boy. He was twelve years old when, in 2014, he was killed in a park near his home. Tamir was playing in a gazebo with a toy gun that a friend had just handed him. He was murdered, like all too many Black boys and men, by a police officer.

How could Tamir's mother, Samaria Rice, bear this unbearable horror? How could she find even "a whisper of equanimity amidst the trumpets of [her] rage, grief, horror and desolation"?[1] I do not know her, or how she coped, or what her life has been like in the years since her son's murder. However, I do know that Samaria Rice became a powerful activist in the struggle against police brutality and racial injustice. She was instrumental in turning the gazebo where her son was killed into a gathering place of remembrance. Instead of having it destroyed, as was the initial impulse, the gazebo was transformed into a physical space of community art, healing, awareness, and enlightenment. She turned the darkest place on earth into a divine abode.

Tamir's mother has much to teach us about the power of equanimity. The word equanimity itself comes from the Latin *aequus,* meaning "equal" or "even," and *animus,* meaning intellect, consciousness, courage, spirit, passion, vehemence, and wrath. Samaria shows us that equanimity is not passivity, not numbing out or shutting down or turning away from. Equanimity is both evenness and passion; balance and vehemence. Equanimity makes space for our rage, outrage, and despair and, as Samaria shows us, invites us to transmute that passion into wise action. We can draw upon Samaria's wisdom and inspiration as a mother who, in the midst of terror and horror, was able to lift up love and healing.

The meditation teacher Ruth King reflects on the practice of equanimity in a racialized world:

> As we walk through the minefields of social injustice and hardship, we may want to call on the strength of these elemental inner resources for balance and equipoise. For example, there are times when we will need to stand our ground, strong like a mountain, and observe what emerges. And there are times when we may need to add a spark of fiery truth to a situation. Other times, we may need to open and allow more space around the tightness of our worries, or let go and be held by an ocean of love.[2]

Our families are asked to hold and seek answers to painfully complex questions: How can we help our children understand that the people charged with protecting them may instead kill them? How can we help Black children breathe when the cultural knee is on their neck?

Knowing that our children's minds and bodies are under attack, our practice can support us in turning not only our homes—but also our very bodies—into sites of refuge and resistance to white supremacy and anti-Blackness. Resmaa Menakem, the author of the groundbreaking book on healing racialized trauma, *My Grandmother's Hands,* notes that the innate capacity for healing trauma lives in the bodies of individual people and can be spread within families and through communities.[3]

We can work to help our children's bodies, minds, and nervous systems relax enough so that they may begin to hold the painful realities and contradictions of Black life in the African Diaspora and develop some foundational tools to navigate it. We can teach our children about intergenerational trauma so that the light of awareness illuminates their path through the darkness, and we can teach them the basics of body awareness and somatic healing through practices like breathing, singing, humming, chanting, dancing, cooking, playing, braiding hair, and being in community. We can learn the specifics from Black scholars and dharma teachers who are using their deeply embodied knowing to manifest healing in our beloved communities.

The four heavenly abodes, sometimes called the four immeasurables due to their far-reaching capacity, is one such practice that can help our Black community do the healing it needs.

METTA: LOVING-KINDNESS

Metta is a word that reflects the many faces of love: friendliness, kindliness, warmth, good will, and, most commonly, loving-kindness. *Metta* is the state of mind that cares for and wishes well without judgment, conditions, or expectations.

I recently saw a young Black man being arrested on a street corner at the mouth of the Santa Monica pier in Los Angeles. He could have been my son or your brother. He was sitting silently on the curb, handcuffed, staring off into the middle distance, flanked by police officers on walkie-talkies. There were many spectators on this crowded stretch of street. Among them, one stood out: a middle-aged Black woman who could have been my sister or my neighbor. Her carriage was stiff, rigid with adrenaline and watchfulness, as she held her phone out in front of her, conspicuously filming the scene. As she walked slowly past, the cops told her to "keep it moving." She said, "I'm watching you."

She was speaking to the cops, warning them: you are being witnessed; I see you. Your actions—be they routine or deadly—are being recorded.

She was also speaking to the young man, loving him: you are being witnessed; I see you. She was telling him: you are being seen through the eyes of love, whoever you are, whatever they claim you did, you are loved, and I am doing my small, brave part to protect you and your precious life; I could be your mother or your auntie, you could be my son, we are bound together, you and I. I will not turn away.

As I passed, feeling helpless, angry, and deeply moved, I was overcome with the collective grief of mothers of Black boys in America. In that bleak moment, I turned to dharma practice. I offered the young man *metta;* I offered the woman *metta.* May you be safe and protected from all harm and danger, may you be honored and respected, may you find peace and release, may you be loved and share love. I offered *metta* to myself and to all the mothers who love Black children and fear for their lives every day. May we be safe, may our families be safe, may we know the ease of well-being. In my triggered, activated state, I cannot say that my impulse was to offer *metta* to the police officers—may your kind heart awaken—but I expect that one day, with continued, diligent mindfulness practice, I will have the stability and spaciousness of mind and heart to leave no one out of the circle of my loving-kindness.

KARUNA: COMPASSION

Karuna is translated as compassion and is defined in the classical Buddhist texts as the quivering or trembling of the heart in the face of suffering; compassion is considered to be the heart's noblest quality. Compassion is a multifaceted response to pain. It includes kindness, empathy, courage, equanimity, and generosity.

In this way, compassion in the Buddhist context is both active and a call to action.

As parents of Black children, we can turn our compassion toward our own selves in difficult times. We have all the worries, concerns, and wishes that parents of children of any race have. We all want our kids to be safe, happy, and healthy, to live with ease, to do well in school, to pursue their passions. However, we who are parenting Black children have other questions that lurk, questions that often have to do with the threat of physical and emotional violence against our children.

It is an act of compassion to connect with and acknowledge our pain. In this way, we can sit in the center of our suffering and allow it to teach us. We can start by facing the reality of our feelings: "This is grief, this is rage, this is outrage, this is injustice, this is despair . . ." We can then acknowledge that we are not alone: "Other parents of Black children have felt this way too. I am one of many." Finally, we can offer ourselves kindness and support: "How can I be kind to myself in this moment? How can I support myself? My child?"

Cultivating compassion for ourselves and our children— individual and collective—is an act of love. Our families, our world, and we ourselves dearly need our compassion.

MUDITA: JOY IN THE JOY OF OTHERS

The Dalai Lama says, "The more we care for the happiness of others, the greater our own sense of well-being becomes. Cultivating a close, warm-hearted feeling for others automatically puts the mind at ease. This helps remove whatever fears or insecurities we may have and gives us the strength to cope with any obstacles we encounter."[4]

Mudita, or sympathetic joy, is the invitation for us to rejoice in happiness—our own and others'. *Mudita* is the feeling that arises when you hear a baby's hearty laugh and feel that very same laughter bubbling up inside you too. You smile, you feel uplifted, you feel lighter. *Mudita* is joy that is shared, connected, affirming; joy that is untouched by envy, jealousy, or frustration. This joy encourages us to seek and see the good in others and ourselves and to celebrate it.

For parents of Black children in a wider world that often censures rather than celebrates them, the cultivation of *mudita* is an especially powerful practice. When we cultivate *mudita,* we are practicing joy; we are inviting more and more joy into our lives, our hearts, and our homes.

You can practice *mudita* by sitting quietly and lovingly holding the image of your child (or anyone else you wish) in your mind's eye.* See your child happy, smiling, flourishing, joyful. See them at ease, in alignment, healthy, and whole. Allow in the pleasure of seeing your child thriving; feel what this pleasure feels like in your body and being. Is it a warmth in your chest? The corners of your lips tipped up into a smile? A tingling sense of relaxation? You can let your mind wander over the many gifts, large or small, that grace your child's life, even if they exist alongside sufferings they may also experience.

When you are ready, you may silently repeat these phrases (or any variation that resonates with you), pausing between each phrase to allow the reverberations of these words to be deeply felt:

> Your joy brings me joy
> I'm happy that you're happy
> May your happiness continue
> May your happiness increase
> May your good fortune shine

---

*This practice is inspired by parenting specialist Taylor Ross, of The Practice of Parenting.

The dharma comes alive in our homes and in our hearts when we turn parenting our children into the path of practice. When we deliberately develop equanimity, loving-kindness, compassion, and joy, we turn our hearts, minds, and homes into heavenly abodes. Our 10,000 joys and 10,000 sorrows become fuel for enlightenment, liberation, and freedom for ourselves, for our children, and for all beings.

NOTES

1 Ram Dass, from his "Letter to Rachel's Parents."
2 King, Ruth. "How to Be Equanimous in a Racialized World," *Lion's Roar,* July 16, 2020, www.lionsroar.com/how-to-be-equanimous-in-a-racialized-world/.
3 Menakem, Resmaa. *My Grandmother's Hands: Racialized Trauma and the Pathway to Mending Our Hearts and Bodies* (Las Vegas: Central Recovery Press, 2017).
4 Gyatso, Tenzin, the Fourteenth Dalai Lama. "Compassion and the Individual." His Holiness the 14th Dalai Lama of Tibet. www.dalailama.com/messages/compassion-and-human-values/compassion.

COMING HOME TO
EMBODIED NONDUALITY

by Anouk Aimée Shambrook

WALKING INTO THE DINING HALL at Spirit Rock Meditation Center in October of 2019, I am stunned to see a room full of people of African descent. This gathering of Black Buddhist teachers has brought together two dimensions of my life that rarely overlap: my love of Buddhist teachings and my love of Black people. As an African American mixed-race daughter of immigrants, I hadn't realized how deeply the experience would impact me. My tears flow freely.

This is not my typical experience in Vajrayana Buddhist gatherings. Usually, I am one of maybe two Black people sitting in a sea of white people. At the Black Buddhist teachers gathering, we sit on cushions in a comfortable meditation center, knowing that #BlackLivesMatter, knowing that *if we have to keep saying it out loud,* it's because it isn't so for the majority of the US population. We sit and breathe, knowing that George Floyd can't. Breonna Taylor can't. Tamir Rice can't. We breathe for them, to remember what racist institutions want us to forget daily.

Although biologically speaking, there is no truly existing thing as a "race,"[1] the *impact* of the illusion of race and the resulting racism is devastating. When confronted with outright or unconscious racism within my spiritual community, I attempt to sustain the perspective of the teachings while staying utterly open to the wounds I experience. This helps me honor my vulnerability and activation, while remembering that this does not define the whole that I am. My goal is always liberation from suffering.

It has been a long journey coming back home in the deepest sense: coming home to my true nature and my wholeness.

THE ALIEN

My journey began in Orange County, southern California, where I grew up in the only Black family in an otherwise totally white town. In high school, when another Black family moved to town, the Ku Klux Klan burned a cross on their lawn. Visiting the land of my father's family—Cork, Ireland—I was considered Black and obviously didn't fit in. Visiting the land of my mother's family—Haiti—the consensus was flipped: I was considered white. Not being able to speak the native Kreyòl language didn't help any. I felt like an alien who didn't fit in anywhere.

It wasn't until I moved to Manhattan that I found a sense of home—where Black folks made eye contact and nodded as we passed each other on the street. Finally, there was a shared recognition of both my Blackness and my humanness.

During my time at Columbia College as a physics major, I learned about some of the mind-bending parallels between quantum physics and Eastern mysticism. Who would've thought

I could find a sense of belonging in awe of the vastness of the universe? I delved into the study of deep space as I earned my PhD in astrophysics and became a NASA fellow, coming to know a larger perspective than what we're used to in our daily lives on Earth.

DISCONNECTION VS. CONNECTION

Focused on the vastness of the universe, I was not giving any attention to the universe within my body. Having experienced trauma as a child and then being raised with the idea of "mind over matter," I didn't pay attention to the early warning signs when my health became unbalanced. I didn't realize I wasn't at home, even in my own body. I only began to recognize this disconnection after I became severely ill. It took years to learn about the cumulative effect of trauma. Trauma can be described as separating our awareness from our body. Over time, I came to understand that when I cut myself off from my body, I cut myself off from the wholeness of who I am. Out of habit, we tend to identify with the sense of separation. Healing trauma is thus a process of reidentifying with our wholeness.

Part of my healing began in 1995 when the Tibetan Buddhist Dzogchen teacher Chagdud Rinpoche introduced me *experientially* to a profound wholeness and grace that had always been within me, but had gone unrecognized. We call this many things: divinity, love, unity, feeling one with everything, embodied nonduality. Although it is essential to who we are, we are often disconnected from this deepest sense of home, which takes a toll.

CONNECTION AND EMBODIED NONDUALITY

Embodied nonduality is a tactile truth that breaks through all concepts and cultural trappings, and allows us to revel in our true nature. This natural state is an experience most of us have had at one time or another, at least briefly. You may relate to it as feeling connected with everything, being fully present in your body, and feeling relaxed with an open mind and heart. Perhaps you remember being a child in awe, or being in nature feeling deeply connected. Artists and athletes may experience it as being "in the flow"; or "in the zone" for others when journeying with psychedelics or in the moment of orgasm.

As Toni Morrison says, "If you surrendered to the air, you could ride it."[2]

We can develop a visceral feeling for that which cannot be captured in words. For instance, I often experience this natural state when I'm in the ocean.

> *My floating body completely surrenders to the gentle waves of the ocean moving through me. My limbs, hair, and torso sway slowly like kelp. Over time, my muscles and mind relax more deeply, drinking in the sheer beauty until it feels like the water inside my body merges with the water outside my body. I feel a part of the whole. In this fluid moment, I am free, no longer hijacked by the thinking mind. My heart softens and expands, and a burden is lifted.*

The truth of nonduality is ancestral wisdom. It's our true nature.* It still exists in many of our Indigenous African traditions and worldviews.[3] "Ubuntu" in Zulu is often translated as "I am, because *we are.*"

---

*In the Buddhist Dzogchen tradition, this nonduality is sometimes called our nonconceptual self-knowing timeless awareness. It is ineffable, open, spontaneously present, and one with everything. In contrast, most of us usually experience a sense of duality: a separation between "me" as a subject and "the rest of the universe" as an object.

WHY IS IT IMPORTANT?

Ever felt like much of the time you're living life from an externally driven, checklist-like place? Tapping into nonduality is a way to begin tasting the freedom and fundamental connectedness that is right here, *all the time*. It's powerful. We suffer on so many levels from disconnection—some levels that we're conscious of and deeper levels of which we're not even aware. There are so many things in our lives that we cannot control, yet we have this amazing capacity to shift in awareness *every* moment. This shift can completely change our lives.

For some of us, an experiential introduction to awareness can be all that's needed to know in all circumstances, beyond any doubt, your true nature, your refuge, your home. For most of us, myself definitely included, it's a journey! But it's *non*linear. That's the tricky bit for a scientist like me.

OBSTACLES TO EXPERIENCING NONDUALITY

Even though we have the potential to access our true nature all the time, there are plenty of obstacles to doing so. Out of habit, most of us get distracted and enticed by our perception of the world around us. How often do we have the courage to let go of not only our social conventions but also the very concepts that bind us to our so-called reality? Do we dare to live without reference points?

Initially, despite teachings to the contrary, I considered this kind of awareness like an object "out there" to attain. I grasped at it. I was pretty disconnected from my body and it felt like a *momentary* experience of my mind expanding, letting go of concepts, and feeling beyond time. For years, my experience of awareness was highly dependent on special conditions, such as meditating in the presence of my teachers. But I couldn't simply "drop in" at will.

As Black people, we often grapple with *additional* obstacles to coming back to our true nature. The trauma of the relentless rejection of our humanity and the denial of our reality can make us feel under attack. We often lack an embodied sense of safety, making relaxation, trust, and openness feel counterintuitive. With the collective history of trauma that our bodies carry,[4] we may not trust that oneness is our true nature and birthright. Yet our bodies can also be a doorway back to our wholeness.

FREEING THE BODY TO FREE THE MIND

It has been a long road coming home to my very human body, a body that is feminine, Black, beautiful, and vulnerable. Finding safe spaces with other Black folks, as well as healing trauma, has been essential in helping me come home to my body, and ultimately, the wholeness of who I am.

When I became seriously ill a second time and needed surgery, I sought the advice of my teacher, Lama Drimed, since I understood the body, mind, emotions, and spirit to be connected. He suggested I go to Kiskeya (the island of Haiti and the Dominican Republic). He recognized that somehow connecting with the land of my cultural heritage could support my physical healing *and* spiritual practice. The suggestion shocked me, for it was the first time my teacher explicitly brought in my heritage as a potential support for my spiritual growth. For years, I had been told to *just focus on my practice* when I brought up how white our spiritual community was. My concerns about racism in those earlier years were dismissed as a distraction.

So, taking his suggestion, I made the radical move to the coast of the Dominican Republic and began my daily meditation in the ocean. Since the mind and body are connected, the fragmentation of my mind impacted my body, and vice versa. And both impacted my depth of connection with my heart. Working first with my mind, I practiced seeing how I unconsciously spent so much energy trying to push away the parts of my personality that I didn't like. By embracing those shadow sides as aspects of me that needed compassion, I began to come back home to wholeness and taste liberation. I used daily encounters and conflicts to learn that *how I related* to my ego determined whether I suffered or was free. This allowed me to relax more deeply into awareness, into the simple feeling of being.

Then I began working directly with my body to heal past trauma. Part of this process was learning to hear my body's deeper wisdom by tuning in to its sensations (and not just my *ideas* about the sensations, or my *emotional reactions* to those sensations).[5] This, combined with connecting deeply with nature and surrendering in dance, enabled me to gradually re-*member*— put the pieces of myself back together. In doing so, I found myself dropping ever more deeply into the field of awareness that permeates everything.

Over time, I have come to understand the experience of awareness to be more like a dimmer switch rather than an on-off function. In retrospect, as profound as my initial experiences of nonduality were, I slowly realized there were many dimensions of my being that I was excluding. Expansive though my experience of awareness was, it wasn't *fully embodied;* it didn't readily include my physical sensations, emotions, environment, or how I related to others. And part of the reason for this was my personal trauma and intergenerational racial trauma. It took time to shift from meditating *on* the body, to meditating *as* the body. In the alchemy of dance, psychological work, and trauma therapy, I began including more of myself—even my earthy, warm, steamy, breathy body! As I did this, awareness acted like a medicine, offering liberation. Gradually, layers of unconscious defenses around my heart began to melt. Love has begun to feel less dependent on conditions and can shine through me far more often, with greater freedom. This is incredibly powerful. Finally I am arriving home in both my body and the fullness of my heart.

MY JOURNEY TO A MORE DEEPLY EMBODIED NONDUALITY

When I started my meditation retreat in the Dominican Republic, I had a lot of momentum of "doing." It took a long time to relax my thinking mind. To *slow down*. To sink my mind into my heart, into its source. To come back into my body. To come back fully into the present moment. For the initial years of my retreat, I longed for structure—something I could hold on to for a sense of progress. What is it like to take awareness and nonduality itself as the path?

As Dzongsar Khyentse Rinpoche said, "Awareness has no handrails."[6]

My teachers encouraged me to do "research and development" in my seven years of Vajrayana and Dzogchen meditation retreats, exploring what I found to be particularly juicy doorways to awareness. Ultimately, my body has become like a weather vane. When I feel my body contracted, it's a sign that a part of me not only needs my attention, but has slyly distracted me, yet again, from remembering to rest as awareness. As I become more relaxed and open, my relationship with different experiences is shifting. I still feel happy, sad, fearful, or angry, but sometimes those encounters don't grip me as long as they used to in the past.

I continue to come home to my Black body, even as I also know myself as something more fundamental than all my human characteristics. Day by day, my heart is becoming more tender in the midst of unconscious microaggressions and intentional racist violence. I am more able to open to the joys as well as oppression. The hurts don't stop coming, but they just don't have the same impact. I am beginning to develop a bit more courage to look in an unflinching way and be open *to the whole range of my experience.* In other words, **we're not doing a spiritual bypass** (trying to prematurely transcend basic human needs, feelings, and sociopolitical realities through the use of spiritual practices).[7] This is a key distinction: though our true nature is not defined by our identities, it includes the whole experience of our lives! I strive to shine through my Blackness with a presence beyond any category.

I would like to express my gratitude—beyond words—to my teachers Chagdud Rinpoche, Dzongsar Khyentse Rinpoche, and Lama Drimed Norbu.[*] I also would like to thank Noliwe Alexander, Myokei Caine-Barrett, Konda Mason, and Rev. angel Kyodo williams, who organized the Black Buddhist teachers retreat at Spirit Rock, where we could breathe for those who no longer can.

> *That afternoon at Spirit Rock, as I looked at the faces of my new Black spiritual community, I completely surrendered to the gentle waves moving through me. Over time, my muscles and mind relaxed more deeply. I felt part of a whole. My heart softened and expanded. . . . I was home.*

May the merit of our journey together support all displaced people who are seeking a true home.

NOTES

1 I. Kendi, *How to Be an Antiracist* (New York: One World, 2019); Megan Gannon, "Race Is a Social Construct, Scientists Argue,"

---

[*]And Yogi space travelers who explored the inner universe, like Yeshe Tsogyal and the fourteenth-century Tibetan mystic Longchenpa.

Scientific American, February 5, 2016, www.scientificamerican.com
/article/race-is-a-social-construct-scientists-argue/.

2 T. Morrison, *Song of Solomon* (New York: Knopf, 1977).

3 J. Olupona, "The Spirituality of Africa," interview by A. Chiorazzi,
Harvard Divinity School, October 7, 2015.

4 T-N. Coates, *Between the World and Me* (New York: One World,
2015); R. Menakem, *My Grandmother's Hands: Racialized Trauma
and the Pathway to Mending Our Hearts and Bodies* (Las Vegas:
Central Recovery Press, 2017).

5 L. Grabbe and E. Miller-Karas, "The Trauma Resiliency Model: A
'Bottom-Up' Intervention for Trauma Psychotherapy," *Journal of the
American Psychiatric Nurses Association* 24, no. 1 (2018): 76–84.

6 Dzongsar Jamyang Khyentse Rinpoche, personal communication,
August 2016.

7 J. Welwood, *Toward a Psychology of Awakening: Buddhism, Psychotherapy, and the Path of Personal and Spiritual Transformation*
(Boston: Shambhala, 2000).

SADHANA OF AWAKENED MELANIN

Devotional Practices to Help Transform Self and Other

by Justin F. Miles, dharma name Shiwa Chuwo

THE ANCESTRAL HOME OF ALL things is Afrika. It is where the first humans began to ask questions about how to find contentment in a world that offers no stability or predictable comfort. As Afrikans, we are called to reclaim and affirm our relationship with the cosmology shared by all humans and what that relationship looks like through an Afrikan-centered lens. Buddhism offers a rational view of humanity rooted in the Earth, the community, and the body that invites us to explore what it means to be a human, born with this body, this skin, and at this time. It does not ask us to discard our conditioned sense of self, but instead to live a meaningful and purposeful life as we are found. Buddhism also asks us to live this life with and for others, and to do so to explore the limitations of solidifying our experience of the world around us. Loosening our grip on our projections reveals a natural spaciousness experienced as an awakened unconditional heartmind of wisdom, compassion, and skillfulness. What this means is that the nature of our Afrikan selves and the myriad ways it manifests in our everyday lives—our culture, society, body, and mind—are useful and worthy as inherent tools of enlightenment. To bring this about, we must shine the light of wisdom through the lens of our Afrikanness to determine for ourselves what enlightened Afrikan society looks like.

When I began contemplating writing and adapting these practices, I remember wondering how the various truths outlined in the Buddha-dharma were being taught to me so that I did not see enlightenment only through the lens of Asia and Europe, but also through the lineage of my ancestors. What I found is that there were no teachings or teachers that attempted to include the history and legacy of Afrikan people in the Buddha-dharma; and because I was unwilling to wait for someone to do it, I began to write. These practices are an attempt at gathering our awareness around our absolute value as humans and our relative value as Afrikans, and with that I offer them as a collective experiment for all who are interested to take part in.

The following practices are a part of a longer liturgy known as the Sadhana of Awakened Melanin. They can be practiced together or separately to account for time limitations or the need to connect with the experience of one or more of the practices.

Prior to engaging in any of these practices, I suggest a period of a concentration meditation practice such as Samatha in order to still the bodymind and allow for more contemplation and integration of the meaning.

The Sadhana of Awakened Melanin consists of four devotional practices that help to polish the Buddha-nature in all Afrikan descent sentient beings. Each practice is a stand-alone piece, or you could do them all together.

- Invocation to the Divine

- Libation in Celebration of the Universal Lineage of Warriorship

- Four Reminders for Afrikan Descent People

- A Declaration of Victory

COMMENTARY: LIBATION IN CELEBRATION OF THE UNIVERSAL LINEAGE OF WARRIORSHIP

The main purpose of this liturgy is to acknowledge all warrior cultures, particularly those contained within our own family lineages. This is also a celebration, as we can take delight that we come from strong, healthy, and dignified warrior clans. These warriors who aided us and others in their human journeys all had a connection with basic goodness and manifested this connection in many ways. We recognize the warriors of whatever land we currently inhabit as well as those abroad. We pour libations, water or *amrita,* as a symbol of purity, or purifying ego and other obscurations that stand in the way of us becoming warriors ourselves. Through fearlessness and gentleness, the energy of all father and mother lineages, our ancestors created the possibility for us, as well as the world, to overcome the suffering caused by the ignorance of our true nature.

> Through the power of your blessings, may we manifest
>   wisdom, compassion, and discipline
> so that we may follow your example in all spheres of life
> awakening all whom we encounter through skillful means
> a noble heart of compassion and authentic presence

> father and mother lineages, recognize us your children
> as the dawn (gong) of the Great Eastern Sun
> invoking your energy, we take the form of those who have
>   gone before
> and raise the banner of Enlightened Society
> in the name of the unbroken Universal Lineage of
>   Warriorship

When invoking the energy of your ancestral warriors, it is important to genuinely feel their presence and allow whatever goodness, dignity, compassion, generosity, or other impactful quality they bestowed on the world to arise in your body and heartmind. Feel that they are present, have always been so, and will always be so. However, the wisdom, compassion, and discipline that manifest in the warrior's life will do so only to the extent that we incorporate the generous blessings of our ancestral lineages into every sphere of our lives. Those are the absolute tools, the teachings of our collective human experience; equanimity, ultimate Bodhicitta, unconditional compassion, authentic presence, all are the universal teachings of warriorship worldwide. We should try to practice what we have learned from our collective lineages in the areas of body, speech, mind, creativity, family, community, environment, and the spiritual realms. We are all descendants of father and mother lineages, patriarchal and matriarchal, who embody the principles of bravery, nourishment, etc. Every living generation is the dawn of the Great Eastern Sun celebrating the arrival of a new warrior clan who will build upon the foundation of the previous generation and promote wakefulness in the name of basic goodness.

Discussion of the Yoruban Ashe Principle

This practice brings together two warrior lineages: the Ifa tradition of West Afrika and the Shambhala warrior lineage. Shambhala teachings were originally conceived by Chögyam Trungpa as secular teachings to achieve enlightened communities. In 2000 the Sakyong Mipham reframed these teachings as Shambhala Buddhism. I take from these teachings and bring them home to our cultural and racialized experiences as Black Afrikans exploring Buddhism and/or Shambhala in the West.

> We pour in remembrance to those ancestors, foremothers
>   and forefathers
> in all our homelands, originators of the races and cultures of
>   basic goodness
> and we all say: Ashe!

When we say Ashe, we cut through our conceptual mind and affirm the presence of our ancestors, experience confidence, and feel energized.

The pouring of libations is a ritual that is Afrikan in origin. It is similar to a *lhasang* in that it invokes the energy of an ancestral force whose energy we recognize as being no different from our own fundamental nature. Instead of the element of fire, we use the element of water as a symbol of inherent purity. When the elder pours the water into the vessel or the earth, it symbolizes joining our pure nature with that of our ancestors.

When we say Ashe, it is similar to the way that we refer to the Black Ashe, the symbol of primordial confidence. According to the Ifa practitioners of West Afrika, Ashe is the primordial creative force of all, and out of it arises form, both male and female. When we say Ashe, we do so with vigor and power, cutting through conceptual mind and proclaiming that we are all connected at our nature. It is a way for us to proclaim our absolute and relative togetherness.

> We pour in remembrance to those ancestors destroyed in
>   atrocities, wars, enslavement, oppression, and so on
> May their bloodshed never be forgotten
> and we all say: Ashe!

We pour again to remember those who have lost their lives in times when ignorance was valued over warriorship.

> We pour in remembrance to those ancestors of this land on
>   which we reside
> The native, enslaved, and migrant caretakers and warriors of
>   this place
> and we all say: Ashe!

We pour a third time to remember that we stand on borrowed land and live a precious life because of another's sacrifice.

The Calling of the Warriors

> We pour in remembrance of those ancestors,
> our heroes and sheroes, whose influence in our lives
> planted the seeds of courage, compassion, and wisdom
> the Bodhisattva warrior's path of aspiring and entering
> O noble ones, we call out your names
> to honor your accomplishments
> that we may continue your legacy
> of sanity and vision for all sentient beings

Here we invoke the collective energy of our ancestors by calling their names, bringing them into our immediate existence, making their wisdom, kindness, and power our own. Our ancestors now share a common space and become each other's ancestors. Here we stand as a clan; we are all the Mukpo clan, but as humans we are also a universal clan of warriors who recognize that we are not alone, and who long to share the spirit of universal warriorship with all.

> In complete remembrance of the warriors throughout time
>   and space
> of our own lineage and others
> who embody the principles of awakened heart, fearlessness,
>   the transcendent actions

and so forth
named and unnamed
born and yet to be born, we pour three times to the unbro-
    ken Universal Lineage of Warriorship
in the past, present, and future
Ashe! Ashe! Ashe!

To close the ceremony, we remember all warriors who have existed, exist presently, or will exist as those who embrace and live the principles of Enlightened Society. We should begin meditation practice afterward, resting with a renewed sense of dignity and awakened energy.

This ends the commentary on the Libation in Celebration of the Universal Lineage of Warriorship.

The rituals begin. You can do just one of these, or all of them together. These rituals are to help us see more clearly, to cultivate compassion for ourselves and others, and to help us transform our lives. They polish the compassion and wisdom seed that we all have within us, no matter our past actions or deeds. Rituals, *pujas* in Buddhism and the Shambhala tradition, are devotional practices. I have adapted them for the Afrikan Diaspora communities.

A FOURFOLD *PUJA:* A DEVOTIONAL PRACTICE (IT CAN BE RECITED TOGETHER AND EACH SECTION CAN BE A STAND-ALONE RITUAL)

Invocation to the Divine

The teacher/leader of the practice rings the gong three times.

The teacher/leader says aloud:

THE FOUR BLESSINGS

Blessings may come from many places: the divine, our ancestors, teachers, loved ones, and even from within our own
nature. Regardless of what you believe, asking to be granted
a blessing is asking for growth in body, speech, and mind,
not just because we wish for it but because we are willing
to practice with devotion and exertion. Watering the seed of
what is innate and ever present will naturally reap the fruits
of wisdom and compassion.

Done in call-and-response (the teacher/leader says a line and
everyone together responds):

Grant your blessing so that my mind may be one with
    the truth
Grant your blessing so that truth may progress along
    the path
Grant your blessing so that the path may clarify confusion
Grant your blessing so that confusion may dawn as wisdom

This is an adaptation of a traditional Buddhist liturgy known as
the Four Dharmas of Gampopa.

The teacher/leader now takes us through the following contemplation (5 minutes):

Close your eyes and invite the divine (whatever you consider
to be divine: your god, higher power, deity, ancestor, etc.) to
be present with you right now. Feel their presence around
and within you: front, back, sides, underneath, above, and
within. Engage in this feeling contemplation, returning again
and again to this experience of sacredness.

The teacher/leader rings the gong.

The teacher/leader says the following words:

THE DIVINE

And then together everyone in unison says the following:

> Let all divine and sacred beings be present
> Inside
> Between
> And as all things
> The alpha and the omega are never in different times
> Only now
> If my divine is real, then my divine is now
> If my divine is now and my mind is elsewhere, then my
>   divine is not realized, it is assumed
> The mind of greed, passion, fear, anger, pride, jealousy,
>   doubt, and ignorance is elsewhere
> The mind that sees the divine in all beings is relaxed and
>   attentive
> The mind that sees the divine between all beings is relaxed
>   and attentive
> The mind that sees the divine in all things is relaxed and
>   attentive
> All else is talk and ideas
> Which have never built families, schools, communities, cul-
>   tures, or friendships
> The basis for these things is awareness of ever-present
>   goodness
> Therefore, let all divine beings be present, but let us be pres-
>   ent with all divine beings.

The teacher/leader rings the gong.

The teacher/leader says the following:

> Rest in the presence of the collective energy of all divine pres-
> ent in the space. Do not talk or listen for messages. Rest in the

feeling. Do not describe it. Just feel within, between, and as all things. Arise with an integrated sense of divine presence.

This text was conceived by Justin Miles, dharma name Shiwa Chuwo, on March 26, 2015, while on retreat at Casa Werma in Pátzcuaro, Mexico.

Libation in Celebration of the Universal Lineage of Warriorship

The teacher/leader says the stanza below in monotone:

> When the confidence which is primordially free
> Was followed and delighted in
> Countless multitudes of warriors arose.

(O>o)

This symbol denotes a drum roll that takes place throughout the piece every time you see the symbol. Someone will do a drum roll.

Begin drumming slowly for the first three syllables then steadily. The teacher/leader says the following word:

REJOICING

And then together everyone in unison says the following:

> In remembrance and celebration
> of the human manifestations of basic goodness
> both here on this land and throughout the world
> we pour libation to those ancestors who through their
> fearlessness and gentleness
> helped to liberate all sentient beings from ignorance and
> suffering
> so that Enlightened Society could manifest in the ten
> directions

Through the power of your blessings may we manifest
    wisdom, compassion, and discipline so that we may
    follow your example in all spheres of life
awakening all whom we encounter through skillful means
a noble heart of compassion and authentic presence
father and mother lineages, recognize us your children
as the dawn (gong) of the Great Afrikan Sun
invoking your energy we take the form of those who have
    gone before
and raise the banner of Enlightened Society
in the name of the unbroken Universal Lineage of
    Warriorship

(O>o)

The teacher/leader says the following word:

REMEMBRANCE

And then together everyone in unison says the following:

We pour in remembrance to those ancestors, foremothers
    and forefathers
in all our homelands, originators of the races and cultures of
    basic goodness
and we all say: Ashe! (The teacher/leader rings the gong.)

We pour in remembrance to those ancestors destroyed in
    atrocities, wars, enslavement, oppression, and so on
May their bloodshed never be forgotten
and we all say: Ashe! (The teacher/leader rings the gong.)

We pour in remembrance to those ancestors of this land on
    which we reside
The native, enslaved, and migrant caretakers and warriors of
    this place
and we all say: Ashe! (The teacher/leader rings the gong.)

We pour in remembrance of those ancestors,
our heroes and sheroes, whose influence in our lives
planted the seeds of courage, compassion, and wisdom
the Bodhisattva warrior's path of aspiring and entering
O noble ones, we call out your names
to honor your accomplishments
that we may continue your legacy
of sanity and vision for all sentient beings

We pour in remembrance of the three Buddhas
Past, Present, Future
Dipankara, Shakyamuni, Maitreya

Note for the following practice: The gong should be rung steadily throughout this part, and water should be poured for each name, for about 2 minutes, or until the calling of names dies down. It should be left to the senior teacher or student present as to when the calling of names should cease. After all names have been called, rest in the presence of your ancestors, contemplating their influence in your life.

The teacher/leader says the following words:

ANCESTOR RETRIEVAL

Call out the name of your ancestors, or anyone who had
a profound impact on your life who is no longer living, to
invoke their energy of compassion, courage, and wisdom.
After any name is said, all should say Ashe!

The teacher/leader rings the gong three times (to end the above practice).

Done in call-and-response. (The teacher/leader says a line and everyone together responds. The teacher/leader begins with a drawn-out "innnn" and then begins the call-and-response of each line.)

Innnn complete remembrance of the warriors throughout
    time and space
of our own lineage and others
who embody the principles of awakened heart, fearlessness,
    the transcendent actions
and so forth
named and unnamed
born and yet to be born, we pour three times to the unbro-
    ken Universal Lineage of Warriorship
in the past, present, and future

The mantra Ashe is begun by the teacher/leader. And after every
Ashe, the teacher/leader rings the gong. Everyone joins in the
mantra, repeating Ashe together. During the mantra recitation,
everyone who wants to has the opportunity to go to the shrine
and give thanks to their ancestors—by bowing and/or prostrat-
ing and offering water and ash.
After everyone who wants to has been to the shrine, the teacher/
leader rings the gong three times.
The teacher/leader says the following words:

HOMAGE TO THE ANCESTORS

And then together everyone in unison says the following in
monotone:

They who have neither beginning nor end
Who possess the glory of countless warriors throughout time
    immemorial
Who possess unquestionable confidence
We pay homage at the feet of our Afrikan ancestors.

Mothers and fathers of the circle of life
Caretakers of humanity
The first kings, queens, soldiers, healers, mystics, sages, teach-
    ers, and travelers

Originators of invention and all that has come into existence
Protector of mystery
Creator of all the Earth's children
I pay homage to the ancestral sovereigns and living embodi-
ments of Afrikan liberation

The teacher/leader says the following words:

WARRIORS OF THE MOTHER LINEAGE

And then together everyone in unison says the following in
monotone:

Queen Hatshepsut, Queen Zenobia, Amanirenas, Queen
Mother Yaa Asantewaa, Queen Nanny of the Maroons,
Carlota Lucumí, Queen Nzinga Mbande, Nyabingi Priest-
esses Muhumusa and Kaigirwa, Aborigine Tarenorerer,
Harriet Tubman, Ella Baker, Angela Davis, Assata Shakur,
Kathleen Cleaver, Maxine Waters, Mary Seacole, Claudia
Jones, Marie-Joseph Angélique, Rosa Parks, and Viola
Desmond

The teacher/leader says the following words:

WARRIORS OF THE FATHER LINEAGE

And then together everyone in unison says the following in
monotone:

Thutmose III, Piye, King of Kush, Hannibal, Mansa Musa,
Abu Yusuf Ya'qub al-Mansur, Sonni Ali, Shaka Zulu,
Ignatius Sancho, Olaudah Equiano, Marcus Garvey, John
Henrik Clarke, Jomo Kenyatta, Mathieu da Costa, Thomas
Peters, William Hall, Malcolm X, Patrice Lumumba, Martin
Luther King Jr., Huey Newton, Bobby Seale, Kwame Nkru-
mah, Fred Hampton, Steve Biko, Julius Nyerere, and Nelson
Mandela

The teacher/leader says the following words:

THE ANCIENT EMPIRES OF

And then together everyone in unison says the following:

Ta Seti, Kemet, Songhay, Kush, Ghana, Mali, and Axum

All of these are evidence of our eternal greatness, fearlessness, gentleness, infinite wisdom, and boundless compassion.

All of these are evidence of victory in the face of ignorance, arrogance, hate, and confusion.

All of these are evidence of how to live our lives in the face of violence, oppression, fear, and doubt.

All of these are evidence of how to organize our families, cultures, and societies.

I pay homage to those who guide us from this life and the next.

Radiating the light of strength, stillness, and love
The transcendent actions of generosity, discipline, exertion, patience, concentration, and wisdom.
Kings and queens of all that we encounter
May the heart of our people remain victorious.

This liturgy is an adaptation of the Shambhala Homage originally created by the Venerable Chögyam Trungpa Rinpoche with the aim of acknowledging the place of Afrikan people among the family of all beings and furthering the mission of creating a global Enlightened Society. Adapted by Shiwa Chuwo/Mind Right Meditation Center, 2016.

Four Reminders for Afrikan Descent People

This is a teaching that originates from the great Buddhist Master Padmasambhava, who brought Buddhism from India to Tibet. Originally called the Four Reversals, they are teachings that turn the mind to our precious birth, the inevitability of death, that actions have consequences, and living with uncertainty and/or the defects of life. Here I adapt them for the Afrikan community.

THREE FACES OF THE SACRED (INNER, INTIMATE, INFINITE)

- Bring your motivation/intention to mind for 1 minute.
- Practice a calming of the mind meditation for 15 minutes. (The teacher/leader can lead this.)
- Contemplate the Four Thoughts for 10 minutes (a little over 2 minutes for each thought).

THE FOUR THOUGHTS THAT TURN THE MIND TOWARD SANITY

The whole practice is done in call-and-response.
The teacher/leader says the following words:

PRECIOUS AFRIKAN/BLACK BIRTH

Done in call-and-response (the teacher/leader says a line and everyone together responds):

> Despite the seeming insanity in our homes, communities, and place of birth
> and historical mistreatment of our people
> I am fortunate to be born an Afrikan/Black person in this human body and at this time
> It did not have to be so

This life is so precious and easily lost
That to be of benefit to my people
I must live with sanity and practice awakening to
    my nature

The teacher/leader rings the gong and then says the following words:

IMPERMANENCE AND DEATH

Done in call-and-response (the teacher/leader says a line and everyone together responds):

All things that have a beginning have an end
All things including myself are coming into and fading from
    existence in every moment
The state of our bodies, our families, our communities,
    nation, and homeland are all temporal
Which means that our situations can and will change
Knowing this, I will awaken to sanity with the blessed time
I have been given and use my time to be of benefit
to my people.

The teacher/leader rings the gong and then says the following word:

KARMA

Done in call-and-response (the teacher/leader says a line and everyone together responds):

Through my actions I influence the direction of my own life
    and the future of my people
This is what is known as karma
Karma is not magical
It is the reaping of seeds that I have planted in my mind
through my actions, speech, and thoughts that result in caus-
    ing myself and others suffering

To live a sane life and to create sanity in the lives of others
I will speak, think, and act from my nature: fundamental
  goodness

The teacher/leader rings the gong and then says the following words:

DEFECTS OF MUNDANE EXISTENCE

Done in call-and-response (the teacher/leader says a line and everyone together responds):

Our people have been convinced that happiness exists in
  another place and in another time
The search for stability through material gain, intelligence,
  and spiritual materialism is never-ending
I will never find true happiness there
The attachment to pleasure seeking, aggression, and self-
  ignorance is never-ending as well
I will never find happiness there either
Searching for happiness where there is none is an insane
  effort
Instead I will give up the search
And strive to awaken to the happiness that is well-being

Adapted by Shiwa Chuwo from the teaching known as "The Four Thoughts That Turn the Mind."

A Declaration of Victory

The teacher/leader rings the gong three times.
The teacher/leader says the following words:

LIBERATION OF THE MIND

Done in call-and-response (the teacher/leader says a line and everyone together responds):

On this day
I declare victory over all perceived enemies
My mind and others
Family, friends, police, government, nations,
Cultures, religions, and races
All at one time or another have been perceived as enemies

When the mind of aggression is unexamined
Ignorance takes root and enemies arise
When the mind of aggression is examined
Liberation is revealed as the natural state of things

There are no enemies
Only minds
Either clear or confused
Processed or unprocessed
Restful or anxious
I do not suffer because of enemies
I suffer because I do not examine the nature of
    perception

With a body of clay
Mind like the sky
Energy like water through bamboo
Free from fixation
I will rest watchfully in uncreated awareness
Where no enemies have ever arisen

If there are enemies there is no victory
The only way to win is to declare true victory
To declare victory means you have never lost
Because your nature has never fought

The teacher/leader rings the gong and says the following words:

LISTENING TO THE MIND

Done in call-and-response (the teacher/leader says a line and everyone together responds):

When you feel disturbed, relax
Victory spontaneously arises from the mind of peacefulness
When you feel disturbed, do not act on impulse
Knowing when and how to move comes from spaciousness,
    not intelligence
Practice being, then behaving
When you feel disturbed by hope, fear, doubt, regret, shame,
    anger,
or other afflicting emotions
Acknowledge it
See it
Own it
But do not see it as the fundamental nature of things
Do not become what you are not
In fact, you cannot become what you are not
That is why victory has already been declared
It is a matter of seeing that your nature has never been
    disturbed
It was never created, so it could never be destroyed
Never be defiled
Never be stained
Never be bought
Never be co-opted
Never be tricked
Never be harmed

The teacher/leader rings the gong and says the following words:

PURE MIND

Done in call-and-response (the teacher/leader says a line and everyone together responds):

No matter your trauma, your pain, or your suffering
Your basic nature is kind, wise, peaceful, and intelligent
It has always been so and will always be so

Proclaiming victory, I will turn my attention toward staying
   wakeful of my nature
Toward avoidant situations and people
Knowing that my essence is enough
To overcome any obstacle
Real or imagined

As a society we win
Not by who we can defeat
But by concentrating our efforts on forging a relationship
with what has never been defeated in ourselves or in others
We perceive loss when we distrust our and others' nature
We perceive defeat when we do not see the goodness in those
who are confused about their good nature
We perceive revenge when we forget that we are conquered
   only when we surrender to ignorance
And even then conquered in perception only

Unexplored perception
Pretending to know when we do not know
Knowing without looking
Is the heart of ignorance
Ignorance is the heart of suffering
Suffering is the condition of dissatisfaction
Dissatisfaction leads to passion, aggression, and prejudice

The teacher/leader rings the gong and says the following words:

THE POISONS

And then together everyone in unison says the following:

> Those three poisons cause all beings around the world to
>   behave like animals
> toward themselves and others
>
> Greed, hatred, and delusion will keep us on the wheel of life
>
> Bring our ignorance to the path, explore it, see beyond all
>   fixations
> And ignorance will stop obscuring our nature—it will
>   become the antidote to all false views
>
> If we are worried about our physical health, the antidote is
>   found in ignorance
> If we are worried about our mental health, the antidote is
>   found in ignorance
> If we are worried about our families and communities, the
>   antidote is found in ignorance
> If we are worried about any ism, the antidote is found in
>   ignorance
> If we are worried about war, the antidote is found in
>   ignorance

The teacher/leader rings the gong and says the following words:

BUDDHA-NATURE

And then together everyone in unison says the following:

> Therefore begin looking there, not for answers, but to prac-
>   tice looking with our original eyes
> Before our identities and conditioning
> When we were just so

Directly experiencing our nature is the heart of a right mind
Let us develop a right mind
Let us build our families and communities on right mind
Let us forge relationships with all beings based on
    right mind
Let us engage the suffering and problems of the world
    with a right mind
A mind righted is never wronged
A wronged mind is never righted

Above all, be brave enough to relax, look, do not be afraid,
    do not solidify your ideas,
Learn from everything, smile, laugh, be curious, and let your
    heart care about the most disgusting of situations
No matter the hand you're dealt, let love be every card played
Even if it does not feel good to you or others
All of us are confused
And only the most confused deny this truth
All of us are enlightened, right now in every moment since
    before your birth
And only the most distracted deny this truth

Do not be a believer
Test these words in your everyday life
Do not be a talker
Let your body be your tongue
Know your nature as a secret but share it with everyone
For it is theirs already
Speak to them from the sanity that lies within them
Practice these words until they become living truth
Develop ultimate confidence in them through diligent
    contentment
Recall them in times of hesitance and aggression
Returning over and over again
Declaring victory as the natural state of things

The teacher/leader rings the gong three times.

The teacher/leader says the following words:

DEDICATION OF MERIT

And then together everyone in unison says the following:

> By this merit may our people be liberated.
> May it defeat the enemy, ignorance of self and other.
> From the struggles of desire, aggression, and prejudice
> From the ocean of suffering, may it free all Afrikans.

This was written by Shiwa Chuwo on March 23, 2018, in Baltimore, Maryland, and is an adaptation from a traditional Dedication of Merit chant.

PART TWO

Black Liberation

THERE IS A BALM

Black Liberation Theology and the Contemporary Struggle

by Andrea Murray-Lichtman, MSW, LCSW,
and Ashton Murray, M.Div.

"Here," she said, "in this here place, we flesh; flesh that weeps, laughs; flesh that dances on bare feet in grass. Love it. Love it hard. Yonder they do not love your flesh. They despise it."

—BABY SUGGS HOLY, *Beloved*

WHAT DOES IT MEAN TO be despised flesh? Flesh that can be bought or sold, raped or lynched, disenfranchised or systematically othered, or denigrated? Baby Suggs Holy, the unchurched preacher in Toni Morrison's *Beloved,* says that we are to love such flesh. It is in the loving of the despised flesh, that the flesh is redeemed and made whole. Her sermon in "the Clearing," a hush harbor of protection for enslaved Black people, weaves together seeds of African spirituality, Christianity, and Black Consciousness into a tapestry of meaning-making for Black people across the African Diaspora. This system of meaning-making, a faithful grappling with what it means to be Black in a world that despises Blackness, gave birth to Black Liberation theology.

Jeremiah, a prophet in the Old Testament of the Bible, tortured by the ailments of his people, stated, "Since my people are crushed, I am crushed; I mourn, and horror grips me. Is there no balm in Gilead? Is there no physician there? Why then is there no healing for the wound of my people?" (Jeremiah 8:21–22, NIV) Amid globalized poverty and poor health inequitably impacting Black and brown communities, globalized mass incarceration disproportionately impacting Black and brown bodies, globalized rejection and demonization of Black and brown refugees fleeing persecution, and globalized racism, there is a cry rising: Is there no balm in Gilead? This chapter will wrestle with the contemporary crisis of Black people and will present Black Liberation theology and the message of Jesus Christ as a balm for the wounds and renewal of the soul for Black people.

"Is there a balm in Gilead?" This question is salient for all religions but particularly for Christianity, which arguably, offers Jesus Christ as the answer to the "cries in the wilderness" from biblical prophets of old. Prophets and messengers who foretold of a Messiah who would redeem the nation took refuge in the claim of redemption through Christianity. Historically Christianity was present in parts of Africa and had found refuge there long before mass enslavement and colonization by Europeans. Africa's presence in both the Old and New Testaments, therefore, offered Black people across the Diaspora a prophetic symbol of hope despite the oppression that they faced.

This hope persisted despite European enslavers and colonizers co-opting the promise of deliverance and resurrection found in the holy scriptures, especially in the message of Christ, to fit an individualistic, European-centered worldview that, as Baby Suggs Holy said, despised Black flesh. While the powers of the world may have despised Black flesh, Black people across the Diaspora found hope and strength in verses like Psalm 68:31, which stated that "Princes shall come out of Egypt; Ethiopia shall soon stretch out her hands unto God" (KJV). Verses like these gave rise to the "Ethiopian movement," which began as a way to resist colonialism in Africa and later spread through North America as Black people globally pushed back against oppression (Paris, 1994).

Just as Baby Suggs Holy admonished, Black people of every nation across the Diaspora kept the flame of hope alive. Though in most cases unlearned in the language of inhumanness, Black people translated Europeanized Christianity given as a means of social control and an anchor to the bottom of society for Black bodies. They instead took up Christianity as a form of social resistance. It was evidenced by Harriet Tubman, Black Moses, who led enslaved Africans to the promised land of freedom. Marimba Ani, in *Let the Circle Be Unbroken,* says, "Oppressed by dehumanizing circumstances we [Black people] still found something in which to recognize enough of ourselves to revitalize our souls—to create new selves" (Ani, 1980, 14). Black people took their humanity and Christianity and translated it into a transcendent Black theology that recognized the similarities between their struggles and the Christ struggle for liberty. In the Christ story that upset oppressive systems, Black people found the directive to overthrow oppression. Though it was not coined, this liberating theology became the essence of their Christian belief.

Since the seventeenth century, Black people have wrestled with a wilderness of oppression; it morphs into many forms, but retains dangerous implications for Black people. The cries in the wilderness are still rising: "Is there no balm in Gilead?" Black Liberation theology calls Black Christians in the twenty-first century to become the Jeremiahs who deny the individualistic religious dogma that separates, tunnel focuses on the hereafter, and denies contemporary injustice. Instead, Black Liberation theology offers a theology that fights injustice on behalf of those who are racialized and marginalized. The struggle for every racialized and marginalized body must become the struggle that Black people are "crushed by," "horrified by," and for which a cry of anguish rises to secure the balm that can heal and bring liberty.

While Blackness is not a monolith, slavery, colonialism, and neocolonialism have negatively impacted Black people globally and call for strategic essentialism (Spivak, 1990) to fight injustice. At its core, Black Liberation theology (coined by James Cone) speaks to the biopolitical (politics that affect bodies) realities of Black life across the Diaspora. Black Liberation theology offers a theological reflection on the topics of the extraction of Black bodies from Africa, the Middle Passage, the realities of enslavement (i.e., constriction, beating/maiming, forced labor, the auction block, etc.), systemic racial terror (i.e., lynching, rape, state-sponsored terrorism), and the denial of access to goods and services. This messy experience of being the despised flesh offered Black people, those extracted from the continent and those living under colonialism on the continent, an opportunity to take the European Christianity of their oppressors and mold it into a God talk that reflected their daily realities. According to Charles Long (1986), these creators of Black Liberation theologies were not blank slates but were instead informed by the idea of Africa as both a historical reality and as a religious image. As they attempted to make sense of themselves and their involuntary presence in the locations that they found themselves in, they birthed a theology that was informed by both European Christianity and the traditional religions of Africa. For example, Vodun (a.k.a. Voodoo) in Haitian and Louisianan cultures, Santería in Cuban cultures, and Sango in Trinidad and Tobago represent the creation of meaning-making systems that combine elements of both Christianity and African traditional religions to create a praxis of resistance to the systemic debasement that they endured at the hands of white supremacy (Floyd-Thomas, 2016). Simply put, Black Liberation theology provided a systematic language to help Black people suffering from the radical evil of white supremacy.

Christian Black Liberation theology has broad claims and goals. As a political theological movement, it begins with a reflection on the state of affairs of Black people specifically, and the state of oppression within social systems generally. Theologically, Black Liberation theology considers both the nature of God and God's expression and desire for liberation of the oppressed through Jesus. It grapples with what Frederick Douglass called the "seemingly" inconsistency between slaveholding Christianity and the Christianity of Christ. In wrestling with that inconsistency, Black Liberation theology provides Black people with language for how to understand their suffering while not being held captive by it. It is a call to action for the collective of Black people. James Cone (1970) argued that the central claim of Black Liberation theology is the concern of the existential crisis of oppressed people. Unlike European Christianity, Black Liberation theology is sourced from the Black experience, Black history, Black culture, and revelation, scripture, and tradition. Cone (1970) argued that there is no "good news" unless it is centered on, and arises from, the oppressed community. For Cone, faith in God necessitates the active participation of a just

world. South African anti-apartheid activist Steve Biko describes
Black Liberation theology as "it seeks to relate God and Christ
once more to the black man and his daily problems. It wants to
describe Christ as a fighting God, not a passive God who allows
a lie to rest unchallenged. It grapples with existential problems
and does not claim to be a theology of absolutes" (Biko, 2002,
94). From North America to South Africa, Black Liberation theology has historically provided Black people with the tools to
not only demand deliverance from bondage, but also claim their
humanity and dignity.

James Cone argued that when the word of God was made
flesh (John 1:14) in the body of a poor, politically dispossessed
person who found themselves living under the boot of Roman
colonization, God put God's self on the side of every marginalized person and group throughout time. Cone writes, "Until
we can see the cross and the lynching tree together, until we can
identify Christ with a 'recrucified' black body hanging from a
lynching tree, there can be no genuine understanding of Christian identity" (Cone, 2011, xiv). For Cone, and many adherents
of Black Liberation theology, Christ was lynched on a cross by
a racist state that despised his flesh the same way that the state
despises Black flesh. This kinship with Jesus, forged through
shared suffering due to asymmetrical political and social power,
has undergirded Black people's unwavering call for justice. In
Eric Garner's* cry, "I can't breathe," Black people can hear Jesus's
cry on the cross, "I thirst." The promise of Jesus's remark that
"today you will be with me in paradise" (Luke 23:43) is similarly
found in songs like "No More Auction Block for Me," a song
that originated in communities of formerly enslaved people who
had escaped to Canada. Jesus's resurrection, his overcoming the
subjugation and denigration at the hands of the state, becomes
Black people's liberation from oppression and vice versa. Black
Liberation theology's promise to Black people is simple while

provocative: any system that would wish to destroy you will fail. Through the resurrection of Jesus, God shows a liberating preference for the marginalized and downtrodden that overwhelms and shocks the powers of the world as we know it.

As Black people know, liberation is not always simple or easy, nor does it always look like what one might expect. In *Sisters in the Wilderness,* Delores Williams complicates the idea of liberation and salvation by suggesting that perhaps, like the biblical character Hagar, we find salvation in wilderness experiences. Just as many self-liberated people found freedom from slavery in the woods and swamps as they ran north, Black Liberation theology posits that while unjust systems may exist, survival is possible. Throughout history, while walking through the wilderness of their experiences, Black people have always been prophetic people, speaking for a future free from oppression despite their current realities. This is the task for Black people in the twenty-first century, to continue to prophetically call for change despite the wilderness around us. This call for change will embrace the work of being the voice and hands for those who are "the least among us," those racialized and marginalized. While the wilderness seems to crush from each side with globalized crises, inequities, and disparities, Black Liberation theology offers an indefatigable balm of hope. This hope springs forth with life, waters parched places, and demands that we call for change. By doing so, we join the great cloud of ancestral witnesses that have gone before us. By loving our Black flesh, loving it hard despite a world that despises it, we claim our humanity and dignity and move the world a bit closer to God's justice.

---

*Eric Garner was an African American man who fell victim to police brutality in Staten Island, New York, in 2014. Garner could be heard screaming, "I can't breathe," as he was placed in an illegal chokehold by officers in the NYPD. New York City's medical examiner found that the chokehold was the cause of Garner's death.

REFERENCES

Ani, M. (1980). *Let the Circle Be Unbroken: The Implications of African Spirituality in the Diaspora.* New York: Nkonimfo Publications.

Baker, A., Goodman, J., and Mueller, B. (2015, June 13). "Beyond the Chokehold: The Path to Eric Garner's Death." *New York Times.* www .nytimes.com/2015/06/14/nyregion/eric-garner-police-chokehold -staten-island.html.

Biko, S. (2002). *I Write What I Like: A Selection of His Writings.* Chicago: University of Chicago Press.

Cone, J. H. (1970). *A Black Theology of Liberation.* Maryknoll, NY: Orbis Books.

Cone, J. H. (2011). *The Cross and the Lynching Tree.* Maryknoll, NY: Orbis Books.

Floyd-Thomas, J. M. (2016). "Towards a Religious History of the Black Atlantic: Charles H. Long's Significations and New World Slavery." *Journal of Religious History* 42(1): 3–24. https://doi .org/10.1111/1467-9809.12409.

Long, C. H. (1986). *Significations: Signs, Symbols, and Images in the Interpretation of Religion.* Aurora, CO: Davies Group.

Morrison, T. (1987). *Beloved.* New York: Knopf.

Paris, P. J. (1994). *The Spirituality of African Peoples: The Search for a Common Moral Discourse.* Minneapolis, MN: Fortress Press.

Spivak, G. C. (1990). *The Post-Colonial Critic: Interviews, Strategies, Dialogues.* New York: Routledge.

Williams, D. S. (1993). *Sisters in the Wilderness: The Challenge of Womanist God-Talk.* Maryknoll, NY: Orbis Books.

AFRICA, ISLAM, AND LIBERATION

by Nisa Muhammad

Emulate the Blacks, for among them are three lords
of the people of Paradise: Luqmān the Sage, the Negus,
and Bilāl the Muezzin.

—SAYING ATTRIBUTED TO THE PROPHET MUHAMMAD

IN THE LATE EIGHTEENTH CENTURY, a group of Muslims
dissatisfied with the kidnappings and violence against Africans
became sufficiently strong to wrest control of the ruling dynasty
of Futa Toro (middle valley of the Senegal River) and create a
new state called the Almamate (Robinson 1975). They nomi-
nated Abdul-Qadir Kan as their leader, a man of about fifty years
old. He had the military training they needed, but most important the Islamic education as a Qur'an teacher and a specialist in

Maliki law. He was called Almamy, the Pular form of al-imam (Robinson 1973). In 1776, a momentous year for revolutions, he began the liberation of all enslaved people. In addition to liberation, he began to establish Islamic institutions of government that offered freedom, justice, and equality. In 1785, the Almamy negotiated his first trade agreement with the French in St. Louis. They were eager to reestablish their commerce of enslaved people from the upper valley of Senegal, bound primarily for the transatlantic trade (Ware 2014). Almamy was clear about Islamic law. Muslims were not to be enslaved. These men and women were keepers of the divine words of Allah contained in the Qur'an. They were the walking Qur'an. There was no question in his mind; the Almamy would release all of the "walking Qur'ans." The people living in the Futa now were Muslims. Maybe not all by practice but all by principle and were therefore off-limits to the French. In 1788, he displayed his determination: he had a French slave convoy searched by his soldiers, who freed the almost ninety men from Futa whom they found among the captives (Diouf 2013).

The enslavement of Muslims by their rulers reached epidemic proportions during the eighteenth century, when roughly half of the total volume of the Atlantic slave trade was conducted (Ware 2014). Abdul-Qadir Kan offered freedom to any enslaved person who would recite even a verse of the Qur'an. Regardless if it was recited backward, or mispronounced. They didn't have to know the entire book. Just knowing one verse was enough to set them free. In 1787, he stopped slave ships along the Senegal River. Europeans responded with bribes and more presents. He sent them all back, adding that he would not only hinder the route of the slave ships for that year but as long as he should live; and that if the whites attempted any depredations on his subjects in consequence of his determination, he would retaliate (Ware 2014).

The Almamy understood that as these believers were embodied exemplars of the Qur'an, their enslavement was not merely a
violation of Islamic law but had a more profound significance. It
was also the desecration of the Book of God. This understanding
started a dramatic revolutionary movement led by an African
Muslim leader committed to Islamic principles. His work continued until the early 1800s when he was captured. The Almamy
used Islam to liberate enslaved Africans and should be remembered as having destroyed the institution of slavery in the newly
established Islamic republic.

ISLAM COMES TO AFRICA

The northeastern part of the African continent, more precisely
Ethiopia, then known as Abyssinia, is significant in the early history of Islam. It was in Ethiopia that the nascent Muslim community fleeing the Meccans' persecutions found its first refuge
around 615 CE (Al-Deen, Hibbard, and Saud 2013). They lived
there for seven years before the Muslims left Mecca for Medina.
Mecca is the birthplace of Bilāl, the first muezzin, the caller to
prayer. Islam continued to spread in Africa in the early seventh
century from the east and the north long before the first visitors
from the west arrived (Levtzion and Pouwels 2000). The carriers
navigated through the vast and empty spaces of Africa to the
kingdoms where Indigenous people live. They spread Islam from
the Indian Ocean to the vast deserts of North and West Africa.
The ocean separating Africa from the rest of the world and the
deserts of Africa had been an obstacle for earlier people to traverse (Levtzion and Pouwels 2000). The carriers of Islam came
with the knowledge base and advanced navigational skills. As a
result, they were able to traverse the deserts into regions with a
high population.

From the north, Islam spread in three directions. Men bringing the word of Islam, many of them merchants, crossed the Red Sea and occupied coastal towns. Afterward, some navigated up the Nile River to Sudan, where they made settlements, while others crossed the Sahara Desert to the Maghrib (Levtzion and Pouwels 2000). In the early eleventh century, Arab nomads moved toward the south from Egypt and then across the Sahara to West Africa (Wright 2019). These nomads transformed the lives of people from their traditional religious approaches to Islam. This expansion of Islam over many centuries was mainly the result of the combined actions of itinerant merchants, rulers, militants, charismatic scholars, and religious families (Al-Deen, Hibbard, and Saud 2013). These messengers led to the Islamization of Sudan and other North African countries such as Egypt. As they continued with the spread of Islam, other Arabs from Egypt and Arabia established towns along the coasts of the Red Sea as well as in other regions on the east coast of Africa. During the twelfth century, the battle between Islam and Christianity intensified. Islam was rapidly replacing Indigenous Christianity and other religions they came across. By the sixteenth century, Christianity had lost ground. For example, in Egypt, the Coptic Christians had been reduced to less than 15 percent (Levtzion and Pouwels 2000). In West Africa as well, the majority had been converted to Islam.

As Islam steadily gained ground in Africa, their efforts were met with resistance in the horn of Africa. The battle remained undecided as most people chose to stick to their traditional religions and, in some cases, Christianity. The laws existing in these regions did not support the growth of Islam. Ethiopia remained a Christian state, even as the Muslim population had snowballed (Levtzion and Pouwels 2000). The emperor made strict laws that made it difficult for Muslims to interact with the local community. On the East African coast, Arabs met the Indigenous Bantu people who were firmly attached to their religion and could not be quickly converted (Mazrui 1988).

ISLAM AND AFRICAN LIFESTYLES

Islam impacted African lifestyles in many ways for more than a millennium. Interactions between early Muslims and native Africans resulted in the merging new tribes such as the Swahili on the East African coast. These communities have blended Islamic lifestyles with African lifestyles. Islam not only enriched African lifestyles but was also enhanced (Gilliland 1987). Traditional shrines became mosques. Islam wanted to replace the African traditional religion without clashes. This change was easy because Islam had minimal requirements. Muslims were permitted to keep their names and wear the same clothing. The new Muslims were only required to recite the testimony of faith (*shahādah*), and gradually, their lifestyles changed over time. As with any religion, Islam in Africa had a variety of followers—the devout, the sincere, the casual believers, the fundamentalists, the lightly touched, and the mystics (Diouf 2013).

Instead of abandoning their African ways, Africans accepted Islam but still held on to some African beliefs. For example, the existence of natural invisible spirits that have superpowers is an essential part of many African cultures. Islam, on the other hand, allows for belief in the presence of such creatures, commonly known as *jinn* (Ware 2014). Also, some African practices such as polygamy are permitted in Islam, though Islam limited wives to four.

The occurrence of new things that formerly did not exist made people's practice of Islamic lifestyles easy. For example, when there were epidemics of new diseases such as smallpox and cholera, which never existed before, people were desperate.

They tried new practices that never existed before in an attempt
to manage the conditions (Gilliland 1987).

ISLAM AS AN AFRICAN RELIGION

Noted Islamic scholar Dr. Ali Mazrui's documentary *The Africans: A Triple Heritage* showed how the single God concept
was not new in Africa. Akhenaten, 2,000 years before Muhammad, worshipped one God: the Sun. In Islam, the lunar calendar
became important. Senegal is significant for Muslims. The poor
who cannot afford to make pilgrimage to Mecca head to Touba's
Grand Magal Mosque, where Sheikh Amadu Bamba is buried.
He is revered for calling the country back to traditional Islam
like the Prophet did and uniting the country during colonization.
He founded the Mourīdiyya brotherhood that focuses on the
Qur'an, Sunnah, and Ṣūfīsm.

Africa is the continent with the highest Muslim population.
According to the Pew Research Center, more than 27 percent
of the world's 1.6 billion Muslims live in Africa. Their research
also showed that the population of Muslims living north of the
Sahara is far less than those living outside Africa. The study
states that those in the south are twice those in the north.

Sudan alone has more Muslims than Jordan, Palestine, and
Syria combined. There are more than eighty million Muslims in
Nigeria alone compared to thirty-five million who live in Saudi
Arabia. Sparsely populated countries of Africa, such as Somalia
and Niger, have 98 percent Muslim populations. In this context,
they narrowly outpace countries like Saudi Arabia and Pakistan,
which have 97 percent Muslim populations. If you were to traverse Africa from the eastern part of Somalia to the western-
most part of Senegal, you would pass through almost entirely
Muslim communities that have practiced Islam for nearly a
millennium. Dr. Mazrui viewed Africa as a confluence between

Islamic civilizations, Western civilizations, and African civilizations (Mazrui 1986). Islam can be found all over Africa; it is the faith of millions all over the continent. There is no part of the African continent where you cannot find Muslims. Islam has shaped the African continent in many different ways (Mazrui et al. 2006). About one in every five Muslims (in total, between 400 million and 450 million of them) lives on the African continent (Al-Deen, Hibbard, and Saud 2013). Nigeria, which is the country with the highest population in Africa, has more Muslims than any other country, including Egypt. South Africa was the last to be visited by the liberating message of Islam.

ISLAM COMES TO THE DIASPORA

For hundreds of years, slavery was an entrenched economic and racist system in America. The transatlantic slave trade constituted the most massive deportation of human beings in history and was a determining factor in the world economy of the eighteenth and nineteenth centuries. Millions of Africans were torn from their homes, transported to North America, South America, and the Caribbean, and enslaved. The Trans-Atlantic Slave Trade Database has records of almost 43,600 slaving voyages, which forced 12.5 million Africans aboard European and American slave ships over 350 years between the sixteenth and nineteenth centuries; approximately 10.7 million survivors of the Middle Passage disembarked in the New World (National Endowment for the Humanities 2010). The database estimates that up to 30 percent of the enslaved Africans were Muslims.

Slavery stripped them of their humanity and forbade the practice of Islam. In spite of their wretched conditions, Muslim parents tried to pass Islam to their children, but found it very hard. The majority of Muslim children turned out to be Christians because as they came to the New World, they saw the festivals of the Christians in the churches, with the abundance of patriarchs, clergymen, music, and the beauty of dances (Diouf 2013). The children looked at their parents' faith as different and strange, missing the pomp and circumstance Christianity offered. An exception to this loss of connection to Islam is the autobiography of Omar ibn Said, who was born around 1770 in Futa Toro. Since 1831, when Said first recorded his autobiography as a fifteen-page manuscript in Arabic, it has undergone multiple translations, and the original manuscript was unlocated for many years (Jameson 1925).

Fast forward to the early 1900s, and Islam comes from several sources to a people who have been stripped of their humanity, a people who were told when to eat, when to sleep, when to work, when to go to the bathroom, when to procreate, when to do everything, and then were told they were free. After they were told they were free, they were given nothing to be free with.

They were given the opportunity to be sharecroppers for their previous enslavers, which was one degree above slavery and kept them in perpetual debt. Hearing the liberating words of Islam, hundreds, probably thousands, of African American men and women joined the Ahmadiyya movement headed by Mufti Muhammad Sadiq that brought the first English translation of the Qur'an to America (Curtis 2009). Many other Black Muslims formed their Islamic group. In 1927, Noble Drew Ali started the Moorish Science Temple. He was followed by Master Fard Muhammad, who started the Nation of Islam in 1930 in Black Bottom, Detroit. There he found Elijah Poole, who later became the Honorable Elijah Muhammad and went on to lead the Nation of Islam. In 1934, Shaykh Daoud Ahmed Faisal, an African American emigrant from the Caribbean, and his wife Mother Khadijah leased a brownstone at 143 State Street in Brooklyn Heights for his Islamic Mission of America (Curtis 2009). Imam Al-Hajj Wali Akram founded the First Cleveland Mosque in 1937; it started with his involvement with visiting Muslim missionaries. After they left, he became the imam of the city's new Muslim community.

The Nation of Islam presented the most extensive and most widespread expression of the liberating force of Islam. Malcolm X was a star student whose life transformed from a petty criminal to national representative. He preached far and wide the message of Islam's liberating abilities. In the late 1950s, the Nation of Islam became the best known Muslim organization in the United States (Curtis 2009). Malcolm X's messages of Islam and liberation spread across America.

> The common goal of 22 million Afro-Americans is respect as human beings, the God-given right to be a human being. Our common goal is to obtain the human rights that America has been denying us. We can never get civil rights in America until our human rights are first restored. We will never be recognized as citizens there until we are first recognized as humans. (X 1964)

When Malcolm X left the Nation of Islam, his commitment to his faith and the liberation of his people grew stronger. However, in 1965, he was rebuked by Said Ramadan, the director-general of the Islamic Centre in Geneva, Switzerland. "How could a man of your spirit, intellect, and worldwide outlook," asked Ramadan, "fail to see in Islam its main characteristic, from its earliest days, as a message that confirms beyond doubt the ethnological oneness and quality of all races, thus striking at the very root of the monstrosity of racial discrimination?" (DeCaro 1997). Ramadan expressed several concerns he had in an invitation letter to Malcolm X to speak at the center. Malcolm X "responded that being an African American, he felt his 'first responsibility' was to 'my 22 million fellow Black Americans who suffer the same indignities because of their color as I do.' Further, Malcolm stated that he did not believe his 'personal problem' with racism could be solved until it was solved for all African Americans" (DeCaro 1997).

Malcolm was the Black Prince; he was the hope of Muslims around the world. He traveled to Africa three times and met with all of the continent's prominent leaders. He was invited to serve in the governments of Egypt, Ghana, and Algeria. That love for Malcolm, his work, his love of Islam, and how it liberates continues today.

Islam is the second-largest religion in the world after Christianity, with about 1.8 billion Muslims worldwide. Islam is an Arabic word that literally means "submission (to God)" and Muslim refers to "one who submits (to God)."

THERE ARE FIVE PILLARS OF ISLAM:

- The *shahādah* [the testimony of the unity of God and the prophethood of Muhammad];
- The *ṣalāt* [ritual prayer];
- The *zakāt* [alms];
- *ṣawm* [the fast of Ramadan; Muslims fast from dawn to sunset]; and
- The Hajj (pilgrimage to Mecca).

Africa is as important to Islam as Mecca. It is where the first Muslims went to flee religious persecution, and they were welcomed by an African king. They stayed there for seven years before the Muslims migrated to Medina. Africa welcomed the liberating messages of Islam and saw how easy it fit into their African lifestyle. There are more Muslims in Africa than anywhere else in the world.

> O mankind! We created you from a single (pair) of a male and a female, and made you into nations and tribes, that ye may know each other (not that ye may despise (each other).
>
> —QUR'AN 49:13

REFERENCES

Al-Deen, Aminah, Scott W. Hibbard, and Laith Saud. 2013. *An Introduction to Islam in the 21st century.* Wiley.

Curtis, Edward E. 2009. *Muslims in America: A Short History.* Oxford University Press.

DeCaro, Louis A. 1997. *On the Side of My People: A Religious Life of Malcolm X.* NYU Press.

Diouf, Sylviane. 2013. *Servants of Allah: African Muslims Enslaved in the Americas.* NYU Press.

Gilliland, Dean S. 1987. "African Religion Meets Islam: Religious Change in Northern Nigeria." *Islamic Studies* 26 (2): 207–210.

Jameson, John Franklin, ed. 1925. "Summary of Autobiography of Omar Ibn Said, Slave in North Carolina, 1831." *American Historical Review* 30 (4) (July): 787–795. https://docsouth.unc.edu/nc/omarsaid/summary.html.

Levtzion, Nehemia, and Randall Lee Pouwels. 2000. *The History of Islam in Africa.* Ohio University Press.

Mazrui, Ali A. 1988. "African Islam and Competitive Religion: Between Revivalism and Expansion." *Third World Quarterly* 10 (2): 499–518. https://doi.org/10.1080/01436598808420069.

Mazrui, Ali Al'Amin. 1986. *The Africans: A Triple Heritage.* Little, Brown.

Mazrui, Ali Al'Amin, Shalahudin Kafrawi, and Ruzima Sebuharara. 2006. *Islam: Between Globalization and Counter-Terrorism.* Africa World Press.

National Endowment for the Humanities. 2010. "Trans-Atlantic Slave Trade—Database." www.slavevoyages.org/voyage/database.

Robinson, David. 1973. "Abdul Qadir and Shaykh Umar: A Continuing Tradition of Islamic Leadership in Futa Toro." *International Journal of African Historical Studies* 6 (2): 286.

Robinson, David. 1975. "The Islamic Revolution of Futa Toro." *International Journal of African Historical Studies* 8 (2): 185.

Ware, Rudolph T. 2014. *The Walking Qur'an: Islamic Education, Embodied Knowledge, and History in West Africa.* University of North Carolina Press.

Wright, James S. 2019. "Beyond Timbuktu: An Intellectual History of Muslim West Africa—Ousmane Oumar Kane." *Journal of Islamic Faith and Practice* 2 (1). https://doi.org/10.18060/23277.

X, Malcolm. n.d. "Malcolm X Quotes and Facts: Find the Info You Need Here!" Accessed May 19, 2020. www.easybib.com/guides/quotes-facts -stats/malcolm-x/.

THE WISDOM OF RASTAFARI

Key Moments That Led to the Uprising of the Rastafari Movement in the Mid-1970s until Now

by Elisha Precilla

I WOULD LIKE TO MAKE it clear that Rastafari is not a religion, a racialist idea, a cult, a drug trafficking gang, or some political philosophy. Rastafari is reality. It is a radically intentional decision to emancipate one's self from the legal, political, and social restrictions of Babylon (which is the police, politicians, people with power over Black people). There have been many different and derogatory ideas projected onto the Rasta man/woman from the "outside."

Advocating for the liberation of all Black people, Jamaican activist and publisher Marcus Garvey sparked the consciousness of many living in colonial Jamaica. During his career he founded the Universal Negro Improvement Association.

> Our desire is for a place in the world; not to disturb the tranquillity of other men, but to lay down our burden and rest our weary backs and feet by the banks of Niger and sing our songs and chant our hymns to the God of Ethiopia.[1]

When Ethiopian King Haile Selassie I and Empress Menen were crowned in 1930, Garvey's expanding followers did not take this as a coincidence, but a revolutionary symbol of redemption.

Selassie I himself never claimed to be anything other than the emperor, yet his visit to Jamaica in 1966 made history. Thousands gathered in spell-like awe to witness, in flesh, the divinity of a living man as the "son of God." I'd like to note that not all Rastas today believe that Selassie I is literally the "son of God," but a manifestation of the divinity of the Black man, as king.

The early Rastas' vision of revival grew when it was reported that Selassie I would grant many acres of his fertile land to the Western Black people.

Although the vision to unite Black people in Africa had never been materialized, Garvey had already secured the hearts and minds of countless Black people around the world and, most importantly, changed their self-conceptions.

A QUANTUM LEAP

The rise of the Rastafari movement itself is a "quantum leap," fascinating and rarely heard of within a single generation. Many early Rastas were the offspring of first-generation West Indians.

Coming to (or born in) England, Black youths were promised the opportunity of a good education, a respectable, well-paid job, and the chance to integrate as an equal member of society.

Black youths realized their experiences were not what they were set out to be when they began to experience prejudice and bullying from their native peers, schoolteachers, the police, and so on. Understandably, this led to resentment of and rebellion against the system.

It was difficult for parents to truly empathize with their children's torment, as elders were generally "less visible" to the natives. The older generation usually kept to themselves in churches or in each other's homes. Most of those who were employed would not outwardly defend themselves against mistreatment in the workplace, in avoidance of the consequences.

Although disapproval began to build in West Indian households, due to parents' inability to understand their youth's situation, this did not deter the Rasta youth. The general feel toward the older generation was one of pity. They were believed to be in a state of brainwashing, misguided by Babylon (the system), and still unable to see their true power as Africans.

Rastafari is essentially a break in the cycle.

THE LOCS

For the early Rasta, locs signaled a certain level of consciousness. They were a way for brothers and sisters to identify with each other. However, for the scornful spectator, locs were the symbol of idleness and terror. Black youths received constant, unjustifiable, and brutally violent interventions from the police. (Those with locs were often referred to as "the dreadful ones," so for this reason, some may not refer to locs as dreads as it can be considered a slur.)

Because of the societal pressures on women to reflect a specific image of "beauty," the Rasta women's locs are an especially powerful affirmation.

> When a woman put on a dread, it is with deep thought. She don't just dread. She don't just stop comb her hair. If you get up one day and say, "Well, I going and dread," that is a threat to society. It is a threat whether you are a working-class woman or a middle-class woman. If a woman put on a dread, it means it is in defiance of what has been already ordained as beautiful, clean, upright.[2]

Although I'd like to note that it is also believed you don't need to wear locs to harness true Rasta values, because at the same time, Rastafari is much more than the physical.

> You don't haffi dread to be Rasta
> This is not a dread locs thing
> Divine conception of the heart.[3]

BABYLON

As previously mentioned, the term "Babylon" is a way to refer to politicians, employers, financiers, the law, and so on. In the earlier days of the Rastafari movement, pressure from Babylon was at a height. The main personification of Babylon, and the cause of everyday suffering for Rasta, were the police.

> Them just respond to the needs of Babylon; wear "the badge of brutality."[4]

In the inner cities of England, Rastas were routinely harassed and beaten by the police. They were sensationalized in the news, causing fear and judgment among society and sometimes leading to a self-fulfilling prophecy. Although many wanted a job, the employment system was so institutionally racialized at this time, that it was made almost impossible. This rejection from society meant that Black youths spent a lot of time on the street.

In 1986 the "Public Order Act" was introduced in the UK. This was made to abolish public offenses such as riot. However, police used it casually, deliberately antagonizing specific individuals in inner-city communities, and then arresting them for something as minuscule as "using their hands to talk," declaring it was a threat to cause violent harm.

> The police were provoking people by calling them monkeys and wogs. And they're only young. Fourteen, sixteen to seventeen-year-olds.
>
> —R. JAMES, youth and community worker, in 1987[5]

In Jamaica, Rastas who chose to live remotely and naturally, off the earth, were often raided by the police. Many were accused of plotting attacks for being in possession of their farming tools. The police would commit dehumanizing acts such as "trimming"—forcefully cutting off one's locs.

After many years of discrimination and harassment against Black people, the Rastas set out to be independent from a system that is designed to treat one as inferior, subsequently disconnecting from all forms of oppression and exploitation.

> I and I never in no labor ting where you get up and you say you're going to work for an established organization, cah all of the "isms," dem are problematic. Capitalism, socialism, every kind of ism! I and I ah deal with people and livity, seen?
>
> —DR. KADAMAWE KNIFE[6]

RASTA LIVITY

The Rasta livity is what can be described as the right way of living in order to connect the Rastas back to the truth of who they are. One of the main ways that Rastas maintain the proper livity is to grow the food that they eat.

> It's like you plant your blessing. It make you more in tune.
>
> —RAS STIMULANT[7]

This is called "ital" food (derived from "vital"), which mostly consists of organically grown fruits and vegetables and is considered the most natural way for a person to sustain their livity. Rastas avoid harmful substances such as alcohol and tobacco. Animal products are not to be consumed either, as it is deemed unnecessary for one to take a life in order to maintain theirs. Processed foods like white sugar are also avoided. Rastas see these products as poisonous tools that Babylon uses to keep the Black person down, as they often lead to health conditions such as obesity, deterioration of mental health, and alcoholism. Although some are less lenient than others with these practices. Marijuana is closely associated with Rastas due to their use of the organically grown herb for its mystical healing properties. However, some Rastas are beginning to see the health risks of smoking and are turning to the use of the herb in alternative forms, such as oil.

> Rum is a part of the metal that they are using on our people to keep us in darkness. . . . It help to create crime and it help to destroy family. . . . Them nuh need the gun, them nuh need the jail, them nuh need no form of weapon more.
>
> —PROF-I[8]

As a part of this livity, many Rastas start their own business ventures in farming, arts, ital cuisine, carpentry, and so on.

> So the fundamental difference you ah go see between the Rastaman and the man who trod under the order of the West is that we hold a culture of independence.
>
> —DR. KADAMAWE KNIFE[9]

Although I must note that Rastas who do seek mainstream employment to support their families are generally not scrutinized by their peers, as long as they are not causing suffering to the earth or others because of the work they do.

Although the two are innately different, I find a connection here to the traditional Buddhist teaching of the Eightfold Path. Those who take a Buddhist way of life try to follow this path as a guidance to the right way of living. A part of the Eightfold Path is to practice "Right Livelihood."

> To practice Right Livelihood, you have to find a way to earn your living without transgressing your ideals of love and compassion.
>
> —THICH NHAT HANH[10]

LOVE AND I-NITY

Like many other words in the Rastas' vocabulary, the word "unity" is often adapted to communicate a deeper message. Changing the "u" in "unity" to an "i" is representative of the Rastafari concept of "I and I"—a way to refer to the oneness of all life and Jah (God) within it.

There are many new terminologies for those who remind people of the importance of protecting nature. However, Rastas believe that as a people, they have existed in every ancient society, coming forward in this time as "Rasta." Music has been a medium through which the message of Rastafari has reached the world. Many reggae artists execute these values profoundly, providing a voice, a source of identity, and a tool of survival for many.

"Sun Is Shining" by singer Bob Marley goes as follows:

> When the morning gather the rainbow,
> Want you to know I'm a rainbow too,
> To the rescue, here I am[11]

This could be taken as a reference to "The Warriors of the Rainbow," a legend of an ancient environmentalist tribe.

Rastas are an example of a people who challenge the status quo, live as one with nature, and stand against all forms of oppression, promoting love, peace, and equality for all.

NIYABINGHI

The name Niyabinghi comes from a legendary African drummer and warrior queen. A Niyabinghi event is when Rastas come together to set up camp at a location in the bush. Here they give praise and thanks to the "Most High," reason with one another, drum, dance, and chant words of upliftment. The people will stay for as long as four days.

> The concept of coming together, just to do good. No buying, no selling, no rush, no timing, no nuttin. You just gather, show love, share food, eat, praise the Most High, and then you go back into the world.
>
> —RAS IYAH[12]

> There is three drums. . . . The *funde* is the one that tells you to do good. Do good to mankind, do good to everybody. . . . The three instruments remind you of who you are and where you came from.
>
> —RAS FLAKO TAFARI[13]

In an interview in 1978, Bob Marley was asked why his music had "changed recently" and if it was because he had stopped "fighting." To which he responded:

> I was at home with my people, so I didn't need to be fighting no more. . . . I was in the camp, and there was no war.[14]

It makes sense to say that the Niyabinghi camp is a space for Rastas to seek refuge from the pressures of Babylon, hold a meditation in the sound of the drums, and become charged with the spiritual strength to defend one's self on the outside.

A LINK TO THE SANGHA

Although many may not have the means to travel to the tropics in order to find a Niyabinghi, one could find something similar in a local sangha (a group of people who come together to practice Buddhist teachings). The sangha will often organize retreats, where they live communally (often in the countryside). Here they hold group meditation, chant, share experiences, take walks in nature, hold periods of silence, nourish with plant-based food, and share the responsibility of cooking, cleaning, and so on, like a family. I must note that you do not need to consider yourself a Buddhist to be part of a sangha.

Although the two events are inherently different, becoming a part of a sangha—specifically one for "People of Color"—can be freeing for the Black person. Being a part of a community where one is not a minority is important here, as it offers a sense of permission, allowing one to feel more deeply involved, find connection, and flourish from one's experience. This sangha can then equip one with intangible tools for liberation.

> Taking refuge in Buddha, Dharma, and Sangha is a fundamental practice in Buddhism. These are universal values that transcend sectarian and cultural boundaries.
>
> —THICH NHAT HANH[15]

CONCLUSION

Finally, I believe taking a Rastafari way of life can emancipate the Black person, particularly the one who does not live in Africa. Although we are African by genetics, being physically torn from our roots has given us a totally different experience of the world than our African native brothers and sisters. The West Indian born and living Rasta will also experience separate struggles than their London-living counterpart. Yet the principle of Rastafari remains the same. Rastafari connects the Black person back to the wisdom already within their DNA through the proper discipline and livity. Although Africa may never be able to literally accommodate all Black people across the world, taking this way of life enables one to reconnect with their true self no matter where they are in the world.

Rastas have created their own Africa, free from the political state of the material Africa. This Africa is of the mind; it guides us on the path to emancipation and can never be taken away. Our spirit will always reside in the Motherland.

NOTES

1 Quoted in Leonard E. Barrett, *The Rastafarians* (Boston: Beacon Press, 1997).

2 A Rasta woman, 1988, quoted in *Omega Rising Women in Rastafari,* Jaylarno (reggae DJ), YouTube, 2013, www.youtube.com /watch?v=onalpomCEGU&t=816s.

3 Morgan Heritage, "Don't Haffi Dread," VP Records, 1999.

4 A Rasta quoted in Ernest Cashmore, *Rastaman* (London: Unwin Paperbacks, 1979).

5 Saffron Saffron, *Chapeltown, Leeds, UK: June 1987—Documentary about Riots after the Arrest of Marcus Skellington,* YouTube, 2019, www.youtube.com/watch? v=cJdC0jYGEv0.

6 Laura Maier, *Rastafari as a Sustainable Lifestyle: Messages from Jamaica,* YouTube, 2015, www.youtube.com/watch?v=KiPs3iUeax0.

7 I Never Knew TV, *Spirituality, Discipline, and Healthy Lifestyle: Rastafari Teachings,* YouTube, 2017, www.youtube.com/watch?v =LmFmNjIsXHE&t=163s.

8 I Never Knew TV, *Alcohol Is Destroying Black People | Prof-I,* YouTube, 2018, www.youtube.com/watch?v=l8NZY3xebAI.

9 Laura Maier, *Rastafari as a Sustainable Lifestyle.*

10 Thich Nhat Hanh, *The Heart of the Buddha's Teaching* (New York: Broadway Books, 1998).

11 Bob Marley, "Sun Is Shining," Tuff Gong, Island Records, 1970.

12 I Never Knew TV, *Chanting Rastafari | Documentary* [the story of Nyahbinghi], YouTube, 2016, www.youtube.com/watch?v=aYP _hfjrGf8.

13 I Never Knew TV, *Chanting Rastafari.*

14 Bob Marley Fan, *Bob Marley—Interview in Norway—1978— Subtitles Video,* YouTube, 2016, www.youtube.com/watch?v =_EFOtZrY1Wc.

15 Thich Nhat Hanh, *The Heart of the Buddha's Teaching.*

VAJRAYANA BUDDHISM

A Path to Healing and Liberation for People of African Descent

by Karla Jackson-Brewer, MS

TIBETANS, LIKE MANY WHO HAVE been forced to flee their country and arrive on distant shores as refugees, entered these new spaces holding on to their history, culture, and spirituality. Not so dissimilarly, people of African descent created Diaspora as a result of a forced migration. They too were initially supported by tribal histories, culture, and spirituality. Colonization, enslavement, and racist oppression created a breach in their connection to traditional African wisdoms and spiritual practices. Cultural and spiritual syncretism, and a strong ability to survive and adapt, fostered the continuation of many of the core beliefs that are visible and activated in African Diasporic communities.

Tibetan refugees, on the other hand, have been able to be the preservers of their traditions and spiritual practices. Outside of the colonized space of Tibet, they have been able to continue the lineage of teachers, wisdom holders, and spiritual practices that have proven themselves to be beneficial not only for Tibetans, but for people throughout the world.

In the West, Buddhism has been introduced through a white lens. Most of the Tibetan teachers and refugee communities have been supported by white folks. Most of the first students of the Vajrayana Tibetan teachers were white. At the time Buddhism entered America, Black communities were involved in political and social liberation struggles, and were working to reclaim our own history, culture, and spiritual practices and wisdoms. One of the outcomes of these sociopolitical dynamics has been that white folks have become the predominant face of Buddhist teachings and institutions. Thanks to the efforts of African American teachers like angel Kyodo williams, Zenju Earthlyn Manuel, Ruth King, Jan Willis, Lama Rod Owens, and many, many others, Buddhism is being challenged to confront and transform its racism, inequity, and bias.

Some people of African descent may believe that Buddhism is too foreign, too different from our Christian or Muslim roots. Some have experienced a coldness, or unwelcoming energy, in Buddhist practice spaces as they attempted to explore or learn about Buddhism. Some left believing that this system had nothing to offer them. Others did not see enough people who looked like them or who could provide the translation of ancient teachings that could benefit their lives. Where are the Black Buddhist practitioners?

In October 2019, a group of 300 Buddhists of Black African descent, teachers and Buddhist practitioners, gathered at Spirit Rock Meditation Center in California. People of many ages, genders, and Buddhist traditions—the embodiment of Buddhist principles in beautiful Black faces. This is a testament to the reality that Buddhism has something precious to offer Black people. It provides a path to liberation. It provides a path that includes meditation practices that are so needed in this time of stress, conflict, and environmental upheaval, around the globe. It offers us a way to truly transform our world. There are numerous schools of Buddhism, which all ascribe to its core tenets—the Four Noble Truths, the Eightfold Path, relative and absolute truth, and a process of liberation. The focus here is Vajrayana (Tibetan) Buddhism.

Vajrayana Buddhism arose around the seventh century AD. It includes aspects of both Sutrayana and Mahayana Buddhism.* It incorporates a Yogic tradition and the knowledge that enlightenment can occur in one lifetime. Vajrayana is often referred to as the "swift path" in Buddhism, primarily because it supports the fact that enlightenment, realization of one's true Buddha-nature, can happen in one lifetime. Vajrayana was strongly influenced by Buddhist Tantra† around the eighth century AD. Tantric Buddhism is the practice of embracing all aspects of life, incorporating them into the path, by seeing the true nature of reality in all things. In Buddhism, the basic understanding of the true nature of anything in the universe, including humans, is referred to as "emptiness awareness," or the awareness that all phenomena, everything in the universe, is void of inherent existence.

---

*The earliest manifestation of Buddhism is called Sutrayana. In short, it focuses on what the Buddha taught. It is a path that encouraged renunciation of the world (monasticism). The next manifestation of Buddhism is called Mahayana Buddhism. Mahayana encompasses Sutrayana, and stresses compassion for all beings, the development of Bodhicitta, and the Bodhisattva.

†Miranda Shaw's *Passionate Enlightenment* is an excellent resource for more information on Tantra.

The word "Tantra" translates as continuum, continuity. The continuity of awareness and luminosity that runs through everything, the union that flows through everything. When practicing Tantra and Vajrayana Buddhism, one is recognizing the interdependence of all things and maintaining the vision of all things in their luminous empty expression. The continuity, the continuum, is this recognition of the luminous manifestation in all things whether we consider them negative, dirty, and ugly; or positive, clean, and beautiful. The essence that flows through all, so to speak, is luminosity. Therefore, all experiences in life may be taken on the path and provide an opportunity to recognize the true nature of things. An analogy used to help us understand interdependence is the lotus growing out of the mud in the river or lake. There is a relationship between the mud that supports the roots and nourishes the lotus into a beautiful flower. This analogy also informs us that Tantric Vajrayana Buddhism is a path of transformation. By challenging the dualistic thinking that the mud is impure and the flower is pure, you can experience the continuity of luminosity through meditation. One can transform one's muddy, encumbered, messy self into a lotus representing the oneness of all things. Vajrayana Buddhism supports that our ordinary lives reveal wisdom, and through inspiration and recognition of wisdom, we can achieve liberation. Buddhism is a way of living, a path that provides numerous strategies and technologies that ultimately lead to liberation from suffering.

During the eighth century, there was an eruption of the principle of the sacred feminine in Vajrayana Buddhism. Tantric practices in Vajrayana Buddhism supported the interaction, the complementarity of the feminine and masculine principles. This is commonly expressed as the interaction between wisdom, represented by the feminine, and skillful means and compassion, represented by the masculine. Neither one is superior to the other, as there is a continual flow between them. They are not inherently different if one recognizes their true nature. The feminine and masculine principles are tools that support one's transformation through practice.

In Tantric Vajrayana Buddhism, practitioners work with the sensory world; we are working with our senses and our emotions rather than denying them or trying to conquer them. Tantra and Vajrayana Buddhism are rich with symbols, colors, sound, scent, taste, rituals, and mantras. Tantra teaches us that emotion, like all things, will arise; however, we do not need to either run from emotion or be overly attached to it. We can observe and recognize the inherent wisdom within emotion. Buddhism is a path that speaks frequently of nonattachment. That does not mean ignoring sensation, or denying feelings; rather, one is encouraged to observe and recognize the true nature of the emotion. We see the continuum of luminosity in our own experience.

Reciting mantra, a practice of sounding sacred syllables, affects our environment and our whole being. People familiar with reciting the syllable Om often experience a peaceful and calming energy. The effect of mantra is not dissimilar to the experience of hearing and singing Black Gospel music. We are moved by the power of sound.

As Black people, we are confronted with the challenges of oppression. Our very lives are physically threatened and harmed with a regularity that is staggering. The coping mechanisms we've developed can entangle us in a web of reactivity. It is difficult to just exist, to actually live with a sense of belongingness, in many of the countries where we reside. The emotional residue of our lives can be overwhelming. Vajrayana Buddhism offers a remedy for this.

Vajrayana Buddhism provides tools to work with events, feelings, and reactions in the world. It provides a spiritual remedy that, when used with regularity, has the potential for bringing us into an enlightened state. Spiritual practices that incorporate working with an enlightened expression of Source, sometimes referred to as deity practice, bring us into direct experience of our Buddha-nature. We can experience, if only for a nanosecond, the embodiment of that enlightened energy. Vajrayana supports embodied experience of Source.

An example of Vajrayana Buddhist practices that can be supportive of Black people's liberation is mandala practice. Mandala is a Sanskrit word that means circle, group, or association. A traditional mandala has a center with four quadrants that are enclosed in a circle. Mandalas are in African art, in nature, and in spiritual imagery. A mandala is a map toward spiritual enlightenment and psychological health.* In practice, a mandala creates a sacred space for transformation to occur. In Vajrayana we can use the mandala principle and deity practice to work intensely on spiritual, physical, and emotional transformation. Within Vajrayana Buddhism, five encumbered, or unevolved, emotional states—ignorance, anger, pride (poverty mentality), craving, and envy—block the experience of one's true nature. It is easy to see how these five emotional states, which can manifest in a host of ways, can disrupt the flow of life, and the experience of ease and peace. In Vajrayana Buddhism, we are not trying to be rid of these emotional states; we are transforming them, more specifically lessening the charge they carry, to be able to see the inherent expression of the five wisdoms—spaciousness, "mirror-like wisdom" (clarity), equanimity, the wisdom of discernment, and all-accomplishing wisdom. These wisdoms are liberating. They free us from the contraction of the encumbered emotions. The five encumbered expressions are a part of the human experience and create a lot of suffering. Just notice how envy causes

---

*For more information on mandalas, see *Wisdom Rising: Journey into the Mandala of the Empowered Feminine* by Tsultrim Allione and the work of Carl Jung.

pain and suffering. In Vajrayana Buddhism these states are not seen as essentially negative; we do not need to conquer them. We only need to transform them and see them in their enlightened expression.

For example, if we are angry, it is easy to hold on to that anger, sometimes for days. There is much suffering created through the expression of anger. Once angry words are spoken, it is nearly impossible to erase their effect. Anger creates contraction. The contraction blocks our ability to be open, and to access clarity (mirror-like wisdom). The term "mirror-like" functions as a metaphor to help us see that a mirror is unchanged by anything it reflects. We see the moon reflected in the lake, but we know that the lake is not holding the moon. The wisdom associated with anger is clarity. Clarity reduces our reactive response to events and supports a deeper understanding of causes and effects of emotional expression. Clarity supports our experience of greater peace. This process of transformation takes place through mandala practices; and when we shift from an encumbered emotional expression to the wisdom expression, the transformation happens on spiritual, energetic, and physical levels. We move inside the mandala, through the center and the four quadrants to activate transformation.

Another Vajrayana Buddhist practice that has so much healing to offer Black people is the practice of Chöd. In short, Chöd is a practice that was developed by an eleventh-century Tibetan woman named Machig Labdrön.* Chöd, translated from the Tibetan, means to cut. What are we cutting? We are cutting our clinging to the concept of a self that is inherently different and distinct from any other thing in the universe. Although in

---

*For more information and a biography of Machig Labdrön, read Tsultrim Allione's *Women of Wisdom* and Jerome Edou's *Machig Labdrön and the Foundations of Chöd.*

our everyday world this may seem to be the case, in the absolute understanding of reality, it is not. Chöd is a practice that uses sacred instruments: a double-headed drum, called a *damaru,* and a bell. In pre-colonial Tibet, Chöd was used as a healing practice. Chöd practitioners would travel to villages and heal epidemics and illnesses in humans and animals. Chöd is also a powerful practice for confronting and transforming what blocks one on an emotional, energetic, and physical level. There is much evidence today that supports the efficacy of Chöd as a healing practice. The underlying philosophy that Machig taught is that things that block our enlightenment, or our lives, can be transformed through the action of offering rather than fighting or attempting to conquer.

Lama Tsultrim Allione developed a more accessible practice for Westerners, based on Chöd. The practice is called Feeding Your Demons™. For many, the idea of feeding demons is horrifying. Why would you feed something that is negative? Wouldn't it just become stronger? The answer is no. Machig used the term "demon" to represent all things that block us, that block our enlightenment. Today, we can see how addictions, fears, beliefs, illnesses, or worries muck up our lives and block our experience of happiness and peace. In this context, demons are not the constructions of Hollywood movies, or even the devil. They are our unresolved issues. Feeding Your Demons™ takes the practice of Chöd and combines it with techniques of Western psychology based on the Gestalt therapy technique of interacting with aspects of your psyche, and your dreams, through conversation with those images. Externalizing a feeling gives us an opportunity to examine it outside of ourselves. By forming it into a being, we create a more concrete image of what internally may feel too amorphous. By asking questions in this process, all of the answers are located in our own psyches.

For example, if you are afraid of the dark, you can use Feeding Your Demons (Tara Mandala) FYD™ to locate where you are holding the energy of this fear in your body. In a five-step process, you can interact with this fear and learn what it really needs, and how it would feel when it gets what it really needs. The process has you moving between your perspective and the demon's perspective to access information. This information is transformed into a nectar that feeds the demon until complete satisfaction. Once satisfied, an ally is invited to appear who provides information on the specific help it offers.* When you offer to anyone or anything exactly what it needs, the energy relaxes. The struggle dissipates. Think about a time when you were really thirsty. Your throat is dry and raspy; all you can focus on is quenching that thirst. You might not be able to think so clearly because you are so focused on satisfying your thirst. You take that first sip of cool, refreshing liquid, and your whole being, your whole body relaxes. This is the effect of Chöd. These practices effectively end suffering, whether it be physical, mental, emotional, or spiritual.

Vajrayana Buddhism has so much to offer Black people in the support of our liberation and ultimate freedom. I invite you to explore Buddhism in general, and Vajrayana specifically. I am not asking you to give up your spiritual traditions. Buddhist practices can enhance our connection to our spiritual life and provide tools and techniques that can truly transform the suffering we experience. Vajrayana Buddhism is a spiritual path that supports liberation on both an individual and a community level. Vajrayana Buddhism has the ability to transform the world.

---

*For more detailed information regarding the Feeding Your Demons™ practice, go to www.taramandala.org, and see Tsultrim Allione, *Feeding Your Demons: Ancient Wisdom for Resolving Inner Conflict.*

KWANZAA IN CANADA

by Dr. Afua Cooper

AFRICAN CANADIANS AND BLACKS around the world celebrate Kwanzaa, a cultural holiday, from December 26 to January 1. Celebrants commemorate the history and culture, and the survival, struggles, resilience, and triumphs, of Black families and communities. Kwanzaa was born within the struggle of African Americans during the civil rights era.

In 1966, Maulana Karenga, an American professor of Black studies, devised and held the first Kwanzaa celebrations in North America. The word Kwanzaa is taken from the Ki-Swahili language, spoken in East and Central Africa, and means "first fruits." It is modeled on the various African first fruits or harvest festivals and, as such, is a time of thanksgiving. Karenga chose the Nguzo Saba, or seven principles, as a method for restoring a knowledge of African culture to Blacks around the world.

SEVEN PRINCIPLES

Each day of Kwanzaa "first fruits" is named after one of the Nguzo Saba (the seven principles):

First Day: Umoja

This means unity. *Umoja* reminds us that even though Canadian Blacks come from diverse backgrounds and ethnicities, we are all one. One example of unity is Tiamoyo, a camp for Black youth founded by Joanne Atherly.

Second Day: Kujichagulia

This means self-determination. Only African Canadians can decide what is best for them. An example of *kujichagulia* is the building of the Jamaican Canadian Community Centre in Toronto.

Third Day: Ujima

This means working together and taking responsibility for the problems that afflict Black families and communities. An example of *ujima* in African Canada is the building of schools by Black teachers and parents in nineteenth-century Ontario when the separate school act of 1850 denied many Black children access to education.

Fourth Day: Ujamaa

This means building cooperative economies. The Afri-Can Food-Basket initiative founded by Xola is an expression of *ujamaa*. It is a nonprofit organization that has been at the forefront of championing food justice and food sovereignty for Toronto's African, Caribbean, Black (ACB) community since 1995.

Fifth Day: Nia

This means purpose. One example of *nia* is the founding in 1851 of the *Voice of the Fugitive,* Canada's first Black newspaper, by abolitionists Mary Bibb and Henry Bibb.

Sixth Day: Kuumba

This means creativity. Black Canadian artists have exemplified this: Deborah Cox's music and lyrics are *kuumba*, Althea Prince's stories are *kuumba*, and Vivine Scarlett's dance rhythms are *kuumba*.

Seventh Day: Imani

Imani means faith. Through *imani*, Harriet Tubman led more than 300 enslaved Americans into freedom. Many of these escapees came to live in Canada.

The Nguzo Saba stresses communitarian values, which are the foundation of African culture and traditions.

SEVEN SYMBOLS

There are also seven symbols of Kwanzaa; these express the multiple meanings of Kwanzaa. Before the celebrations begin on December 26, the symbols are arranged on a Kwanzaa table. The symbols are:

1. The *mkeka* is a mat made of straw or fabric. The other symbols are placed on it. The *mkeka* acts as a foundation of our history and traditions.

2. The *mazao* are fruits and vegetables, and symbolize the earth's fertility and abundance.

3. The *muhindi,* or ears of corn, represent growth, life, and prosperity. An ear of corn is placed on the *mkeka*

for each child in the family or each child present at the dinners.

4. The **kikombe cha umoja** or unity cup symbolizes *umoja*. At the dinners on the first and last days of Kwanzaa, each celebrant takes a sip from the *kikombe*.

5. The **kinara,** or candleholder, is placed in the middle of the table. The *kinara* acts as a "groundation" for the seven candles that are placed in it, thus bringing the seven principles into a unified whole. The *kinara* is important because, in addition to being a celebration of first fruits, Kwanzaa is also a festival of light.

6. The **mishumaa saba** are the seven candles. Each candle represents each principle and day of Kwanzaa. Three red candles are on the left, three green candles on the right, and in the center, a black candle. The colors of the candles are symbolic:

   • Red stands for the blood and energy of Africans.

   • Green symbolizes hope and love.

   • Black represents the Black faces of Africans and African descendant peoples.

   These are the colors of the *bandera,* or Pan-African flag, and have the same meaning. On the first evening of Kwanzaa, at dinnertime, the black candle is lit; on each successive evening, the other candles are lit. Around the lighted candles, people eat and talk about the day's happenings. Most importantly, they talk about the meaning of a particular principle and its practical application to everyday life.

7. The **zawadi,** or gifts, are given to children on the day of *imani* (faith). It is encouraged that gifts be

homemade to express *kuumba* (creativity) and *ujima* (working together and taking responsibility).

FOOD, FAMILY, AND FEAST

Each day of Kwanzaa is a celebration of Black cuisine.

Preparing and partaking of the food together reinforces the bond and identity of Africans. At day's end, families gather to nurture themselves with food and each other's words.

On the sixth day of Kwanzaa, *kuumba* (creativity), there is a great feast or *karamu*. The Kwanzaa Committee of Toronto usually hosts a *karamu*. Because it is such a huge feast, the *karamu* is held in a community center, a church hall, or a large restaurant. Some favorite dishes of the *karamu* are stewed snapper, Congo rice and peas, fried chicken, baked potato pie, corn bread and callaloo, jollof rice, and vegetable ital stew.

At the *karamu*, celebrants express *kuumba* in dances, songs, artwork, speeches, and the viewing of films. In commemorating the past, we remember the Black sheroes and heroes.

Some African Canadian sheroes (past and present) that we celebrate and remember include: Marie-Joseph Angélique, Mary Bibb, Chloe Cooley, Rose Fortune, Sylvia Stark, Mattie Hayes, Viola Blackman, Rosemary Brown, Mary Ann Shadd Cary, Portia White, Monifa Owusu, and Juanita Westmoreland-Traoré. Civil rights activist Viola Desmond, Canada's own Rosa Parks, who refused to leave a white-only section of a cinema in New Glasgow in 1946, is on the 2018 Canadian $10 bill.

Kwanzaa is a holiday that stresses the importance of family and community. Women, as keepers of our history, tradition, and culture, play a central role in Kwanzaa. In addition, women are the ones primarily responsible for the preparation of food necessary for the sustenance and maintenance of life. Also, in Black Canada, women have been at the forefront of community building.

RESOURCES FOR THIS STORY

MULTIMEDIA

Worlds of Fire (in Motion), poems by Afua Cooper, CD, Slam Productions, 2002.

The Meaning of Kwanzaa: Values to Live by Throughout the Year, by Akwatu Khenti, Kushitic Inspirations, phone: 416-281-6041, 2000.

BOOKS

Kwanzaa: An Everyday Resource and Instructional Guide, by David A. Anderson, Gumbs and Thomas, 1992.

Kwanzaa: A Celebration of Family, Community and Culture, by Maulana Karenga, University of Sankore Press, 1998.

Seven Candles for Kwanzaa, by Andrea Davis Pinkney, Dial Books, 1993.

The Story of Kwanzaa, by Donna L. Washington, HarperCollins, 1996.

This feature was first published on section15.ca's predecessor site CoolWomen.

AFRICANITY

An Interview with an African Elder Priestess

by Valerie Mason-John (Vimalasara)

To be who you are is true liberation; walk your own pace—
and your own step.

—MAMA YAA

MAMA YAA IS AN AFRICAN elder and priestess. She has studied several of the main religions. I had the good fortune to be
on an African descent retreat, led by the elder Malidoma Patrice
Somé. She brought a case full of spirits in bottles. None for consuming, the spirits were for rubbing in the crown of our heads
and poured onto the earth. So we could be in touch with our
ancestral lineage and the strength of the intoxicating spirits.

Small and fierce, Mama Yaa told me you have everything you need. Expand, the world needs all of us right now. Keep on teaching, beyond your comfort zone. Let the ancestors guide you. Mama Yaa debunked enlightenment as the ultimate goal, and reminded me that African tradition is about interconnectedness and uplifting the whole community.

ENLIGHTENMENT IS THE THING THESE DAYS. HOW DO WE GAIN ENLIGHTENMENT THROUGH THE BLACK EXPERIENCE, MAMA YAA?

For the African to walk in our own pace—that is liberation freed from others' and the injected system of what is right and what is wrong. However, when I think of enlightenment, it's a European construct. When you look it up, you see a lot of European faces. I think of Africanity, which is *umoja,* unity: people together, and building and supporting each other. That is the concept of a well-lived life.

WHAT WOULD IT TAKE FOR BLACK PEOPLE TO FIND TRUE FREEDOM AND LIBERATION?

I don't think liberation for the masses is attainable in the Americas in this system. This system wasn't developed for Africans—it's for the improvement of white Europeans. Of course, liberation is attainable and has been attained by many individuals who have taken their freedom without apology. And there continues to be many who are claiming their liberation without apology. Community ancestors like Marcus Garvey and his wife, Amy Jacques Garvey, men like Malcolm X, and women like Harriet Tubman achieved this too. In the African Diaspora we must be aware that other people have defined us, and have put the words onto what our experience is.

WHAT IS IT THAT HELPED YOU TRANSFORM YOUR OWN LIFE?

What is it that helped you transform your own life?

I was raised as a Garveyite. I have always been aware of who I am from my little childhood in the 1940s. I am African. I was raised in segregation, in the Boston ghetto, which was a blessing. All I saw was Black people being themselves. I was raised in that loving womb in my early years growing up. There wasn't anything I needed to transform. I just needed to continue on the path that was set. I knew I was a child of God and I was deserving of certain things. This was part of the catechism of growing up under the teachings of a man like Garvey. I spent a lot of time with my grandparents. They were rock solid Africans. They grew up in a slave colony in the West Indies. The only stories I heard or recountings of their pasts were to introduce me to my family lines. Also, by living their lives in front of me and showing me examples of how to live, they kept the ugliness of the American experience from my consciousness until I was in my late teen years.

WHAT IS ANCESTRALIZATION AND WHY IS IT IMPORTANT FOR OUR COMMUNITIES?

Ancestralization is something that happens when families get together. It is natural to talk about people who are no longer with us—to talk about them, give them a drink, hang their pictures, talk to them. Films like *Harriet* are part of ancestralization. It's nice of Hollywood to catch up to the wonder of our past, but many of my community have been studying the truth for a long time.

When I was growing up in the neighborhood, on most evenings, the men would gather together on the corner. They would gather after work to drink beer or hard liquor. I noticed they had a habit of pouring liquor on the ground before drinking. I got curious and asked them what they were doing. It was explained to me that this was a traditional habit from Africa. It was a remembrance of those who were no longer with us. Looking back, none of these men had a direct connection to Africa in their experience; it was just something that had been passed down from generation to generation.

This practice that many of us still have makes us understand that there is a continuation of life. At these gathering times, there were often stories told of people who were no longer with us. It was a continuation of life whether in the body or not. In African tradition, even after your demise you are still present in the African community. It's a natural thing—because we believe there is a continuation of living and that we are eternal and cannot be extinguished.

WHAT TEACHINGS DO YOU HAVE TO OFFER? AND WHAT TRADITION DO THEY COME FROM?

I've studied everything I had access to: Christianity, Pentecostalism, Islam, Theosophy, and African American traditionalism. I've studied jazz music and the drums as a religion, because they cleanse the heart and clear the mind, which is what religion is supposed to help us do. True African drummers are priests; they are healers. They know when the deity is coming. It's important for those of us in the Diaspora to link back to some of the traditional religions and their American offshoots like Santería, Hoodoo, and Vodoun.

The Bible is one of the richest grimoires I have ever read of anything that I have picked up in a European structure. When we African prisoners of war were brought to this country, we had to syncretize our religion with the Catholic Church and Christianity. The text is full of witchcraft and drama. I find the same things often in textbooks of Vodoun and Hoodoo and metaphysical magic.

WHAT OTHER ORGANIZATIONS OR SPIRITUAL TRADITIONS, IF ANY, DO YOU BELONG TO?

I was a Mason. Masonry was practiced by men in my family. I found a Masonic practice out of France that acknowledged all genders. This was completely necessary for being part of the Masons while living in the sleazy environment of the USA, where the police have complete license to kill my children. For me, Masonry helps me to be on the square and be on the straight and narrow, and within ritual. This practice encourages me to bring in all the other trainings I have had in terms of my understanding of the continuation of life. I have learned how to stand up straight in my body, and march with the correct step in life and not go crazy. It helps me to remember my true position and rank at all times and have a workable plan. We need something to keep us standing straight when the police are killing our children at will. Masonry has been an important piece of my maturing and staying alive in this country. When you study Masonry, you will learn that its origin is ancient KMT, the ancient name for Egypt.

I've been part of the Akan religion too. The Akan trained me to be a priest. With the teaching of the Akan drums, you have no idea; it just has to be experienced. We reconnect to the African soil and have connections with the deities. This has opened me up to a new way of experiencing myself through the ancestral line. Many deities are ancestors; they were human and deified because of their compassionate and courageous acts.

IN YOUR VIEW, HOW IMPORTANT ARE "SHAMANS"? HOW DO YOU DESCRIBE YOURSELF?

Shaman is not an African word; in Africa we are priests. We live a life dedicated to the deities and the concepts that they represent. My spirit represents the mothering concept in humans, with the responsibility of developing a clear and clarified will within each of the children in her care. Being part of an African traditional experience is important. The people of "two spirits" are highly esteemed in some of the traditions, having a special connection in Spirit. Not everyone is born in the same way.

I am a seeker of truth. I want to find out what it's all about—that's why I was put here. I am a student—just getting out of kindergarten. I appreciate you.

Aphorisms from Mama Yaa

"Free your mind—your arse will follow."

"By whatever means necessary."

"When I get around the deeply melaninated—I am free."

PART THREE

Social Justice:
The Revival of an Old Religion

BLACK LIVES MATTER

An Anthem for Intersectional Black Liberation

by Cicely Belle Blain

BLACK LIVES MATTER.

I have heard these three words more than I have heard my own name this year: the year of a halting pandemic, a global Black uprising spurred by the deaths of George Floyd and Breonna Taylor, ongoing protests for Indigenous sovereignty and land rights across Turtle Island, and so much more.

Humanity is bursting at the seams with grief, rage, and uncertainty—those of us whose lives are dedicated to the liberation of the oppressed, even more so. The world, it seems, has woken up to the realities of systemic racism, the violence of capitalism, the inequity of so many current systems. The optimist in me asks: Is this the year it all changes?

But others have asked that question before—Sojourner Truth in 1851; Martin Luther King Jr. in 1968; Alicia Garza in 2013. The question of when and how our liberation comes is the biggest one of every Black activist movement in history. It is the question that unites and divides social justice communities as we come together—and apart—determining the most effective methods for change. Violent or nonviolent? Systemic or personal? Direct or passive? Streets or boardrooms?

As activists, we are fighting against systemic oppression, state-sanctioned violence, dehumanization of our people. And sometimes, we are fighting against each other as we, inhabitants of a white supremacist world, inadvertently perpetuate the very harmful structures we are trying to dismantle. Activism is exhausting, painful, and at times demoralizing. We continue to shout into the void—and hear our cries echo back at us from the cavernous darkness. That optimistic voice within me is quickly quieted.

My reflections on Black Lives Matter begin this way because, in a year like 2020, optimism does not get one very far.

Yet, something keeps me hooked to this movement. That "something" I boil down to be intersectional feminism. A term much overused by corporations pretending to be woke, white women distancing themselves from white feminism, and academics who love long words. A concept that has, for me, been most actualized by the Black Lives Matter movement.

Black Lives Matter is a movement that picks up the torch from previous generations of Black activists. Not only that, Black Lives Matter pushes the boundaries of Black activist collectives in ways that were not possible for those who came before us. While organizing with Black Lives Matter Vancouver, I was frequently asked, "What would MLK think of BLM?"

It's a question that always struck me as strange until I realized that for so many people—Black and non-Black alike—it was hard to fathom a Black Liberation movement that extended beyond the borders of cisgender American masculinity. They asked me this question—perhaps subconsciously—because the idea of a Black Liberation movement led by queer and transgender women and nonbinary people seemed incongruous. Furthermore, the idea of a global Black uprising—one that transcends borders, one that is applicable outside of North America— contrasted with our US-centric understandings of Black activism.

When I founded the second Black Lives Matter chapter in Canada with a group of Black women and femmes, we were, of course, met with resistance. On the surface, this resistance was the (false) assertion that "Black Lives Matter is an American issue!" The movement was founded in the United States by Alicia Garza, Patrisse Cullors, and Opal Tometi in 2013. But neither the sanctity of Black life nor the systemic anti-Blackness we fight against are unique to America.

As with any country formed by or in relationship with European colonialism, Canada has done so based on anti-Black and anti-Indigenous racism. But it doesn't end—or possibly even begin—there. Anti-Blackness is a global phenomenon, exacerbated by the increasingly interconnected nature of our world. As Opal Tometi says, "The reality is that anti-Black racism is everywhere—globalized in large part by the legacy of the enslavement of people of African descent, the colonial legacy and the current neo-colonial relations."[1] Black people I met in Seoul shared remarkably similar stories to Black people I met in London, Amsterdam, Quito, Bordeaux, and Vancouver. While the form and shape of anti-Blackness may differ, the roots and, most importantly, the pain are devastatingly similar.

Beneath the surface, the vitriol, death threats, and general anti-BLM rhetoric were also rooted in misogyny, homophobia, and transphobia. Much of the language directed at us was either patronizing, oversexualizing, fetishizing, tone-policing, or some combination of them all. Leaders who were cis men, of course, received their fair share of racist abuse but never in the same dehumanizing way that Black women and nonbinary leaders did (and still do), especially dark-skinned trans women. I began to notice this was not unique to our experience on the West Coast. The pervasive vilification of BLM leaders across Canada was markedly gendered. It is not dissimilar to how we remember and idolize Martin Luther King Jr., Malcolm X, and Nelson Mandela but forget (or intentionally erase) the contributions of their wives and other significant women and queer folks in Black Liberation movements.

This experience was compounded by lateral violence. While, in principle, many Black folks in Canada (and everywhere) were excited to see the BLM movement's extension across borders, many took issue with the leadership. Not only were we being targeted by non-Black people, but our peers also took issue with the queer- and trans-centered leadership of Black Lives Matter. In my tenure as a BLM activist, this came to a head when we championed an initiative to remove police from Pride.

At this point, a notable fracture happened. Black folks who were previously grateful for, or at least curious about, the Black Liberation movement's possibilities on their shores drew themselves an invisible line of intolerance and refused to cross it. "It's run by a bunch of lesbians!" read one Facebook comment that sticks out in my mind for its inaccuracy and irrelevance.

We came to realize that intersectionality in action was complicated for many to fathom—even if they were part of marginalized groups. As Black Lives Matter Vancouver and Black Lives Matter as a global movement and ideology became publicly more queer- and trans-centered, we came up against resistance on a million more fronts. In the fight for liberation, our alignment with LGBTQ2S+ rights apparently seemed more like a betrayal rather than an expansion of the movement to those who could not extricate themselves from colonial Christian imperialism. In 2017 we planned our first "March on Pride" in Vancouver—a pro-Black, inclusive, anti-police-brutality march through the heart of Vancouver's "gay village."

In *Burning Sugar*,[1] I describe the painful, transformative experience of that march.

> We stood at the foothills of Davie Street; she seemed dormant, unexpecting, pressing snooze on liberation. Rainbow flags fluttered limply in the summer breeze, and despite being in the heart of downtown, the air felt like slumber.
>
> Until we marched.
>
> The street awoke with the clang of our resilience ricocheting off the blank stares and raised eyebrows. They stared, we marched, they stared, we marched.
>
> The rainbow crosswalk lay waiting for us, simultaneously bright and dull, unprepared for the arrival of our Black bodies. We lay down, our limbs splayed, deformed from the centuries of violence rippling in our skin. We had the phone number of a lawyer written on our bodies—the permanent ink stayed for days as a reminder of how unsafe we are. Comrades drew white chalk outlines around us, leaving evidence of a million unsolved crimes.

A fellow activist wrote the following words:

> And so a group of queer, trans, and non-binary Black youth were assailed by our own queer community, white gay men who refused to acknowledge that their feelings of safety were not the same as others', people who thought "Black issues" didn't belong in Pride, police apologists of all stripes, members of the Black community for bringing uncomfortable conversations into their circles, and garden variety suburban white supremacist trolls.[2]

This first march and all the subsequent ones I attended came to be the most powerful moments of my life. Black Lives Matter's intersectional focus and its origins rooted deeply in Black, queer, femme leadership meant it was a movement fiercely committed to those existing within the margins of the margins. In this space, my Black, queer, nonbinary identity was validated and celebrated—something I had not experienced in Black spaces led by cisgender straight folks or queer spaces led by white folks.

Kimberlé Williams Crenshaw, the designer of the intersectionality theory, facilitates a powerful activity in her 2016 TED Talk. She asks the audience to stand up and then to sit down and stay seated as soon as they hear a name they don't recognize. "Eric Garner. Mike Brown. Tamir Rice . . ."[3] she starts with. "Michelle Cusseaux. Tanisha Anderson. Aura Rosser . . ." she continues, and by this point, almost everyone is sitting down.

The second set of names Crenshaw lists are all women. In this talk, and through the evolution of the intersectionality concept that she initially coined in 1989, Crenshaw reminds us of the compounding impacts of racism and sexism on Black women. Even more so for Black trans women experiencing racism, transphobia, and transmisogyny.

The adaptation of academic analysis into practice is what makes the evolution of Black Lives Matter so powerful. A movement that started to draw attention to police violence and the unlawful murders of Black men and boys has in just seven years expanded to shed light on the violence experienced by Black people who are women (cis and trans), nonbinary, queer, living with disabilities, poor, neurodivergent, immigrant, or otherwise marginalized in a white supremacist society. I believe this kind of growth is only possible within a movement led by those very people who are traditionally excluded from not only society at large but even movements that tout themselves as radical.

On May 25, 2020, Minneapolis police killed George Floyd, a rapper, father, and mentor from North Carolina.[4] His death spurred nationwide and then global outrage. The months that followed were remarkable—I remember pinching myself as I spoke on Canadian breakfast television about anti-Blackness and white supremacy. Is this the year it all changes?

Why did George Floyd's death spark such a response? I do not know if I will ever have the answer; for many Black activists, his name is added to a long list of ancestors-gone-too-soon—a list that we have been crying out in the streets since forever. Perhaps the collective frustration and desire for justice as a pandemic exposed the undeniable inequities in our society and capitalism's fragility. What I do know, however, is that 2020 was the year that many Pride societies across Turtle Island did ban police from participating in their future parades. In all the smoke and mirrors of black squares on Instagram and mostly-nonsense "solidarity" statements, something definitely shifted.

Collectively, our ability to talk about—and respond to—racism expanded. I went into (virtual) boardrooms with my Afro picked out and a Black Excellence chain around my neck; I attended 10,000-person-strong protests in otherwise sleepy Vancouver; I picked up magazines with Black trans women on the cover; I applied for funding for Black entrepreneurs; I saw a 1,000 percent increase in traffic on my anti-racism consulting website.[5]

Most powerfully, the world paid attention to the death of Breonna Taylor. Taylor was a twenty-six-year-old health care professional from Kentucky who was shot and killed in her own apartment by Louisville police.[6] Instead of her story being filed away with the others on Crenshaw's list of forgotten women, Justice for Breonna Taylor and Arrest the Killers of Breonna Taylor became everything from war cries to TikTok anthems.

A world in rage over the death of a Black woman is a world waking up. Is this the year it all changes? No, but it is certainly the year something changed. I'm holding on to that.

NOTES

1 Blain, Cicely Belle, *Burning Sugar* (VS Books, an Imprint of Arsenal Pulp Press, 2020).

2 Anonymous, "Ain't I a Queer? A Letter to the Vancouver Pride Society on Black Lives Matter," *Medium*, August 22, 2020, http://medium.com/@moveonover/aint-i-a-queer-af71da502234.

3 Crenshaw, Kimberlé Williams, "The Urgency of Intersectionality," *TED*, November 2016, www.ted.com/talks/kimberle_crenshaw_the_urgency_of_intersectionality.

4 "Mr. George Floyd Jr.—View Obituary & Service Information," Mr. George Floyd Jr. Obituary, www.estesfuneralchapel.com/obituaries/George-Floyd-7/.

5 Yoshida-Butryn, Carly, "B.C. Diversity, Equity and Inclusion Consulting Firm Sees 1,000% Spike in Web Traffic," *CTV News*, June 5, 2020, http://bc.ctvnews.ca/b-c-diversity-equity-and-inclusion-consulting-firm-sees-1-000-spike-in-web-traffic-1.4970032.

6 "Shooting of Breonna Taylor," *Wikipedia*, Wikimedia Foundation, October 14, 2020, http://en.wikipedia.org/wiki/Shooting_of_Breonna_Taylor.

A TWELVE-STEP APPROACH EXPLORING CULTURAL BIAS, RACISM, AND OTHERISM

by Rev. Seiho Mudo Morris

A TWELVE-STEP APPROACH TO CLEARLY seeing and addressing the experience of cultural bias, racism, and otherism that we as persons of African descent and Black Indigenous People of Color experience.

Long ago, the famed Zen master Dōgen Kigen wrote a summation of an insight:

> To study the Buddha Way is to study the self.
> To study the self is to forget the self.
> To forget the self is to be awakened by all things.
> To be awakened by all things is to remove the barrier
>   between self and other.

For me, it has evolved over the years, especially with regard to cultural bias, racism, and otherism. Today I would restate it as:

> To study the Way is to examine cultural bias, racism, and otherism.
> To examine cultural bias, racism, and otherism is to remember our Ancestors.
> To remember our Ancestors is to meet our Generational madness.
> To meet our Generational madness is to heal our individual and collective suffering, through the path of anti-racism.

To journey this path of examining cultural bias, racism, and otherism as a step toward freedom, I combined and then applied two frameworks, mutually supportive and harmonious, toward meeting the difficult circumstances perpetuated by greed, hatred, and delusion. The first is the Twelve Steps, developed by early members of Alcoholics Anonymous Bill Wilson and Dr. Bob Smith, which since their inception have been adapted and used by many, to address a wide range of addictions and adverse behaviors. The other is the Four Noble Truths and the Eightfold Path as taught by Shakyamuni Buddha.

THE FOUR NOBLE TRUTHS OF CULTURAL BIAS, RACISM, AND OTHERISM

The first truth is that cultural bias, racism, and otherism lead to unmanageability and suffering. This is the first truth. It's a way of seeing that's out of balance, wherein nothing beautiful or wise can come of it.

The second truth is people are addicted to the system of cultural bias, racism, and otherism. Because we can be so conditioned, attached, to the cultural bias, racism, and otherism, suffering is compounded.

The third truth is that we open ourselves to the possibility that we can reduce or end our suffering. That through conscious and intentional effort, we can address the insanity of cultural bias, racism, and otherism in such a way that we are free from its toxic nature. This includes the common symptoms of diminishment of personhood. The dissembling of one's character. The dismemberment and delegitimizing of one's life experience in an effort to erase meaningful accomplishments, because of an irrational ideology contrived about and connected to Black and brown bodies.

And the fourth truth is: here's a reliable path that instead of allowing our personhood, our center of gravity, to be in the hands of others explicitly, we can use this intertwined framework of the Eightfold Path and Twelve Steps to offer a different way of being that is far freer than what we've been conditioned to in the past. Freedom from the mindlessness and fecklessness of cultural bias, racism, and otherism is the goal. This is offered as a process rather than an event for us to practice with, in solidarity and togetherness.

THE RELIABLE PATH

1. We admitted that we lack consistent clarity toward cultural bias, racism, and otherism; that, when not addressed, can influence unmanageability and suffering for ourselves and others.

2. We came to believe that Ahimsa, the Eightfold Path, and skillful means is a power greater than cultural bias, racism, and otherism, capable of relieving its dysfunction.

3. We decided to meet and address cultural bias, racism, and otherism through practices and actions rooted in

Ahimsa, the Eightfold Path, and skillful means, as we understand it in the present moment.

4. We made a searching and fearless inventory of our experiences related to cultural bias, racism, and otherism, including our values, examining and exploring how it impacts us individually and collectively.

5. We opened to dialogue, process, and explored the exact nature of cultural bias, racism, and otherism, and how this creates unmanageability and suffering within ourselves and others, rooted in Ahimsa, the Eightfold Path, and skillful means.

6. We consciously and intentionally cultivate our willingness to practice Ahimsa, the Eightfold Path, and skillful means to help relieve us of the unmanageability and suffering, influenced and caused by cultural bias, racism, and otherism.

7. We consciously and intentionally physically, mentally, emotionally, and spiritually, act to address cultural bias, racism, and otherism within ourselves and others, rooted in Ahimsa, the Eightfold Path, and skillful means.

8. We made a list of all persons harmed that we are aware of as a result of cultural bias, racism, and otherism; and became willing to begin a process of healing the wounds caused by cultural bias, racism, and otherism, to the best of our personal ability.

9. We offer clear and direct support, heal and lift up those harmed by cultural bias, racism, and otherism—wherever possible, except when to do so would injure them or others—through Ahimsa, the Eightfold Path, and skillful means.

10. We continued to take personal inventory, and when we noticed the arising of cultural bias, racism, and otherism, within ourselves or others, promptly addressed its occurrence through our values, Ahimsa, the Eightfold Path, and skillful means.

11. We sought through prayer and meditation to improve our conscious contact with and awareness of Ahimsa, the Eightfold Path, and skillful means, cultivating our ability to carry these principles out.

12. Having had a spiritual awakening as a result of these steps, we live and carry this message, reducing the suffering influenced by cultural bias, racism, and otherism. We accomplish this through Ahimsa, the Eightfold Path, and skillful means to the best of our ability in all of our affairs.

How to work the path and turn toward your cultural bias, racism, and otherism.

STEP ONE | *We admitted that we lack consistent clarity toward cultural bias, racism, and otherism; that, when not addressed, can influence unmanageability and suffering for ourselves and others.*

VERSE OF PURIFICATION

All the cultural bias, racism, and otherism, ever conditioned within and projected toward me, since of old, whether consciously or unconsciously, on account of beginning-less fear, conditioning, or misunderstanding, I am now willing to turn toward them, address, and dissolve them all.

We didn't create cultural bias, racism, and otherism, we didn't cause it, and we can't cure it; but we can learn to meet it in such a way that reduces our entanglement, that reduces our experience of harm and suffering.

How? By not merely admitting its presence, but also turning into it, using the Four Truths and the Eightfold Path as an expression of our skillful means, as pieces of a jigsaw puzzle to relieve our suffering.

FOUR TRUTHS

Dukkha | The weather conditions and waves on the surface of the ocean aren't stable, and the water is often choppy. Cultural bias, racism, and otherism are points of consistent unmanageability and suffering because of the conditioned culture of patriarchy and whiteness, whether there is conscious awareness of it or not.

Samudaya | We mistake the waves for the entire ocean. Attachment and compulsion to upholding differences of cultural bias, racism, and otherism are caused by a combination of a distorted sense of self, disconnection from healthy interpersonal relatedness, and lack of sympathy (empathy + positive caring); influenced by pervasive cultural conditioning and bias that are also manifested through various forms of "structural" and "systemic" violence.

Nirodha | There is a way to navigate the ocean. Despite the waves, choppy water, and storms. Despite the repetitive experience of cultural bias, racism, and otherism, there are ways it can be addressed, responded to, diluted, and disrupted that lessen harm and suffering to oneself and so-called others.

Marga | To navigate our way through the waves, storms, and choppy waters, we use the compass of Ahimsa, the Eightfold Path, and skillful means.

STEP TWO | We came to believe that Ahimsa, the Eightfold Path, and skillful means is a power greater than cultural bias, racism, and otherism, capable of relieving its dysfunction.

EIGHTFOLD PATH

Sincere concentration: Alertness, attentiveness, taking notice, and open awareness to the reality of our personal and shared experience.

Sincere mindfulness and presence: Active listening. Looking not only from our perspective but from the other point of view as well.

Sincere effort (ethics): What are my values? Are they clear to me? Ten Precepts

Sincere livelihood: Livelihood that has an awareness of cultural bias or racism, with a willingness toward equality and equity.

Sincere actions: Physical, mental, emotional, and spiritual congruence and moving in the same direction.

Sincere intentions: Goals that lead toward inclusivity and deepening wholesome relationships. Sympathy (empathy + caring). Practices that disrupt the conditioning, norms, and structural and systemic violence.

Sincere speech: Honesty, integrity, and authenticity grounded in kindness. Verbal and behavioral congruence (what we're doing is matching what we're saying).

Sincere understanding: Open-mindedness . . . awakening . . . relating to ourselves and others with a policy of caring, to the best of our current ability.

STEP THREE | We decided to meet and address cultural bias, racism, and otherism through practices and actions rooted in Ahimsa, the Eightfold Path, and skillful means, as we understand it in the present moment.

EIGHTFOLD PATH PUT INTO ACTION

- What could "sincere concentration" look like for me, in a clear and measurable way?

- What could "sincere mindfulness and presence" look like for me, in a clear and measurable way?

- What could "sincere effort (ethics)" look like for me, in a clear and measurable way?

- What could "sincere livelihood" look like for me, in a clear and measurable way?

- What could "sincere actions" look like for me, in a clear and measurable way?

- What could "sincere intentions" look like for me, in a clear and measurable way?

- What could "sincere speech" look like for me, in a clear and measurable way?

- What could "sincere understanding" look like for me, in a clear and measurable way?

STEP FOUR | We made a searching and fearless inventory of our experiences related to cultural bias, racism, and otherism, including our values, examining and exploring how it impacts us individually and collectively.

What are my historical conditioning, cultural biases, or feelings of racism or otherism that can either trigger or influence me?

How do my historical conditioning, cultural biases, or feelings of racism or otherism affect me in real time?

What are the internal or external resources that I could invite myself into, allowing me to meet my historical conditioning, cultural biases, racism, or otherism?

STEP FIVE | *We opened to dialogue, process, and explored the exact nature of cultural bias, racism, and otherism, and how this creates unmanageability and suffering within ourselves and others, rooted in Ahimsa, the Eightfold Path, and skillful means.*

Sincere communication is a powerful meditation practice. It requires the ability to apply courageousness and bravery, unambiguously naming and claiming what is real and present for us, without bypassing, passing over with a minimum of concern, explaining away, or obfuscating the reality of our individual and collective experience. As we engage this practice, it's useful to let go of the "fast food" mentality, engaging patience, and not always come to what some might think of as a satisfactory result or "actionable" plan of action.

STEP SIX | *We consciously and intentionally cultivate our willingness to practice Ahimsa, the Eightfold Path, and skillful means to help relieve us of the unmanageability and suffering, influenced and caused by cultural bias, racism, and otherism.*

We invite meditation and mindfulness practices that support, cultivate, and open spaciousness, in noticing our suffering and that of so-called others; harmed by cultural bias, racism, and otherism. We can do so with the idea and feeling of generosity and ethical conduct in heart and mind.

STEP SEVEN | We consciously and intentionally physically, mentally, emotionally, and spiritually, act to address cultural bias, racism, and otherism within ourselves and others, rooted in Ahimsa, the Eightfold Path, and skillful means.

The most common form of suffering can be what happens in, and what can feel like the isolated space of, our mind. It can be helpful and comforting to approach our individual and collective healing as a "team effort." Positive belief + positive action = faith. It's not enough to have positive beliefs and values. We need to act on them, to improve our own life and if possible that of others. This can allow harm and suffering to be alleviated in very concrete and tangible ways, rather than leaving this undone and incomplete. In this way we can engage a process of disabling the hardship, Big T trauma, and little t trauma that have been a part of the causes and conditions of meeting our life experience that is in harmony with our values.

STEP EIGHT | We made a list of all persons harmed that we are aware of as a result of cultural bias, racism, and otherism; and became willing to begin a process of healing the wounds caused by cultural bias, racism, and otherism, to the best of our personal ability.

PHRASES FOR CULTIVATING BOUNDLESS FRIENDLINESS

May I be without fear and obscuration,
May I be well: physically, mentally, emotionally, and
    spiritually,
May I be friendly and kind,
May I be at ease.

May all oppressed beings be without fear and
    obscuration,

May all oppressed beings be well: physically, mentally,
    emotionally, and spiritually,
May all oppressed beings be friendly and kind,
May all oppressed beings be at ease.

May all beings be without fear and obscuration,
May all beings be well: physically, mentally, emotionally,
    and spiritually,
May all beings be friendly and kind,
May all beings be at ease.

STEP NINE | *We offer clear and direct support, heal and lift up those harmed by cultural bias, racism, and otherism—wherever possible, except when to do so would injure them or others—through Ahimsa, the Eightfold Path, and skillful means.*

The principle of "amends" means to engage in actions that heal the relationships that have been injured or torn, to the best of our ability. This often involves fortitude, compassion, sympathy, directness, clear communication, patience, and equanimity. It challenges us to shift our physical, mental, emotional, and spiritual weight in such a way that it allows us to go forward together, rather than falling back into patterns that can interfere with our ability to live in our present-time experience with completeness and wholesomeness. The ethos of Ahimsa is the ground, root, and foundation of changing how we experience cultural bias, racism, and otherism.

STEP TEN | *We continued to take personal inventory, and when we noticed the arising of cultural bias, racism, and otherism, within ourselves or others, promptly addressed its occurrence through our values, Ahimsa, the Eightfold Path, and skillful means.*

The meditation practice is attentiveness to our present-moment actions, and how they are landing with ourselves and others;

with regards to cultural bias, racism, and otherism. It's a practice of when we notice we're off track or not standing in our values with authenticity and integrity, we take note and return to mindful and caring engagement.

STEP ELEVEN | *We sought through prayer and meditation to improve our conscious contact with and awareness of Ahimsa, the Eightfold Path, and skillful means, cultivating our ability to carry these principles out.*

The practice of prayer is like offering an exhalation. We might say something such as:

> Dear universal loving Presence,
> please protect and provide for us.
> Guide and illuminate the path of our journey.
> Grant us courage, commitment, and strength,
> encouraging us to care and give without reservation.
> Remind us of appreciation, gratitude, our values, and
>   principles,
> and allow our life to be a reflection of universal loving
>   Presence.

We give voice to our aspirations, allowing for a kind of openness. In this way, we help to prepare the ground for us to sit upon, for meditation.

The practice of meditation is like receiving the inhalation. We invite ourselves into stillness through the posture of our body. We attentively sit, breathe, opening our awareness 360 degrees, listening and noticing with a gentle mind. In this way, we intentionally lean into practices that support Ahimsa . . . nonharming mind, the Eightfold Path, and our values.

STEP TWELVE | Having had a spiritual awakening as a result of these steps, we live and carry this message, reducing the suffering influenced by cultural bias, racism, and otherism. We accomplish this through Ahimsa, the Eightfold Path, and skillful means to the best of our ability in all of our affairs.

When we speak of change and growth in our culture, we often say, "Growth is an inside job." This is true, but there's another element that the Buddha spoke of that's incredibly important: community and support.

It's an inside job, with outside help, support, and guidance. Each of us is like a jigsaw puzzle piece, independent, but a part of an interconnecting system and way of being. When we connect our jigsaw puzzle piece to that of another, we create a profound mosaic of beauty, offering something deeper than what we might be able to experience on our own. Dr. Martin Luther King Jr., in his practice of engaging cultural bias, racism, and otherism, looked to the principle of what he described as the "beloved community."

In this aspect of a living meditation practice, there's the principle of generosity and being of service, of which there are three types: the generosity of material resources, fearing-less-ness . . . fearlessness, and the grace of our experience.

In working together, things that can when we're on our own seem immovable, insurmountable, intractable, impenetrable can be changed . . . altered . . . dissolved . . . bettered, not just for the sake of one person, but the entire beloved community. And in this way of being, we get to discover and understand that my personal freedom is somehow connected to your freedom. It's for this reason that we engage good will and creative action, to attain the reality of the beloved community.

THEY CALL YOU
A BODHISATTVA

Homage to Martin Luther King Jr.

by Larry Ward, PhD

FRIENDS ON THE PATH

Out of the many inspirational figures of African American descent, I would like to address Dr. Martin Luther King Jr. I enjoy a vivid memory of him. In 1967, he visited my high school in Cleveland, Ohio. I attended this event around the edges of the crowd and had an encounter that changed my life's trajectory. I remember the walk from my house up St. Clair Avenue to the Glenville High auditorium. As I got closer to the buildings, my body could feel a kind of electricity in the air. I left with a sense of energy and purpose I never had before.

I also choose Martin Luther King Jr. because of his friendship with my Buddhist teacher and friend Thich Nhat Hanh (TNH). In 1967, TNH referred to Dr. King as a *Bodhisattva*. This naming communicated that he witnessed a non-Buddhist American embodying the great goal of Mahayana Buddhism. This means in his view that Dr. King had achieved an "awakened mind and heart through his development of extraordinary compassion and wisdom."[1]

TNH met the Reverend Martin Luther King Jr. for the first time in Chicago. In TNH's words, "From the first moment, I knew I was in the presence of a holy person. Not just his good work but his very being was a source of great inspiration for me. When those who represent a spiritual tradition embody the essence of their tradition, just the way they walk, sit, and smile speaks volumes about the tradition."[2]

At a pivotal 1967 press conference, Dr. King spoke out for the first time against the Vietnam War. In the words of TNH, "That was the day we combined our efforts to work for peace in Vietnam and to fight for civil rights in the US. We agreed that the true enemy of man is not man. Our enemy is not outside of us. Our true enemy is the anger, hatred, and discrimination that is found in the hearts and minds of man. We must identify the real enemy and seek nonviolent ways to remove it."

The last time they would be face-to-face, TNH said to him, **"Martin, do you know something? In Vietnam, they call you a Bodhisattva,** an enlightened being trying to awaken other living beings and help them move toward more compassion and understanding. I'm glad I had the chance to tell him that, because just a few months later he was assassinated in Memphis."

A BODHISATTVA

A Bodhisattva may be described as an ordinary person who embodies the awakening of wisdom and compassion within themselves on behalf of others. And who dedicates their life to end the suffering of all beings. This quality of deep human awareness is described by Dr. King as the realization "that the life that flows through each of us and through everything around us is all connected." In many of his speeches, we can hear a resounding echo to live beyond self-centeredness. Dr. King offered that "An individual has not started living until he can rise above the narrow confines of his individualistic concerns to the broader concerns of all humanity." This capacity for extension of heart and mind to include others beyond boundaries is a profound quality of a Bodhisattva.

This awakening is activated by the mind of love, another name for Bodhicitta. The core of Bodhicitta is to have a good, kind heart that wishes to help others, and one is able to refrain from causing harm to themselves or others. A Bodhisattva aspires to live beyond self-centeredness and beyond the popular scripts of the day. To live such an aspiration is a mind of enlightenment in action. This quality of mind and heart is another description of Bodhicitta. Pema Chödrön calls this the "soft spot of bravery and kindness." The Bodhisattva recognizes that this soft spot is always available, in pain as well as in joy. Dr. King's life and death remains a true witness of a Bodhisattva's mind of the embodiment of love.

However, it is not enough just to know the definition of Bodhisattva. It is and has been of great value in my social and spiritual life to learn from the teachings and actions of many Bodhisattvas. A Bodhisattva as one who acts as a true adult. Today many people who are called adults are not true adults. A true adult is an individual who seeks enlightenment both for themselves and for others. Deep adulthood is the awakened Bodhisattva capacities within each of us. The continuous source of support for the Bodhisattva life of service in the world lies in the quality of their spiritual practices of meditation, contemplation, and prayer.

TODAY'S WORLD

There is no greater moment than this moment to respond to the Bodhisattva call within ourselves. Now is the time to embody this call with fresh, vigorous actions in our thinking, speech, and physical behaviors. We live in a world turned upside down through the afflictions of greed, hate, and ignorance. We face challenges never experienced before by the human species. Dr. King as a Bodhisattva carried within himself a penetrating vision of the interconnectedness of life whether near or far away. In a powerful speech made more than fifty years ago, Dr. King stated our basic challenge. These words seem to ring louder at this very moment of our lives as together we face never imagined dangers and opportunities around this planet.

Dr. King summarized this challenge as follows: "First, we are challenged to develop a world perspective. No individual can live alone, no nation can live alone, and anyone who feels that he can live alone is sleeping through a revolution. The world in which we live is geographically one. The challenge that we face today is to make it one in terms of brotherhood."[3] This illustrates a Bodhisattva's view of what is possible in a society. This social imagination is activated by the insight of what Thich Nhat Hanh calls interbeing, an experience of connectedness and interdependence of all phenomena, both individual and collective, that is described in Dr. King's "Remaining Awake through a Great Revolution."

The true test of a Bodhisattva's awakening is their willingness to consciously learn and grow. This growth in Dr. King's understanding and vision can be seen in his public speeches, especially in the last two years of his life. Despite Dr. King's profound discourse and clear call for deep systemic changes in American economic, political, and cultural life, this radical call has been sanitized through the language of American popular acceptability. There remain many depictions of the Reverend King's life that reduce his life and death to a kind of cheerleader for racial justice in America alone. He saw through the history of America's centuries of racial injustice and recognized the footprints of colonialism, imperialism, and militarism that sustained it.

In the words of Matt Berman, "As he himself said, King was always more than 'I Have a Dream.'" The total spectrum of his active vision is not reducible to a slogan such as "Let freedom ring." His full vision and aspiration was much larger than the safe-for-everyone caricature that is often presented today. The depth and breadth of his message and mission reveals the connection between racial justice and justice for all everywhere. In Dr. King's words, "Beyond the calling of race or nation or creed is this vocation of sonship and brotherhood."

Most Bodhisattvas can go through life unnoticed, working in the background. It is often the fate of more public ones to be met by doom. We have many examples of lives cut short at their peak like Dr. King's. It is important to remember that Bodhisattva qualities of wisdom and compassion lie within all of us. We may show up as teachers, family members, caregivers, emergency responders, friends, social activists, or strangers. Not all or many will achieve fame nor is it their concern.

A Bodhisattva's life, however one may appear, is nevertheless lived out in the real world with its pain and possibility. This "living out" called Dr. King to a life of unimaginable stress and difficulty, which is his service to humanity. His capacity to serve so completely was rooted in his deep faith in the divine nature of the universe and humanity's potentials for deep change. His deep faith was more than creed but a lived experience constantly renewed through his spiritual life. This reveals how a Bodhisattva's compassion remains grounded in the precious insight into life's indivisible unity.

THE CALL

Out of this insight the depth of Dr. King's critique of American society flows through his voice. It highlights Dr. King's radical vision of change for the world, which at this moment is still so very important. This takes us back to one year prior to the date of his assassination. Dr. King's worldview came out clearly in a speech to an overflow crowd of more than 3,000 people at Riverside Church in New York City on April 4, 1967.

The following excerpt illuminates the profound nature of Dr. King's understanding of how a deep transformation is required in America's attitudes, values, habits, and systems: "I knew that I could never again raise my voice against the violence of the oppressed in the ghettos without having first spoken clearly to the greatest purveyor of violence in the world today—my own government." In this speech, Dr. King called for the United States to "undergo a radical revolution of values," saying that "we must rapidly begin the shift from a 'thing-oriented' society to a 'person-oriented' society."

He continued: "When machines and computers, profit motives and property rights are considered more important than people, the giant triplets of racism, materialism, and militarism are incapable of being conquered." Certainly, this posture called into question the American status quo's tolerance, maintenance, and protection of a system of oppression based on colonial models of thought, speech, and action both individual and collective.

To speak such truth to minds, hearts, and systems of power reveals Dr. King's embodiment of the Bodhisattva's deep practice of nonfear. This means the Bodhisattva learns continuously to face their fears and not be debilitated by them. In the words of Judith Lief, "Fear is not a trivial matter. In many ways, it restricts our lives; it imprisons us. Fear is also a tool of oppression.

Because of fear, we do many harmful things, individually and collectively, and people who are hungry for power over others know that and exploit it. We can be made to do things out of fear. Fear has two extremes. At one extreme, we freeze. We are petrified, literally, like a rock. At the other extreme, we panic. How do we find the path through those extremes?"[4]

A Bodhisattva's spiritual practice invites them to face and embrace their fears, understand their fears, and release them through wisdom and compassion in action. Dr. King describes the impact of fear in our lives: "The soft-minded man always fears change. He feels security in the status quo, and he has an almost morbid fear of the new. For him, the greatest pain is the pain of a new idea."[5]

Dr. King's life called me in and out of hiding into my own unique voice. I found myself full of openness to the creation of a new future for America, and deeper still called into the Bodhisattva path of universal care. So, I call you in and out as Dr. King did me and as we must do for one another. In his words, "And so there are things that all of us can do and I urge you to do it with zeal and with vigor."

I conclude this brief description of Dr. King as a Bodhisattva with a quote from TNH. It is a beautiful expression of the Bodhisattva's vow: "We have enough suffering already, so we don't want to make any more. We have enough suffering for us to give rise to awakening. We want to avoid making more suffering, if we can. We want to use the suffering that's already here to help us to wake up, to awaken." And will we wake, for compassion's sake?

NOTES

1 Excerpted from *At Home in the World: Stories from a Monk's Life,* Thich Nhat Hanh (2016), 72–73.

2 Ibid.

3 Matt Berman, www.nationaljournal.com, January 21, 2019.

4 Judith Lief, "Fear and Fearlessness: What the Buddhists Teach," *Lion's Roar,* May 25, 2017.

5 Martin Luther King Jr., *Strength to Love* (1963).

BRINGING MALCOLM X DOWN HOME, TO CANADA— AND TO NOVA SCOTIA

by George Elliott Clarke, Canada's 7th Poet Laureate

WHEN MALCOLM X WAS ASSASSINATED, fifty-five years ago, on February 21, 1965, the anti-imperialist, Black nationalist, intellectual freedom-fighter had just been to Toronto, three weeks before, where he appeared on Canadian Broadcasting Corporation (CBC) Television's *Front Page Challenge*. But that was not his first encounter with Canada.

Indeed, Malcolm's parents—Earl and Louise Little—were both members in the 1920s of the Universal Negro Improvement Association—the world's greatest mobilization of Black people aspiring for true equality and liberty, plus an end to white imperialism in Africa and the Caribbean. They met in Montreal in 1917 and married there in 1919.

In his gangster days as Detroit Red, one should guess that X had occasion to cross over to Windsor, Canada, or at least to look across the Detroit River and wonder about the white-ruled Dominion due *south*—in that locale—of the Dixiecrat-controlled United States.

Like many African Americans, X may have deemed Canada as "Canaan"—the "Promised Land"—at the end of the Under-ground Railroad, delivering freedom plus "milk and honey" for fugitives from and resisters of slavery.

(Martin Luther King Jr. himself idealized this notion in his 1967 CBC Massey Lectures.)

As a pro-human-rights tribune, X formulated the talking point that any place "south of the Canadian border" was a warren of oppression, not only the once-slaveholding South.

Thus, X was deliberately redirecting the Dixie-myopic anti-racism of the civil rights movement to view all of America as practicing white supremacy.

Moreover, X was postulating that anti-Black racism was con-nected to Americo-Euro-Caucasian imperialism versus People of Color in the ex-colonial world.

By referring to Canada, X reminded his audience of the historical internationalism of African American freedom-struggle—and thus its potential alliance with Algerians, Viet-namese, Cubans, and even the "French-Canadians" struggling to defend their language and liberate themselves from their Anglo overlords.

(I've always wondered whether Pierre Vallières, in authoring his memoir *cum* political tract, *White Niggers of America: The Precocious Autobiography of a Québécois "Terrorist"* [1968], was influenced by X's *Autobiography of Malcolm X* [1965]. Certainly, the styles are similar: the unfolding of a life alongside a committed, social analysis, each informing the other. If X demonizes white Americans as reactionaries, so does Vallières damn English Canadians as colonialists vis-à-vis Quebec.)

In his political jeremiad, *Lament for a Nation: The Defeat of Canadian Nationalism* (1965), Canuck *philosophe* George Grant develops the idea, also proposed by X, that America is a diabolical empire, intent on paving over Vietnam—and happy to bully Canada into importing US nuclear missiles.

By the time of his silencing—or, shall we say, "canceling"—by the Nation of Islam in November 1963 (for seemingly gloating over the assassination of President JFK), X had become a major proponent of liberation "by any means necessary"—including armed (guerrilla) struggle, an idea endorsed by the Front de Libération du Québec as well as by the Black Panther Party (BPP) for Self-Defense.

Not only that, but he was now articulating—especially during and after his departure from the Nation of Islam (which now advocated X's ultimate cancellation by assassination)—the need for Black dignity, Black socioeconomic and political power, Black history courses, and a love of the Black body (so long demonized by white supremacist propaganda).

Culturally, too, X influenced Black Canada greatly. Bajan-Canadian scribe Austin C. Clarke interviewed X—in 1963—for Canadian Broadcasting Corporation Radio, which saw the about-to-be-published, debut novelist travel to Harlem to score the scoop.

In 1968, Clarke published a radical pamphlet, *Black Man in a White Land,* which followed X in being issued under a Muslim pseudonym and attacking white (Canadian) racism. Clarke also published a separate pamphlet, that same year, critiquing what he saw as the failure of King's nonviolence protest movement to alter the viciousness of white supremacism. His rebuke of King also likely marks his tacit acceptance of X's analyses.

The Guyanese-born writer—and English Canada's second Black novelist—Jan Carew later published a memoir about his meeting X in London, England, in February 1965, but also about X's travels in Africa and his influence on West Indian intellectuals. See Carew's *Ghosts in Our Blood: With Malcolm X in Africa, England, and the Caribbean* (1994).

In 2013, African Canadian author Graeme Abernethy published his mammoth study, *The Iconography of Malcolm X*, examining X's "afterlife" as a cultural icon constructed of absolutely contradictory—but wonderfully provocative—images and statements.

Writer-activists as diverse as Althea Prince and Desmond Cole reflect X's thought in their letters and works.

For me, X's fundamental thought may be distilled as the requirement that principles and activism be derived from intellectual reflection and constant study; that truth and justice are attained via virtue and courage, praxis, and uncompromising, analytical oratory (the bridge between words and action). And that, when objective facts change, so must analyses keep pace with ethics and tactics, insight and advisories, political philosophies and organizational strategies.

These ideas got picked up by Canada's foremost Black radical of the 1960s, namely, Burnley "Rocky" Jones (1941–2013), who helped establish a Transition Year Program (TYP), focusing on cultural history, for African Nova Scotian and Indigenous students, to prepare them to take regular university classes at Dalhousie University. (The University of Toronto's TYP is modeled on the Dal program.)

Rocky and—his Angela-Davis-fierce wife—Joan (1939–2019) also applied X to the need to set up the Black United Front of Nova Scotia, the Nova Scotia Human Rights Commission, and to help set up the National Black Coalition of Canada. They also spearheaded Black Canadian support for international, anti-racist, and anti-imperialist freedom struggles: anti-war in Vietnam, anti-apartheid in South Africa, backing of decolonization in the Caribbean (including defense of the Cuban Revolution), and acknowledging the links between Canada and Africa (including Nova Scotia and Sierra Leone).

Rocky was the charismatic orator—in the style of X— challenging white supremacism in all its potent forms (cultural, economic, judicial, pedagogical, policing, and sociopolitical), and, as a hunter, was known to carry arms, though not threateningly. His reward—like X's—was to attract persistent, secret-police surveillance, not exposed in the House of Commons until 1993.

For her part, though, Joan Jones (*née* Bonner) was more in the background; she seemed to channel Davis, given her similar look and style, plus her equally uncompromising, critical vision for Black women's empowerment, via scrutinizing and contesting the interlocking oppressions of sex, race, and class.

In addition, it was Joan who tutored Rocky in critical race theory, for she was the one with the household library that she insisted he familiarize himself with when they were still dating.

(Imagine: a Black couple courtship conducted in part through shared reading! A model, really, for all Afro-Romantics!)

Although Rocky and historian James Walker organized TYP at Dalhousie, Joan was the one who insisted that neighborhood Black kids like me actually go to university. Like X and Davis, she believed in the efficacy of education as a means of developing revolutionary—I mean, critically thinking—cadres.

(Indeed, Joan turned her home into a salon: There was always curry on the stove, wine in the fridge, Last Poets on the turntable, and guests like singer Harry Belafonte and writer and actor Walter Borden dropping by for some rice and beans and a congenial, instantaneous symposium on socialism.)

The Joneses also founded Canada's singular chapter of the BPP and hosted Stokely Carmichael (later Kwame Touré) and his wife, the South African–born singer Miriam Makeba, in Halifax, Nova Scotia, in the fall of 1968. In fact, the Joneses met Carmichael and Makeba in Montreal in October 1968 at the Congress of Black Writers, which was really a Who's Who of radicals in the mode of X: C. L. R. James, Walter Rodney, James Forman, and the Joneses themselves.

To sum up, the wisdom that X conveys to us all, especially youth, and that was also exemplified in the sterling examples of Joan Jones and Rocky Jones, is that effective militancy—feminist, anti-racist, anti-imperialist, pro-humanitarian (including environmentalism)—can only succeed—or has the best chance of succeeding—when folks accept to read and study, study and act, write and critique, read and study, organize and act, write and organize.

Many oppressed communities accept the insidious propaganda that our brains are less vital than our brawn and/or our genitals. That our value is only in labor (including sex work and sexual reproduction) and entertainment (athleticism, dance, song), and that our bodies are our essence.

Too many of us are led to think that books, that literacy itself, that "book-learning," are antithetical to liberation struggle.

But X (autodidact intellectual) and Davis (given her earned doctorate from the Humboldt University of Berlin and her career as a university professor)—and, for me, personally, the Joneses—taught and teach us that our true liberation depends upon wielding words, not just weapons, and maybe even always words, more than weapons.

When I was eighteen and unsure about going to university—because I was fearful that I wouldn't measure up and fearful of debt, it was Joan Jones who grabbed me one day, thrust her finger in my face, and said, "You're going to university!" She gave me a job—and that helped to cover my costs.

But she also said to me, "Georgie, when you're sitting in that classroom and you know the answer to the question, or you think you know the answer, always put your hand up. Always speak up! Always speak out!"

I carried that wisdom all the way through to my PhD, and then I passed it on to my daughter—along with my favorite quotation from X: "Only the unasked question is stupid."

X's example is as deathless as our struggles for true freedom and equality, which—in Canada and everywhere—seem endless. But we can only move forward toward achieving the Just Society (I cite Pierre Elliott Trudeau) through developing the economics of sharing and the politics of caring (especially for the environment)—"by any means necessary."

AFRICAN WISDOM
TRADITIONS

Womxn, Embodiment, and
Creative Expression

by Arisika Razak

I AM A SEVENTY-ONE-YEAR-OLD US-BORN African American woman whose African ancestry is uncertain.* However, I take great pride in my African/Diasporic foremothers who were priestesses, healers, agriculturalists, warriors, mothers, leaders, teachers, midwives, and artists. Their traditions survived, and I salute them.

---

*DNA analysis suggests that my ancestry includes peoples of Nigeria (20 percent); Cameroon, the Congo, and other southern Bantu peoples (20 percent); Mali and Ghana (24 percent); Benin and Togo (7 percent); Senegal (3 percent); eastern Bantu peoples (1 percent); England, Scotland, Ireland, and Wales (16 percent); and Indigenous Americas (central) (5 percent).

While Africa is a continent and not a country, many African/ Diasporic scholars have acknowledged commonalities found in African traditional religions. Although not every African religion includes all the following, these commonalities include:

1. Belief in a sentient, ensouled universe containing sacred ancestors, elemental powers, and other-than-human entities who influence human life and well-being;

2. Diverse pantheons of male, female, nongendered, and/or ambiguously gendered deities;

3. Inclusive community-based rituals with drummers, dancers, praise singers, and musicians;

4. Highly trained priesthoods inclusive of womxn;*

5. Embodied worship styles enabling trance, spirit possession, healing, and prophesying; and

6. A rich tradition of sacred kings and queens.

Written by an African/Diasporic scholar and noninitiate, this essay briefly explores how these elements promote womxn's empowerment and Black Liberation struggles.

---

*I do not wish to conflate contemporary Western norms of gender identity with traditional African beliefs, which may emphasize sociospiritual identities rather than sexual orientation or gender identity. However, I do wish to call attention to (a) the ways that traditional (i.e., pre-colonial) African notions of "femininity" and "masculinity" may subvert Western gender binaries; (b) the existence of nongendered or ambiguously gendered beings in African cosmologies that predate and/or anticipate recognition of these embodied realities in the West; and (c) the flexibility of gender in situations where anatomical females may become social males in a patrilineage (see: Amadiume, Ifi, *Male Daughters, Female Husbands: Gender and Sex in an African Society,* Atlantic Highlands, NJ: Zed Ltd., 1987); and (d) the sociocultural construction of gender in cultures where the language is not gendered and men can be "wives" and women husbands (see: Adeeko, Adeleke, "Ko Sohun ti Mbe ti o Nitan (Nothing Is That Lacks a [Hi]Story): On Oyeronke Oyewumi's 'The Invention of Women,'" in Oyewumi, Oyeronke (Ed.), *African Gender Studies: A Reader,* New York: Palgrave Macmillan, 2005, 121–126).

MUSIC AND DANCE IN DIASPORIC TRADITIONS

Growing up during the civil rights and Black Power eras of the 1960s I initially encountered West African goddesses in Harlem's Yoruba Temple.* Their worship included music, dance, and drumming, reminding me of civil rights era congregational singing, which enabled Black people to stand unbowed and resilient during racist attacks.† African methodologies privileged voice, embodiment, female leadership, and liberation—and they became central to Black Liberation struggles.[1]

Abrahamic patriarchal religion's Divine Feminine‡ is nurturing, maternal, and chaste/asexual. Indigenous African goddesses are powerful, sexual, lethal, and protective. The Yoruba *orisa* Oshun is a preeminent healer, trader, and craftswoman. She's also a warrior goddess who leads the *aje,* who punish and kill wrongdoers.[2] A wealthy, sensual, and sexual deity, Oshun embodies

---

*The Yoruba Temple was founded in Harlem in 1960 by the late Baba Efuntola Oseijeman Adefunmi (later Oba [King] Waja Ofuntola Oseijeman Adelabu Adefunmi I), who was the first African American initiated into the Orisa-Vodun priesthood. Initiated in Cuba, Oseijeman rejected Cuba's conflation of Yoruba and Catholic traditions and committed himself to returning the tradition to its African roots. He later founded Oyotunji Village, modeled on traditional Yoruba lifeways in Beaufort County, South Carolina.

†"Sound is a way to extend [your] territory. . . . When . . . the sheriff [entered] mass meetings . . . taking pictures and names . . . we knew our jobs were on the line and maybe more . . . somebody would begin a song. Soon everyone was singing, and we had taken back the air in that space." —Bernice Johnson Reagon in Bill Moyers and Gail Pellett, *The Songs Are Free: Bernice Johnson Reagon and African American Music,* Public Affairs Television, 1991. Distributed by: Films for the Humanities & Sciences. Princeton, NJ: Film Media Group, 1991. https://gailpellettproductions.com/the -songs-are-free-bernice-johnson-reagon-and-african-american-music/. Accessed September 6, 2020.

‡I use this term to refer to culturally constructed qualities, attributes, and endowments assigned to other-than-human entities who are socioculturally deemed "female."

primal, spiritual, female power. Without her involvement, efforts by sixteen (or 400) male deities to create the world failed—and Olodumare (Yoruba Supreme Being) proclaimed that without womxn's participation, nothing men did would succeed.[3]

African goddesses are role models for African womxn, who are rulers, traders, priestesses, artisans, agriculturalists, and market womxn. The Yoruba term *iyalode,* "mother of the outside," refers to womxn who hold independent spiritual and political roles of authority. The *iyalode* was a female chief with her own court—and she exercised social, political, and judicial powers in male assemblies of power.[4]

The Nigerian Igbo ancestral spirit, Abere, could curse or kill wrongdoers. Her decisions could not be challenged, and as a reincarnated ancestor, she supported womxn traders and market womxn.[5] Likewise, Igbo womxn could judge and punish wrong-doers. The pre-colonial rite "sitting on a man"[6] was employed by collectives of womxn when men abused their wives or failed to keep animals from destroying womxn's crops. Womxn sang demeaning songs, beat up men, destroyed their dwellings, and could even kill them.

WOMXN IN AFRICAN/DIASPORIC LIBERATION STRUGGLES

Africa's sacred queens and queen mothers* were also war leaders. The Kushite (Sudanese) queen Amanirenas battled the Romans

---

*In areas where sacred king/queenship still exists, a "queen mother" may be the literal mother of the king, or an elder female relative. Queen mothers are especially prominent among Ghana's Ashanti peoples, who have a matrilineal line of descent. Ashanti queen mothers were co-rulers at every level of governance; in other areas of Africa they were responsible for the welfare of women, and held key roles in succession, inheritance, and warfare.

from 27 BPE to 22 BPE, brokering a peace that lasted almost 200 years. In 1900, Yaa Asantewa (c. 1840–1921), Ghanaian queen mother of Ashantiland's Ejisu people, warred against the British, and her brilliance and bravery are commemorated today. The Ahosi, ceremonial (celibate) wives of the kings of Dahomey (Benin, c. seventeenth to nineteenth centuries), were a female military group renowned for their battle skills and prowess.

In the Diaspora, enslaved African women freed themselves and others. Jamaica's Queen Nanny, herbalist and spiritual practitioner, escaped slavery, establishing a free "Maroon"* settlement (Nannytown, c. 1720). She reputedly freed 800 enslaved Africans, and successfully negotiated with the British for Nannytown's independence.

Traveling with Vodoun† priest Dutty Boukman, Vodoun priestess Cécile Fatiman encouraged enslaved Haitians to revolt. On August 14, 1791, she was possessed by the spirit of Ezili Danto, a fierce female Vodoun *lwa*,‡ sparking the Haitian Revolution, and Haiti's emergence as a free Black republic. In the United States, Harriet Tubman not only escaped from slavery,

---

*"Maroon" settlements (Jamaica) were formed by groups of enslaved Africans who had successfully escaped slavery and formed free communities in difficult-to-access mountainous regions where they were not easily recaptured.

†Vodoun, a.k.a. Vodou, a.k.a. Vodun is the religion of the Fon people who live in Benin, Togo, Ghana, and Nigeria. Their religions traveled with enslaved Africans to Haiti, where they were syncretized with Catholicism, resulting in Haitian Vodun/Voodoo.

‡The *lwa* are deities of the Haitian pantheon, where the worship of selected West African (Fon, Yoruba, Wolof, Bambera, etc.) deities was syncretized with the worship of Catholic saints. See: Osumare, Halifu, "Sacred Dance-Drumming: Reciprocation and Contention within African Belief Systems in the San Francisco-Oakland Bay Area," in Ashcraft-Eason, Lillian, Darnese Martin, and Oyeronke Olademo (Eds.), *Women and New and Africana Religions* (Santa Barbara, CA: ABC-CLIO, LLC, 2010), 123–141.

but repeatedly returned to the South, freeing dozens of enslaved Africans. She is the only US woman known to have commanded troops in battle, liberating more than 700 enslaved Africans from plantations along the Combahee River during the Civil War.

EMBODIED AND INCLUSIVE COMMUNITY-BASED RITUALS: COMPLEMENTARITY IN ACTION

African Indigenous religions viewed the spiritual and material realms as complementary and interpenetrative. The creation of sculpture, the smelting of iron and gold, everyday acts of farming, weaving, pottery-making, and dyeing, and the execution of creative skills in music, dance, and singing all required prayers to the ancestors, the deities, and the spirits of the materials with which one worked.

Traditional religious festivals demonstrated complementarity between male and female spheres of activity. The Yoruba Gelede masquerade honors the awesome female powers, respectfully titled "Our Mothers." It's danced by men, masked and costumed as women. Female Gelede masks depict womxn of power, and womxn donate the head ties and clothes male performers wear.

Although African womxn don't make wooden masks, they create and paint fiber ones.[7] Côte d'Ivorian Senufo men carve masks for the (male) Poro society, but women determine the best mask placement in male shrines. While blacksmithing among the Senufo is a male profession, the wives of Senufo blacksmiths create ceremonial baskets, and the wives of brass-makers create pots.

RANDOM THOUGHTS AND CONCLUSIONS

African traditional religions are grounded in the earthy and the embodied. In West Africa, the "female genital power"[8] of post-menopausal womxn opposes the power of patriarchal elites, destructive spiritual entities, and capitalist organizations. While Côte d'Ivorian Abidji Dipri rituals center on trance-enabled bodily feats by young male initiates, these rites cannot safely take place without secret nighttime ceremonies performed by naked female elders who protect the village with magical potions containing female bodily fluids.[9] Post-menopausal womxn's ritual nudity was used to protest civil war/colonialism in Ghana, Côte d'Ivoire, and Nigeria;[10] as recently as 2014, threats of ritual nudity disrupted oil production in Nigeria.[11]

To venerate Yoruba *orisas*, who are elemental powers/natural forces, is to acknowledge and revere the powers of Nature. Even when Christianity is dominant, traditional beliefs may continue. Kenya's Nobel Prize laureate, Wangari Maathai, was taught by her mother to revere the fig tree and not use it for firewood. As a scientist, she learned that where the fig grew, springs were abundant.[12]

Deities of African traditional religions can be male, female, or ambiguously sexed/gendered. Olodumare, the Yoruba Supreme Being, exists beyond human conceptions of gender. Eshu, Yoruba Divine Trickster, may be male, female, or both. Dahomey's Creator deity, Mawu-Lisa, represents the union of the Moon goddess, Mawu, with the Sun god, Lisa. By honoring diverse genders, African traditional thought anticipates Western acknowledgment of nonbinary gender identities.

Indigenous African beliefs have sustained their descendants through centuries of forced and chosen global migrations. May they continue to do so.

RESOURCES

Achebe, Nwando. "Women and Authority in West African History." In Achebe, Nwando, Samuel Adu-Gyamfi, Joe Alie, et al. *History Text-book: West African Senior School Certificate Examination*. 163–177

(2018), https://wasscehistorytextbook.com/. Accessed September 5, 2020.

Amadiume, Ifi. *Male Daughters, Female Husbands: Gender and Sex in an African Society* (Atlantic Highlands, NJ: Zed Ltd., 1987).

Badejo, Diedre. *Osun Seegesi: The Elegant Deity of Wealth, Power and Femininity* (Trenton, NJ: Africa World Press, 1996).

Drewal, Henry John and Margaret Thompson Drewal. *Gelede: Art and Female Power among the Yoruba* (Bloomington: Indiana University Press, 1990).

Grillo, Laura S. *An Intimate Rebuke: Female Genital Power in Ritual and Politics in West Africa* (Durham, NC: Duke University Press, 2018).

Moyers, Bill and Gail Pellett. *The Songs Are Free: Bernice Johnson Reagon and African American Music*. Public Affairs Television, 1991. Distributed by: Films for the Humanities & Sciences (Princeton, NJ: Film Media Group, 1991). https://gailpellettproductions.com/the -songs-are-free-bernice-johnson-reagon-and-african-american-music/. Accessed September 6, 2020.

Van Allen, Judith. "'Sitting on a Man': Colonialism and the Lost Political Institutions of Igbo Women." *Canadian Journal of African Studies/ Revue Canadienne Des Etudes Africaines* 6, No. 2 (1972): 165–181. Doi:10.2307/484197. Accessed September 5, 2020.

Washington, Teresa N. *Our Mothers, Our Powers, Our Texts: Manifestations of Aje in Africana Literature* (Bloomington: Indiana University Press, 2005).

NOTES

1   Osumare, Halifu. "Sacred Dance-Drumming: Reciprocation and Contention within African Belief Systems in the San Francisco-Oakland Bay Area." In *Women and New and Africana Religions*. Ashcraft-Eason, Lillian, Darnese Martin, and Oyeronke Olademo (Eds.) (Santa Barbara, CA: ABC-CLIO, LLC, 2010), 123–141. (See 123)

2   Washington, Teresa N. "Aje in Yorubaland." *In Our Mothers, Our Powers, Our Texts: Manifestations of Aje in Africana Literature.* Teresa Washington (Bloomington: Indiana University Press, 2005), 13–55.

3 Karenga, Maulana. *Odu Ifa: The Ethical Teachings* (Los Angeles: University of Sankore Press, 1999). 72–75; Abiodun, Rowland. "Hidden Power: Osun the Seventeenth Odu." In *Osun across the Waters: A Yoruba Goddess in Africa and the Americas,* eds. Joseph M. Murphy and Mei-Mei Sanford (Bloomington: Indiana University Press, 2001), 10–33.

4 Achebe, Nwando. "Women and Authority in West African History." In Achebe, Nwando, Samuel Adu-Gyamfi, Joe Alie, et al. *History Textbook: West African Senior School Certificate Examination* (2018), 163–177. https://wasscehistorytextbook.com/. Accessed September 5, 2020.

5 Ibid.

6 Van Allen, Judith. "'Sitting on a Man': Colonialism and the Lost Political Institutions of Igbo Women." *Canadian Journal of African Studies/Revue Canadienne Des Etudes Africaines* 6, No. 2 (1972): 165–181. Doi:10.2307/484197. Accessed September 5, 2020.

7 Aronson, Lisa. "Women in the Arts." In *African Women South of the Sahara.* 2nd Edition. Margaret Jean Hay and Sharon Stichter (Eds.) (New York: Longman Group Limited, 1995).

8 Grillo, Laura S. *An Intimate Rebuke: Female Genital Power in Ritual and Politics in West Africa* (Durham, NC: Duke University Press, 2018).

9 Ibid.

10 Grillo, Laura S. "Catachresis in Côte d'Ivoire: Female Genital Power in Religious Ritual and Political Resistance." *Religion and Gender* 3, No. 2 (2013), 188–206. www.researchgate.net/publication /291224532_Catachresis_in_Cote_d'Ivoire_Female_Genital_Power _in_Religious_Ritual_and_Political_Resistance.

11 Folami, Olakunle Michael. "The Gendered Construction of Reparations: An Exploration of Women's Exclusion from the Niger Delta Reintegration Processes." *Palgrave Communications* 2, 16083 (2016). www.nature.com/articles/palcomms201683. Accessed September 7, 2020; "Nigeria: Half-Nude Women Protest against Shell in Bayelsa." Vanguard/AllAfrica Global Media, January 8, 2014. https://allafrica.com/stories/201401080080.html. Accessed September 5, 2020.

12 Maparyan, Layli. "Spiritualized Sustainability: Wangari Maathai,
    Unbowed and The Green Belt Movement: The Womanist Idea."
    (New York: Routledge, 2012), 254–290.

PURIFICATION AND PROTESTS

The Murder of Black Bodies in America

by Alex Kakuyo

THERE ARE MANY MISCONCEPTIONS AROUND Buddhist retreats, on the source of the healing that's found in them. Spiritual seekers walk into temples expecting a spa weekend. They think they'll eat tasty food, sleep in comfortable beds, and sit happily in the lotus position until some meek, mild-mannered monk taps them on the shoulder and says, "Congratulations, you've attained enlightenment!"

But that's not how it works. Practitioners often sleep on the floor during their stay at a temple. The food is nourishing, but it's not designed to be good. And the act of seated meditation feels like torture for a variety of reasons.

First, Westerners aren't used to sitting on the floor. Our hamstrings are tight, our backs are weak, and it can take several days before we settle into a routine. Then there's the silence. The average American spends eight or more hours each day sitting in front of a screen. A steady stream of music, news, and podcast interviews protects us from silence, protects us from having to be alone with our thoughts.

But we lose those protections during a meditation retreat. There's no cell phone, there's no laptop, there's not even a book to read. There's just us and a resounding quiet that threatens to drive us mad. Because once the distractions have been removed, we can't hide from the trauma that we've been carrying for years.

The confusion we feel when a parent won't say, "I love you," the grief caused by a spouse who was unfaithful, the anger at a boss who won't give us a promotion: it all comes to the surface. And we have to sit with it. We have to sit in the resounding silence of our shame, our hurt, and our anguish until the meditation period ends. Then we get up, walk around for a bit, and then we sit down to do it again.

A Buddhist retreat is a bloodletting. We open our veins and let our trauma leak onto the hardwood floor. We don't call for help. We don't beg the monks to make it stop. Because this is what we came for. We want to hurt. We want to be made pure. And purification doesn't happen without pain.

I've been thinking about this recently as it relates to the murder of George Floyd. Floyd died on May 25, 2020, when officer Derek Chauvin held his knee on the back of Floyd's neck for 9 minutes and 29 seconds while trying to arrest him.[1] During this time, Floyd was handcuffed, lying facedown on the cement, and begging for his life. Ignoring the pleas of onlookers who recorded the event on their phones, Chauvin didn't remove his knee until medics asked him to. Floyd was declared dead a short time later.

In the aftermath of this tragedy, groups like Black Lives Matter led protests against police brutality that spread to all fifty states and several countries around the world. The protests were largely peaceful, but there were some that turned into full-scale riots due to police officers firing tear gas and rubber bullets into the crowds. In Minneapolis, Minnesota, where George Floyd died, things escalated to the point that the Minneapolis third precinct police station was burned to the ground.

In the aftermath, naysayers have asked, What do protests solve? Some people have wondered aloud if groups like Black Lives Matter are creating racial division instead of healing it. This is a wrongheaded reaction, but it's an understandable one.

It's like the reaction people have while engaging in traditional Buddhist practices during a meditation retreat. Often, these individuals have spiritual and mental baggage that they need to work through. The body carries physical trauma and refuses to let it go. The mind carries painful memories that it plays on repeat. And it's not uncommon for people to develop unhealthy habits (drinking, smoking, infidelity, etc.) that increase their suffering.

The practices of bowing, chanting, and seated meditation that one experiences at a retreat help us transmute that suffering into fuel for our practice. Bowing teaches humility. Chanting trains us to use our voices for good. And seated meditation helps us identify positive actions that we can take for the good of all sentient beings. These practices are effective, and practitioners have been using them for thousands of years to heal trauma and realize their own enlightenment. However, they require us to pay a price.

In order to experience the benefits of bowing, we must step outside of our comfort zone and allow ourselves to be vulnerable both mentally and physically as we crouch with our foreheads touching the floor. In order to understand the power of chanting and how it purifies our speech, we must be willing to chant for the benefit of those who have done us harm. And if we want our seated meditation practice to work, we must identify the negative habits that cause us suffering and extricate them from our lives.

In short, it's only when we're willing to let go of our comfort, our grudges, and our negative habits that our mental and spiritual trauma can be healed during a retreat.

Similarly, America has a long history of racial trauma that needs to be healed. The psychic pain of Black bodies being sold on auction blocks, raped in plantation houses, and jailed in for-profit prisons has poisoned this country's mind. And it's our unwillingness to engage in the uncomfortable practices of protest and reconciliation that keeps recovery from taking place.

Like a spiritual seeker who walks into a Buddhist temple, America is waiting for some meek, mild-mannered Black person to give it a certificate that says, "Congratulations, you're not racist!" It wants the feeling of cleanliness that comes through spiritual release, but there's a price that must be paid for purity, and our country won't pay the bill.

It's simple math: how does one pay for slavery without protests? How do they heal the wounds of Jim Crow without riots? How does a country repent for the murder of unarmed black bodies like George Floyd's without burning down a police station? It doesn't.

Like a Buddhist retreat, this period of racial reconciliation isn't a spa weekend. It's a spiritual bloodletting. The United States must open its veins and let more than 400 years of racial trauma leak onto the American flag. This isn't what it came for, but it's what's required. America needs to hurt. It needs to be made pure. And purification doesn't come without protests.

NOTES

1 Nicholas Bogel-Burroughs, "Prosecutors Say Derek Chauvin Knelt on George Floyd for 9 Minutes 29 Seconds, Longer Than Initially Reported," *New York Times*, March 30, 2021, https://www.nytimes.com/2021/03/30/us/derek-chauvin-george-floyd-kneel-9-minutes-29-seconds.html.

WISDOM TEACHINGS FOR OUR BLACK INCARCERATED BROTHERS AND SISTERS

by Audrey Charlton

Some tame with a blunt stick,
with hooks, & with whips
But without blunt or bladed weapons
I was tamed by the one who is Such.

"Doer of No Harm" is my name,
but I used to be a doer of harm.
Today I am true to my name,
for I harm no one at all.

—ANGULIMALA SUTRA (TRANSLATED
BY THANISSARO BHIKKHU)[1]

*We get the worst kind . . . we get the worst inmates in the state
of Alabama. It's the highest-level custody prison there is . . .*
—DONALDSON PRISON GUARD[2]

IN JANUARY 2002, AFTER A couple of years' preparation, twenty inmates at Donaldson silently stepped onto their meditation cushions, sat down, crossed their legs into a modified lotus position, and began the first full Vipassana meditation program held in a state prison in the United States.

> It's amazing. I had to come to prison in order to be free, and it's stupid, I guess, but it happened.
>
> —LK, in an interview with Jenny Phillips[3]

Donaldson was the site of the film *The Dhamma Brothers*, directed by Jenny Phillips during their second meditation program in 2002. Half of the men in the Vipassana program, most serving life sentences, were Black. The racial breakdown in the Donaldson Vipassana programs represents US prison populations generally. In 2017, about 33 percent of the incarcerated population were Black, although they represented 12 percent of the US population. Tragically, more than 60 percent of the women in state prisons have a child under the age of eighteen. Along with imprisoned Black mothers, one in three Black men between the ages of eighteen and thirty are in jail, in prison, on probation, or on parole. That represents an enormous depletion of social capital, an existential disaster at the community level, and deep personal suffering for the men and women, their families and loved ones.

Charles R. Johnson, author and professor, in his essay "Why Buddhism for Black America Now?" reflected on a speech by Martin Luther King Jr. that systemic injustice has resulted in an undercurrent that threatens the Black community. The goal must be to "work on two fronts," both to fight oppression and injustice and to heal the effects. He said, "I'm convinced that in terms of what we traditionally call 'ethics,' the twenty-six-hundred-year-old Dharma of Buddhism must be part of that conversation."[4] For the incarcerated, creating a moral, ethical, and liberating world for themselves is an even more daunting challenge.

> Kenkaiyichi is a twenty-nine-year-old Black man who was sentenced to life imprisonment at the age of fifteen. Through another prisoner, he got connected to Zen Mountain Monastery's prison sangha correspondence program. Along with another Black man, they became study partners and soon started a community (sangha).

> Now, he coordinates a sangha that meets once a week with visiting Zen priests. "Buddhism keeps me from going crazy. Practice allows me to take the edge off being in prison. I see life differently. I actually see things as they are . . . the way it is. [It] appeals to me because it teaches that suffering can be overcome and nothing is permanent. I can acknowledge the pain and suffering. Things happen in prison—drugs, stabbings, gangs, and you get back what you put in. So, pain attaches to you and maybe it is meant to be a test . . . a chance to strengthen you. There are a lot of things in my childhood I'm not yet able to find · closure for . . . but with practice, I'm able to keep peace in my living area. . . . You have to rise above your own predicament."[5]

BUDDHISM

As a nontheistic religion that allows for a variety of beliefs in God, deities, or secularism, Buddhism is unique among the major religions. Most Buddhists, regardless of differences in practices or beliefs, acknowledge a similar moral foundation and a path to liberation from suffering. Steve Hagen, a Zen priest, wrote, "Real Buddhism is not really an 'ism.' It is a process, an awareness, an openness, a spirit of inquiry—not a belief system, or even (as we normally understand it) a religion. It is more accurate to call it 'the teaching of the awakened,' or the buddha-dharma."[6]

Whether we are considering those with life sentences, as in the case of Donaldson, or the 95 percent who will be released back into society, what can the Buddha's teaching offer that can alleviate the suffering of and increase awareness of the positive choices available to our brothers and sisters, particularly our Black brothers and sisters, behind physical prison bars?

THE BUDDHA (SHAKYAMUNI)

> Chris, a social worker, has been a prison sangha volunteer for fifteen years. "Buddhism is tremendous for everybody . . . for African Americans. It is about liberating your mind. Giving prisoners the dharma and benefit of practice, they get what they need. I see the prison pipeline and it's heartbreaking. You have got to liberate yourself from that reality."[7]

The Buddha's life can be read as a teaching parable. His experience of suffering, his perseverance and determination to find the truth of liberation for all humans, and the temptations he faced to take an easy way out inspire a dedicated commitment to follow his example.

After six years as a wandering ascetic, at a point of exhaustion and near death, Siddhartha Gautama, the future Buddha, determined to sit in meditation without rest until he discovered the truth that would release him from suffering. During his meditation, he experienced an awakening to the natural world, to the cause and the remedy for suffering. For more than forty years, he taught what he had come to understand. His teachings, the dharma (or *dhamma*), spread through India and Asia and, in the late nineteenth century, arrived in Europe and North America.

THE DHARMA

At the center of the Buddha's original teaching are the Four Noble Truths: Suffering is a part of the human condition; it has a cause (delusion, greed/craving, anger); a cessation; and a specific Eightfold Path to liberation.

The Eightfold Path is summarized into three essentials of Buddhist training and discipline:

- Ethical conduct (*sila*), based on love and compassion, composed of right speech, right action, and right livelihood;

- Mental discipline (*samadhi*), based on right effort, right mindfulness, and right concentration; and

- Wisdom (*panna*), based on right thought and right understanding.

Ethical conduct is generally practiced through acceptance of a minimum of five precepts: no killing, no stealing, no lying, no sexual misconduct, and no taking of intoxicants. These are guidelines rather than commandments.

Perhaps one of the most challenging and important insights is the delusion of an independent "self." Thich Nhat Hanh asks us to see the clouds in the paper: without rain there are no trees; without trees there is no pulp for paper. We are what he calls "interbeing." Experiencing oneself and all existence from a space of nonduality is to be on the path of compassionate wisdom where there is no essential difference between self and other.

This wisdom teaching of nonduality has an adjunct in the Ngoni Bantu concept of Ubuntu. In parts of southern Africa, the Ubuntu worldview is sometimes expressed in the phrase "I am because we are," meaning that as social beings we come into existence within a field of interdependent social relationships. The idea came to represent a reaffirmation of an African wisdom teaching in post-colonial Africa. With this Ubuntu spirituality, Archbishop Desmond Tutu articulated the healing vision in the Truth and Reconciliation Commission in South Africa. In Buddhism, the understanding of interdependent co-arising—this is because that is—arises with mindful awareness. For incarcerated Black men and women, arriving in an environment that is designed to be punitive and often dehumanizing, being given a number as their new identity, constrained, and cut off from the larger world, what forms can we/they create that would be conducive to their seeing the interconnected quality—the Ubuntu—of life?

Buddhism offers a practice that returns agency to the incarcerated. Despite the tumultuous conditions of their world, they can stay calm and in control of their emotions. It provides a systematic process that allows practitioners to gain direct experience of their own minds through meditation and to understand the mental processes that lead both to the causes of suffering and to liberation from it. For lay practitioners, the everyday support in living a wholesome life comes from the Eightfold Path with its commitment to ethical conduct, mental discipline, and wisdom. Mindfulness meditation is a part of this process.

> The most wholesome action you can perform is to become master of your mind, and that is samādhi.
>
> —S. N. GOENKA[8]

Mindfulness, as described by Jon Kabat-Zinn, is "the awareness that arises from paying attention, on purpose, in the present moment non-judgmentally"[9] and meditation is one of the primary vehicles for teaching this technique. Mindfulness-Based Stress Reduction (MBSR) techniques adapted the mindfulness meditation practices derived from Buddhist teaching to create an entirely secular form of mental discipline leading to stress and pain management. "It often results in apprehending the constantly changing nature of sensations, even highly unpleasant ones, and thus their impermanence," he says. As a result, some of his patients found ways "to be in a different relationship with their pain."[10] From the 1980s, mindfulness and meditation, helped by the MBSR movement, entered the larger mainstream. A variety of MBSR and related programs are offered to prisoners in eight-week programs around the country.

In its thirteenth year at Donaldson, the Vipassana program is unique and challenging to arrange. It requires that some of the prison administration complete a full meditation retreat and that the outside teachers and staff live among and serve the meditation students during the full ten-day period. Participants must begin with vows to undertake the five precepts and maintain "noble silence" during the entire period.[11] What was that experience like for the Vipassana meditators at Donaldson during their marathon ten-day sitting?

> TJ: "Bondage in my eyes stems from the avoidance of reality and the embracing of illusions. Facing life as it really is leads to freedom from the two. . . . Vipassana meditation is a practice I'm using while residing in this contaminated womb. The practice has become one of my most productive tools against a stillborn delivery becoming my fate."[12]

> OR: At forty, OR has already served twenty years for robbery and forgery. He had been an exceptionally bright and sensitive youngster who longed for attention from others. Craving inclusion with his peers, he began to put his energy into criminal activities rather than school and sports. In college, his craving turned to cocaine and "I began to lose everything I had. I dropped out of college and lost a wonderful woman whom I was engaged to marry." In prison OR was filled with despair and remorse for his earlier choices. He became a leader among the Sunni Muslim inmates but said "his daily prayers felt hollow and mechanical." He reported, "[Vipassana's focus on the breath] cinched the deal for me from the very first day. I had enough experience to know with certainty that this was a very effective way of developing focus and concentration of mind. . . . Every day I experienced greater and greater results . . . I began to observe my pain without reacting to it,

and I could see that it was constantly changing. I realized that I could use this in all aspects of my life." After the program ended, OR reported that his prayers and Islamic faith practice took on fresh new meaning, seeing so many parallels in the teachings that he had overlooked.[13]

EJ: "I've always been angry. . . . Anger (and stress management) teaches me to conceal the anger. When I went to Vipassana, sat on the cushion for ten days, that showed . . . how to let it come up and deal with it."[14]

Buddhist mindfulness practice is not about stamping out any of the emotions, even anger, but rather acknowledging emotions with compassionate curiosity. You watch the energetic flow of anger in yourself, using your breath to stabilize the energy, and that creates space between the impulse and the response so you can choose a skillful way of dealing with it rather than having a reactive explosion of the anger energy.

SANGHA

Chris: "Doing this practice reaches such a deep place for them, places we barely know about; there is so much violence in their lives . . . prison can strip you of who you are totally. In the sangha, they can be themselves . . . can keep a [playful and vulnerable] part of themselves alive."[15]

In response to the Venerable Ananda's comment that to be surrounded by admirable company was half the holy life, the Buddha replied, "Having admirable people as friends, companions, and colleagues is actually the whole of the holy life." He made clear that associating with those who pursue the Noble Eightfold Path to learn from and support each other in their awakening is how one lives the wholesome life. Community offers the opportunity to practice the everyday application of ethical conduct and to get feedback. The sangha members support and encourage each other to stay out of trouble.

Rev. Myokei Caine-Barrett, born in Japan to a Japanese mother and an African American father, bridges many worlds. At the Wallace Pack Unit, she faces an improvised altar with its *gohonzon* (scroll), drum to the side, incense bowl, and a lit candle. A circle of men in white prison uniforms are behind her, heads bowed, hands in prayer, all chanting, "*Nam-myoho-renge-kyo*" (I devote my life to the law itself). Chanting is, for the Nichiren Shu practitioners, a form of meditation-like focus, quieting the mind and creating a direct link to the dharma as expounded in the Lotus Sutra. Chanting, she said, is like a snake in a tube or a mugwort in a field of flax. The tube straightens out the snake, and the flax allows the mugwort to grow straight toward the sun. Their lives become aligned with their innate Buddha-nature.[16]

For several years, Roshi Gaelyn Godwin, abbot of the Houston Zen Center, along with Tim Schorre and Royce Johnson, take turns every Monday to make the two-hour drive up to the Ferguson Unit Prison between Houston and Dallas. The prison sangha members report some "powerful experiences" according to the visiting priests who described situations where reactivity was slowed down. In the process of conversations about how they were raised and what they were taught, the men make keen associations with the dharma topics in the sangha meetings. In one sangha conversation about the most serious prohibited acts, including killing parents, Gaelyn saw the distress in the eyes of a few men as she helped them see their own worthiness despite the violence they may have committed. "The Buddha doesn't turn away from any violence."[17]

Prison ministries affect not only the incarcerated but also those who bring the dharma to them. Everyone engaged in prison ministries becomes transformed by this work. Prison is one of society's hardest learning opportunities for people on both sides of the formidable razor-wire fences. Buddha-dharma is one way to transform that experience by examining the delusions of separateness, greed, and anger and by recovering personal agency through ethical conduct and mental discipline. Sangha life in prison serves as an oasis where the seeds of compassion and wisdom can be nourished.

NOTES

1 "Angulimala Sutta: About Angulimala" (MN 86), translated from the Pali by Thanissaro Bhikkhu. *Access to Insight* (BCBS Edition). November 30, 2013. www.accesstoinsight.org/tipitaka/mn/mn.086 .than.html.
2 Quote from the film *The Dhamma Brothers,* 2007.
3 Phillips, Jenny. (2008). *Letters from the Dhamma Brothers* (Pariyatti Press), 77.
4 Johnson, Charles. (2014). *Taming the Ox: Buddhist Stories and Reflections on Politics, Race, Culture, and Spiritual Practice* (Shambhala), 67.
5 Personal interview with Kenkaiyichi, 2020.
6 Hagen, Steve. (2013). *Buddhism Plain and Simple: The Practice of Being Aware, Right Now, Every Day* (Tuttle Publishing), 9.
7 Personal interview with Chris, 2020.
8 Hart, William. (2009). *The Art of Living Vipassana Meditation as Taught by S. N. Goenka* (HarperCollins).
9 Booth, Robert. (2017). "Master of Mindfulness, Jon Kabat-Zinn: 'People Are Losing Their Minds. That Is What We Need to Wake Up To.'" *The Guardian.* October 22, 2017. www.theguardian.com /lifeandstyle/2017/oct/22/mindfulness-jon-kabat-zinn-depression -trump-grenfell.
10 Ibid.
11 Personal interview with current Donaldson staff, 2019.
12 Phillips, *Letters from the Dhamma Brothers,* 35.
13 Ibid., 53–55.

14 Quote from the film *The Dhamma Brothers*.
15 Personal interview with Chris, 2020.
16 Personal interviews, 2019.
17 Personal interview with Gaelyn Godwin, 2019.

EXTINCTION REBELLION

Also a Concern for People
of Color Communities

by Amaragita Pearse

May all beings be
Free from slavery.
May all cages be
Open and empty

—WORDS FROM A SONG BY MOBIUS LOOP

WHAT HUMANS NEED NOW PERHAPS more than ever
before is wisdom and compassion. The increasingly clear scientific evidence is pointing toward human activity having a
lethal effect on the conditions of our beautiful blue planet. Our
connection to and knowledge of our inseparableness from the
sacred web of life is lost as an operational principle. For some

Indigenous communities this was held at the heart of a living culture; now we find it tragically sidelined and forgotten.

Even though we have known for more than thirty years about the effects of carbon dioxide and the threats inherent in "greenhouse gases," we have individually and collectively failed to act.

We are all guilty; we are all innocent. Can we drop into this profound koan? We were all born into a stream of conditioning including our biological survival imperatives. From that place we act and live as those around us do. No one seriously wants to be responsible for making the planet uninhabitable for the majority of species, and yet all but a select few, mainly the few land-loving Indigenous communities, are doing it. The wealthiest countries are at the forefront of the unsustainable use of resources. People of Color communities are already the worst affected by rising sea levels, and severe droughts that stop food production. Climate change is affecting and will continue to affect communities with the least wealth and power. When resources get scarce, the sociopolitical landscape often lurches to the right, with nationalism often taking the form of racism and fascism.

As I reflected more deeply it became clear to me that the "environmental crisis" was actually a spiritual crisis. The fear of our own mortality, and our perception of ourselves as separate from each other and life around us, has given us a relentless quest for comfort, security, and power. With "progress" we have reduced suffering, but without wisdom we are in danger of rendering the planet uninhabitable for all but a select few. Never before has an entire species contemplated its own demise at its own hands. It is a very strange, uncomfortable, and painful place to stand.

How do we enable the vision that allows us to see and understand the big picture? The link between the trees and hedges that we rip up, and the flooding that we are seeing more and more frequently in England. Vulnerable communities all over the world are being affected, losing land, crops, and even countries to the effects of climate change. All of this we can know, but the knowing does not change our actions.

My actions and involvement with the issues changed as a result of a walk with a friend, a two-hour walk in the local woodland. She talked of her own link to Gandhi's nonviolent tradition. She reminded me of people who had taken a stand for something they held dear. I remembered my own connection to Martin Luther King Jr. and watching with my mother news footage in documentary films of water-hoses and dogs being pitted against the nonviolent and sometimes singing protesters. I connected with my place in a historic lineage of people who had been "upstanders" rather than bystanders.

My friend explained exactly why the current timing was critical for the climate emergency. She spoke about a small group of people who had decided to go to Westminster outside the Houses of Parliament in London, UK, and to declare that the government in its failure to act on the science was being criminally negligent. She explained that this group had a theory of change that was based on nonviolent direct action. They were inviting people to come and put their bodies on the line. To get arrested if necessary, and to be willing to spend time in prison. This group was called Extinction Rebellion.

It was this personal invitation from another Person of Color, based in science, that was the catalyst to my becoming a "rebel." In different locations the realities of putting yourself in an arrestable situation are different. In some countries ecoactivists have been targeted and killed. In others the implications of being arrested and going to prison will be different depending on your class or race. There is recognition that because of this in the UK People of Color might be reluctant to get involved. For this reason, there are many roles that can support the cause of bringing the issues into awareness without needing to get arrested. For some like me the issues touched a chord that I could not ignore in spite of the risks. I felt like I had been harpooned! I could no longer do what I had been doing. I felt called to step up to another level of activity and that to not do anything different was to betray myself and the potential of human beings. The more People of Color who are minorities in their nations who become visible in protesting these issues, the more people will be aware that these issues are of concern and of importance to POC communities.

Before this moment I had acted halfheartedly with no real sense that my actions would make a difference. Although my husband has been a keen environmentalist his whole life and has not flown for seven years, I was never able to fully engage actively in environmental issues. We chose to live in a low carbon footprint house, have an electric car, go on marches, and do the usual good citizen environmental things. But instinctively I knew that these individual acts while important were not a significant contribution. As an individual, there was no way of involving myself more deeply with the environmental issues that felt right to me. It was a relief to hear the Extinction Rebellion perspective that it is the bigger players of governments and multinationals that need to be persuaded to take action.

I quickly read everything I could about Extinction Rebellion, their theory of change, their principles and values, and whatever else I could lay my hands on. The most important thing for me was not having to leave my spiritual values to get involved with something political with a small p. I spent many years as a community development worker and activist in the '80s. Eventually I left the world of political activism as the main place of my work and turned to Buddhism as I felt the understanding of why humans act the way they do felt truer. There were also practical teachings to help people act ethically, to become happier and at peace, and to find a perspective on the self and the world that was liberating.

I came to see that without a transformation of consciousness at its deepest level we would perpetrate and have perpetuated much of what we fight against when we wish to challenge what we see as "wrong." As an expression of this I was ordained into the Triratna Buddhist Community.

For me the wisdom lineage of the Buddha exemplifies how we can lead a life of simplicity and freedom. The Buddha left behind his wealth and status and lived simply with two robes and one bowl and begged for his food every day. Yet his teachings were riches beyond measure: the treasury of the human heart when directed with the valuable compass of the truth, the dharma, the way of wisdom. Asking the question "What do humans really need and long for?" has been important for me. We want something to be inspired by, we want to be able to cooperate and collaborate, we want to move beyond the prisons we inhabit. Anywhere there is limitation we see the human spirit seeking to move beyond that. The limitation of economic scarcity, social scarcity, the scarcity and inequality of caste, class, race, gender. We want to be our fullest brightest selves.

The poisons of greed, hatred, and illusion get in the way of realizing with deep awareness our interconnectedness. How our actions will affect future generations, and we do not *feel* that we are part of a web of life—something much bigger than our personal stories of success or failure.

Never before has there been such an existential need for us to move out from the current level of thinking and acting. Extinction Rebellion has given me the means whereby I can put my heart's longing and necessity into action. It has become a beacon for the need for us to wake up to what we are doing to our home. The way we are living is unsustainable, we have to learn to live with less materially, but this is an opportunity to paradoxically live with more. More of a sense of community and kinship with the ecological systems and with each other. This can also be seen as a metaphor for our relationship with ourselves and with our communities. The shift that is, through this crisis, being asked of us as a community of beings is the same shift that the Buddha exemplified was possible at the level of the individual.

I feel proud to be part of a movement that is pushing these important conversations up the agenda. I no longer feel able to simply talk about the need for a transformation of consciousness with people in my Buddhist world. We are asking the hardest questions while asking people to have these conversations in different ways. One of Extinction Rebellion's principles that really spoke to me was that of not blaming or shaming individuals, and I love that the principle has been heard in the mainstream narrative. It is truly revolutionary—not to blame anyone for anything, but to keep pointing to the effects of people's actions, as close to fact based as is humanly possible. It is ultimately the same mindset of acquisition and plunder that fueled colonial takeovers of countries and the enslavement of people. This has also been the relationship to our ecological system. The hunger for material wealth that has destroyed countless lives is now at risk of making our home uninhabitable. As People of Color with awareness of how the colonizing mentality has caused untold suffering, we can choose to be in solidarity with other beings, human and nonhuman, who stand to lose everything if we do not wake up to our senses.

In these new conversations we can begin to bridge the divide between work and play, personal and professional, spiritual and mundane. We can live the whole, the individual and the collective. We are being called to evolve another dimension of consciousness, a dimension where caring for ourselves and caring for the planet are natural expressions of our delight in the beauty of life. By turning toward the most uncomfortable question, by staying with the lack of satisfactory answers, by being willing to act even when we are afraid, we can begin to shake off the chains that bind us to a way of being that does not express the beauty and light of who we are.

COMMITTING TO TRUTH

An Interview with JoAnna Hardy

by Laurie Amodeo

JOANNA HARDY IS AN INSIGHT meditation (Vipassana) practitioner and teacher, founding member of the Meditation Coalition, a teacher's council member at Spirit Rock Meditation Center, visiting retreat teacher at Insight Meditation Society, Vallecitos Mountain Retreat Center, and a collaborator on many online meditation programs. She teaches silent meditation retreats, social-justice-based meditation classes and workshops, and online courses, and does youth work as well as work with private students. Her greatest passion is to teach meditation in communities that are dedicated to seeing the truth of how racism, gender inequality, and oppression go hand in hand with the compassionate action teachings in Buddhism and related perspectives to social and racial justice.

In this interview, JoAnna discusses how she began studying Buddhism and how she brings her practice into her community and social justice work, continuously exploring the relative and absolute nature of reality as keys to true liberation.

Laurie Amodeo: *How did you discover the practice of Buddhism and why did you stay?*

JoAnna Hardy: *I was born a Catholic and I loved contemplation as a kid. Contemplation has always been important to me. I wasn't always contemplating on the wholesome, but was contemplating. I loved doing the rosary, sitting in the pews, I loved the smells, doing my Hail Marys and Our Fathers after confession. All of that I felt really connected to. I also went to Catholic school for eight years.*

Then I started engaging in some Native American practices, some Chumash practices with sweat lodges and Sun Moon Dances, a lot of ceremony. I was studying with a Black female elder that I met who has a center in South L.A. It was a predominantly Black community, which I hadn't experienced yet in my spiritual life. At that time I started to get into these noncognitive, elemental, body-based practices. But they also involved these external sources of belief systems. This teacher that I spent years with engaged in a combination of Hindu and Native American practices. So with both of those influences going there was a lot of devotional practices that took you out of body.

I went to India for a month with that community and cried at the feet of sages. What pulled me away from that was watching multiple friends die of cancer because they had this really externalized guru worship, "You tell me what to do" aspects of their practice. At one point when a final friend died because they took the advice of a guru, believing that the guru would heal them, versus choosing to get chemotherapy and professional medical care, which could have saved her life, I started looking at this ehipassiko teaching of the Buddha that said, "No, see for yourself. Don't look at me. You need to practice, you need to see what happens. Use your own wisdom." There's actually a cause and effect happening here. It's not about somebody fixing it for you.

That was twenty years ago, and I really started getting interested in what that meant. I couldn't place blame anywhere for my unskillful behaviors. I had a lot of personal forgiveness to do, because I'd done a lot of harm over the years, and so I felt invited into this practice that didn't have a whole lot of external expectations. That's how I found Buddhism and then really started to study some of the core teachings like the Satipatthana, the Four Noble Truths, the Eightfold Path. I wasn't interested in the coffee-table books. I was more interested in the suttas and pulling them apart, as dry as they might seem at first. I just wanted to see what might have actually been said by the Buddha. And yes, there are a lot of male-dominant parts in the suttas, and some great expectations. For example, in the Simile of the Saw it talks about a "gentle woman" calling her slave wicked and bashing her over the head with a rolling pin, and this slave according to the sutta is not meant to speak ill of the woman or she is being unskillful. So of course there was questioning, but I felt like the questioning was OK. The questioning did not tell me that I wasn't a good practitioner. I was a good practitioner because I saw change in my life. And I saw a lot of personal trust, and I saw personal empowerment and changes in my relationships. So the proof was in the pudding. This causality, this cause and effect, is real. If I do this, this happens. If I don't do this, this doesn't happen. It's pretty basic, not super complex.

Then it came to the feelings that came up around being, most times, the only Person of Color in the room. Because I was practicing at and later teaching in predominantly white meditation centers and feeling alone, yet also feeling really full with the practice. I also have the knowing that as a Black female-identified teacher, I have to work harder, study more, than my white male counterparts. I've had many experiences of being in front of the room, knowing my shit, and have practitioners ask the white male sitting next to me the question, instead of asking me. It's the way this dominant culture dynamic is conditioned. I've even had practitioners admit it!

What happened for me was having a role in helping to start Against the Stream Buddhist Meditation Society. Being given a lot of space to form and create POC communities, to train POC facilitators, and to be able to help shift some of the demographics. We ended up having a couple of trainings that were POC dominant, so that shifted a lot in the organization, but the organization ended up closing. I learned a lot from the process around my voice and empowerment as a Black female teacher. Rather than people appreciate my movement toward equality, they spoke about the strength of my Blackness. It's definitely not easy.

LA: *Since the closing of Against the Stream you started the Meditation Coalition. What is the Meditation Coalition and what inspired you to create it?*

JH: *When Against the Stream closed, obviously there were a lot of lost people. People had really depended upon regular teachers, regular teachings, a place to go, a place to call home, a place to call their spiritual home, a place they felt* *like they belonged, where they felt seen. Then one day, suddenly that was gone.*

Meditation Coalition came out of that. Our goal has been to offer a place for people to practice. And so myself, Mary Stancavage, and many facilitators kept our classes going.

Meditation Coalition has made a commitment to Buddhism. It's not secular mindfulness, it's not nonviolent communication, it's not anger management. It's a commitment to the Buddhist tenets, precepts, Foundations of Mindfulness, Four Noble Truths, the Eightfold Path. Buddhism is our first commitment. Our second commitment is accessibility. Every space that any facilitator uses needs to be accessible (each group rents its own space). Our goal is to go and teach in the communities that we serve; not to have people have to come to us as the dominant location. We're really wanting to spread out across L.A. so that we can serve lots of different communities, typically the communities where each teacher or facilitator lives. But all those locations need to be accessible to all bodies. That includes hearing impaired and any kind of wheelchair accessibility. Our third commitment is that all teachers and facilitators have a commitment to social justice and have spent time raising their awareness. A big part of this tenet is that they're speaking to and being inclusive of everybody that comes into the room. We're not going to get that perfect, but those are the three core tenets to be a Meditation Coalition group, teacher, or facilitator.

We don't have one single location. We have a group in downtown L.A., the West Side, South L.A., Valley, Hollywood; we have lots of different groups everywhere so that people can be in their own communities to practice. That's the goal.

As we talk about different types of governance, which is not an easy task, what I'd love to see is us being able to thrive with mutual leadership for everybody's different groups. We have a Queer group, a POC group, a Women's POC group, a POC Ally group, Awakening to Whiteness, Undoing Patriarchy, and we have regular nonaffinity groups. They're all dharma based and they all meet in the greater L.A. area. So that's Meditation Coalition. We have a website.

LA: *This combination of bringing in those commitments to Buddhism, accessibility, and social justice awareness, along with the need for community and being able to practice together, feels important in this time we're living in. In a lot of ways we as POC thrive on this. So it sounds like the Meditation Coalition is really working to engage all those aspects in the context of kindness and the recognition that while we're individuals on this path, we are in this together.*

JH: *Yeah, hopefully. And I happen to be one of those people who thinks that what the Buddha came up with was extremely good! So in a way I'm exploring, how can we help keep that going? And what is the mindfulness practice, really, and what are the Four Foundations of Mindfulness, really? One of my favorite teachings is the refrain in the Satipatthana Sutta, which is a contemplation on the internal and external experience. Do we know what's going on inside, and can we see what's going on outside? Skin out, skin in. Those two need to work together. And you know it's hard, especially for Americans because there's so much individuation in this culture, and so much of "How can I get by and how can I be well?" and that's important too.*

LA: *True, our individual and familial needs are paramount for most of us. It can be challenging to go beyond that. At the same time it's hard not to acknowledge that there are so many issues that we as a society need to address. In your* *experience, how do social justice activism and meditation come together?*

JH: *There are spiritual communities where a lot of people like to be at a safe distance from social justice issues, or from talking about climate chaos, or from whatever issue that we're calling social justice, human justice. That distancing may feel like, "Oh, I can engage on social media, and feel really good about voting, and I can go to a march, then I feel like I'm involved, but don't bring it in to my sangha or my spiritual world." You know what I mean? What I think the practice asks from us, though, is to get closer than that. Now, I'm not saying that the majority of us will ever ever know what it's like to have a child taken away from us at four years old and put in an ICE [Immigration and Customs Enforcement] camp. But what is it like to be more engaged than just reading about it, or talking about it with friends? How close can I get to this issue or this person? True mindfulness asks for us to really get in close. We do it from our bodies. It's sensation-based, from a place that doesn't have aversion or doesn't have delusion involved. When we can do this, I think we just have a much better realistic chance of responding well. And our response is coming from a place that is not based in fear.*

Having a conversation with somebody face-to-face that's in a lot of pain is a lot easier when we're willing to acknowledge the truth of what's really going on. Of course part of it is going to be about how we vote, and those kind of things. But even that can create such a separation. To not really engage with homeless people, to not really engage with incarcerated or post-incarcerated people, to not really engage with people that are hungry, to not really engage with children. I'm not saying all people can or get to do that for a living. And some people live in cities where that can never happen because

*they're just so segregated. For me it's so much more about,
how close can I get? So again it goes from the internal to the
external. If I'm not willing to get close inside, and be really
vulnerable and intimate with what's going on, I also can't do
that on the outside. I recognize that I have a lot of privileges.
Yet it just doesn't feel like a life fully lived until there's some
closeness.*

LA: *And even some discomfort.*

JH: *That's right, and most people really don't want that.*

LA: *Let's talk more about being out of our comfort zones as a
dharmic practice. As Black people in this society, we often
find ourselves in situations where we might experience
discomfort.*

JH: *I'm constantly teaching about the two truths—relative and
the ultimate—and I'm not alone in doing so. The Buddha was
not a self-help guru. He was not talking about us just getting
by or feeling stress-free or being pain-free. He was talking
about a real act of ultimately and radically letting go. And
much of that comes in the guise of our identities. So what is
identity? Identity, from what I can see, is not spoken about
in the suttas. Yet at the same time there is an acknowledgment of ultimate freedom being completely letting go of this
idea of a fixed and permanent self. Simultaneously there's the
acknowledgment that there is also the relative self that eats,
drinks, moves, and has a skin color and economic status, that
has an abled body or doesn't, and what all that means. We
can't ignore that. The question I'm bringing into my teaching
lately is, what is ultimate liberation? What is awakening? It's
an awakening to the paradox of both of those things and
everything in between. That the second we think it's any one
or the other, then we're kind of screwed.*

I work with many activist communities and they can get overly involved in the relative, which creates a lot of stress and burnout. Then on the other side when people overlook the relative and get into the spiritual bypassing aspects, it becomes easy to miss each other, then a lot of "othering" happens. For me, the harder one is the spiritual bypassing. That annoys me a lot more than getting stuck in the relative realm of "This is really hard," you know? So that's when I find myself talking with a lot of people about how do we see from one viewpoint to another viewpoint? How are we really opening up? How are we creating possibilities for being in proximity with each other? How are we creating possibilities for authenticity? Really allowing ourselves to see what's happening and again pushing that edge of discomfort.

What I usually do in my meditation groups is introduce a specific topic. Whether it's homelessness, post-incarceration, prison reform, immigration, etc. Things that affect predominantly Black and brown people. I will bring that to the group as our main topic, oftentimes with a guest speaker, and the whole time that we're talking about it we're also engaging with our internal experience around it. How can we stay, how can we stay, how can we stay uncomfortable . . . stay? So it's nice in real time to be able to do that with other people that are also on this path. A lot of those people in the groups are activists, organizers, allies, or want to become involved with what's going on socially in the world, the climate—there's so much to talk about. But then how do we keep practicing in it? When I say practice, I mean really using the Four Foundations of Mindfulness, using the Satipatthana—the internal and external experience—to stay alive, and know that it's going to be painful. The Buddha's teaching never asked us to not engage in discomfort. I mean, that's always been a part of it. So that's how I'm really practicing and have been

Afrikan Wisdom

practicing for a long time. Authentic practice is just feeling more and more real. That word, that specific word.

LA: *Authentic practice versus the spiritual bypassing.*

JH: *Right. Once we've engaged at all in some kind of real in-depth practice, it's hard to turn away. You can't pretend for very long. What are we gonna do? Eventually, we realize, staying separate doesn't work. That's where I feel like maybe People of Color engage far more in community or the sense of community in order to feel and understand spiritual practice. It's not possible to do it alone. Who even wants to?*

PART FOUR

Decolonizing Mindfulness

AFRICAN MINDFULNESS

by Olusola Adebiyi a.k.a. Sola Story

TO BEGIN A CHAPTER CALLED African Mindfulness presents a challenge that might at first not seem obvious. The challenge is this: "Mindfulness" is a new phenomenon of what amounts to a modern "Western" world adaptation of inductions to meditation and spiritual practices arising out of the ancient "Eastern" world. Not from the "African" world; however, this chapter is about "African" mindfulness, so, what about that world?

A Google search using the specific words "African" "mindfulness" generates online hits about twenty-first-century mindfulness programs and their impact on modern-day Africa. I personally found nothing online on ancient and traditional African continental "mindfulness": no histories, anecdotes, or any other substantial information. In fact, trying to locate anything at all in the mindfulness field arising out of Africa returns us to the aforementioned results.

Also, quick question: have you, the reader, ever seen or read any books or watched any documentaries about that subject? I'd be excited to learn that you have!

So, what is the reason for this invisibility? Why could I not find information on African mindfulness as a discipline? I had to ask myself, "Is it because it does not exist, that there are no Indigenous African mindfulness practices?" or "Am I looking for the wrong thing in the wrong place and therefore asking the wrong questions?"

Let me visit the "Eastern" world for a moment. The ancient cultures there once romanticized in the Western imagination as "the Orient" have long (especially Asia) been associated with techniques to encourage calmness and peace. Their literature and art form part of the "Western" understanding of the essence of what it means to be a warrior, a statesperson, or a monk; this is further romanticized through narratives such as descriptions of solitary monks with prodigious skills, amazing powers, and deep wisdom. Some of these narratives were formed by earlier intrepid European travelers to the Orient and the eyewitness accounts they gave on their return.

I decided to look online for Asian mindfulness, knowing that "mindfulness" as a Western invention originates from Asian traditions. I discovered that while there was much on how mindfulness is used in varying Asian traditions, especially Buddhist, I also discovered that these traditions were not "mindfulness" per se; they had their own names, such as Vipassana, Zen meditation techniques, and so on. Perhaps, then, I might extrapolate this success and find it in Africa too, Narratives of elevated attitudes, notions of sublime art, and enlightened practices: can we find "mindfulness" there too among the most ancient people on earth?

On that, here's an interesting thought about "Eastern" traditions and Africa. We all know that the Asian cultural heritage is very ancient; however, the origins of this inspiring heritage are considered "ambiguous" in standard historical texts. It has been theorized that very early Indian classic texts such as the Upanishads, which contain the oldest parts of the Vedic scriptures, were created by an earlier pre-Aryan civilization in Indus Kush. What was or, rather, who were that pre-Aryan Indus Kushite civilization? Writers such as Runoko Rashidi[1] have compiled compelling and plentiful evidence of an African anteriority in the development of ancient "Eastern" practices, showing that the people of African Kush, Nubian Kush, neighbors and contemporaries of the African civilization of Kemet (ancient Egypt), are the same Kushite people (big surprise there!) as those of Indus Kush. This is important since the Upanishads contain scriptures about meditation, philosophy, and spiritual knowledge, while the later "Vedas deal with mantras, benedictions, rituals, ceremonies, and sacrifices" (Wikipedia). Therefore, it follows that the people who created these Upanishads are the ancient people of Indus Kush, who were the same people as the Nubian Kush. I mentioned evidence; one would expect to find knowledge of similar complexity, complete with practices that resemble Tantra, Yoga, meditation, and of course "mindfulness," in both the ancient African world and in contemporary iterations. A cursory investigation into the contents of the still-extant ancient scriptures of Kemet, Nubia, Ethiopia (Kush), and Mali will reveal that ancient knowledge. However, does it also exist within contemporary African practices, as the inheritance of a very under-discoursed "out of Africa" ancient heritage?

Now to me and my own experience as a born-in-the-Diaspora, knowledge-seeking, story-speaking Yoruba man, when I asked my elders the question "What is mindfulness in our culture?" it was a futile quest. As a stand-alone, the question is not really related to their personal experience of Yoruba (properly called Ifa) tradition. However, when I asked them what mindset does a

Babalawo (Ifa diviner) need in order to cast the *opele* (divining chain) effectively, the answers become more revealing. "Well, Ifa is a system in which good character and balance is paramount. The priest of this ancient wisdom tradition, the Babalawo, communicates with Orunmila [the oracular spirit of wisdom] through the Orun [symbolic heaven] and Aiye [symbolic earth] of the divination tray to find how best to create *iwa pele.*"

"What's that?"

"Balance."

"What else, Baba?"

"*Ogbon* [wisdom], *omo mi* [my son]. Also one can include *ife* [love], *ire* [wellness], and *alafia* [peace]."

Here's what Mandaza, a Shona (Zimbabwean people) shaman, has to say: "Gentle peace and a devotion to serve humanity is essential to the heart of a shaman; that a calm presence is a quiet force for healing and, in consoling others, the shaman also is consoled."[2]

It is easy to imagine that the "gentle peace" from the quote above must be achieved through a form of practice. This brings me to the importance of *eemi* (breath) in the understanding of the relationship between it, the *ori* ("head," including intuition and spiritual will), and connection to the *orisa* (or divine communication). When I held the *opele,* an Ifa divination chain, I was asked to "concentrate [apply my *ori*] on the results of the cast, breathe [*eemi*] slowly, and let the image fill your mind [message from *orisa*]," a process that brought me into the present moment, which is one of the primary objectives of mindfulness. Knowing that African spiritual practices highly value a peaceful attitude allows us to extrapolate mindfulness from them, seeing that in these practices breathing to relax and be present is ubiquitous. "African mindfulness" in this context supports the spiritual and social intentions of diverse African peoples' philosophical and existential reasonings. These are oriented on collectivity. The Bantu philosophy of Ubuntu, for example, can be summed up in the statement "I am because we are; we are because I am." This has practical, evolutionary applications and possibilities. It is from the wellspring of collective positive regard that the powerful intention of holistic healing is the subject of many mindfully inducted African rituals and ceremonies.

The warrior's way is alive and kicking in Africa. From Gidigbo in Nigeria to Testa in Ethiopia, mindfulness can be understood as part of the training. Balogun Ojetade in his book *Ori: The Afrikan Warriors' Mindset* says: "Effective concentration means focusing without forcing it. In a strange way, trying to concentrate is a form of inadequate concentration. When your concentration just flows, it results in automatic, instinctive, and ingrained action. When your concentration is forced, however, your analytical mind attempts to control the situation. This disturbs your focus and becomes a distraction itself. Concentration then is the learned skill of passively not reacting to or being impacted by irrelevant stimuli."[3] It is this state of passively not reacting to irrelevant stimuli, which is key to the preparation of African warriors, musicians, and priests, that I am reiterating once again as "African mindfulness." To give an example from my own growth in KaZimba Ngoma, an African martial art: I practice the slow dance movements of Ishakua (self-expression) as a means of uniting body, mind, and breath in a heightened present sense awareness. This is "African movement mindfulness," which I also teach in London. Such movements are common to African warrior traditions and might also include invocations and spiritual songs.

My Ifa guide told me that in the West we are dishonoring *eemi* (breath as a spiritual source of elevation for our *ori*) as we are not concerned with developing *iwa pele* (good spirit led character). That is why our social orientations are based on the unit of the individual, whereas as already stated, African versions have the community as the unit. However, when I asked him about how the archetypical narrative of the mystical monk and their often drastic disciplines and privations manifests in Ifa, he told me that Ifa priests often spend weeks, months, and even years in solitude and silence completing trials and being tested while they remain in a highly receptive, present state or trance, which means they return having had new revelations of spiritual purpose and power, to apply in the service of community healing and guidance toward *iwa pele*. In short, what kind of mental concentration techniques could help a Babalawo remain mentally present for years? The warrior's voice reminds us that "It is this state of passively not reacting to irrelevant stimuli" that is the foundation of African induction practices.

The imagination of the above initiatory iteration of mindfulness evokes my memory of something that stirred a heartfelt resonance in me when I read it. It's about a Wolof man from Senegal who gave us this anecdotal autobiographical insight into his teenage initiation in the book *The Healing Drum*.[4]

He relates that he was asked by his master to sit with his back to an Iroko (cottonwood) tree and just listen. At this stage in his life having practiced drumming from the time he could walk, he felt that he was already a master. Indeed, when it came to rhythms and speed, he was very highly skilled. However, his master was asking him to learn something else. So, feeling reluctant but not daring to disobey, he sat for a day, heard nothing unusual, and was highly frustrated when asked to repeat the exercise again. He sat, he ground his teeth, he pouted, and then finally he heard it. It was the sound of the women pounding grain with their mortars and pestles. This was not unusual, but he simultaneously heard the hammer of the blacksmiths, the axe of the woodcutter, the notes of musicians, and the voices of the market women as a harmonic symphony. He had never heard anything like it, and with that listening he understood that the sound of harmony meant that the village he heard was a well one. Conversely, disharmony or discordant sounds were evidence of psychological, emotional, and spiritual un-wellness, and that it was the responsibility of musicians who could hear this to put right. I include this in order to reiterate that it is rare to find descriptions of the Indigenous practice of what we today call mindfulness in traditional Africa. However, like the boy who heard the "deeper" sound of the village only after he relinquished his frustration and relaxed into the present moment, the techniques that we today call mindfulness are practiced in African contexts learned from masters and always with a specific objective in mind.

The idea of spiritual healing through musical meditative practices is one in which the Shona *n'anga* (healers) from Zimbabwe excel. What they do musically would be called a musical mindfulness induction in twenty-first-century London or any of the metropolises of the Western world. However, for the Shona, the objective is not just present-moment orientation and embodied relaxation that is just a stage in the fulfillment of their intention: the final aim is one of healing, by using music to bridge the veil between the spirit realm and our physical one.

Mbira music is circular in form. As the fundamental melodic and rhythmic cycle of an mbira song repeats, around and around the circle, it draws musician and listeners into a state of meditation. In this state, thoughts and emotions and their associated tension drop away. The resulting state of deep peace allows the mind and body to heal naturally. A feeling of deep relaxation often occurs together with a feeling of being energized. When tension is absent, one's natural vitality and life force can be felt.

These effects cross cultural boundaries and can be felt universally.

—MBIRA[5]

The same description would serve for Malian kora players and uncountably many more too. In fact, the use of artistic modalities like that of the music described above also find life through the medium of African literature. For example, Ayi Kwei Armah dips into the "spirit world" to describe a young man who has been asked to gaze into a bowl of water. The idea is that his mind should become still and then that he should search for visions in the water. "The gazer saw a world in which some, a large number, had a prevalent disease. The disease was an urge to fragment everything. And the disease gave infinite satisfaction to the diseased because it gave them control. There were those with a contrary disease, an urge to unite everything. If that was a disease, the gazer thought, so let it be. But there would be nothing to keep him from choosing it for his own disease, and following its natural course, reaching for its natural aim."[6] That natural aim of stilling the mind is of course compatible with the aims of "mindfulness." However, that is just a stage in the process of achieving the ultimate aim, which like that of the Shona *n'anga,* is healing.

So there is evidence in Indigenous African peoples of mindfulness-type practices that, like those of ancient India and China for example, are aimed at spiritual goals and not relaxation or present-moment awarenesses in and of themselves.

Going forward on a new tack, it is clear that there seems to be a certain degree of obscurity that hides "African mindfulness" from an easily accessible summative view. This is not that surprising as even the historical contributions of Africa and its ancient Diaspora to the development of "Eastern spiritual traditions" have been largely left out of so-called "standard" histories. Unless one knows about the Aboriginal cultures of India, for example, it is likely that we would take "standard" history's perspective that the ancient period of India before the Aryan invasion is "obscure." However, there is a general consensus of knowledge that the early Vedas were written before the

Aryans got there. A potently discomforting question is: "If those early Indians were blonde and blue-eyed, would such academic 'obscurity' about their elevated early past still remain?" I think we'd be watching reruns and reruns of Hollywood films about Indus Kush if there was as much evidence of it being an Aryan (white) culture as there is of it being a Nubian Kushitic one.

Thus, although sociopolitical observations are not natural inclusions to a chapter on mindfulness, they can shed some light on why the practices of Africans have not been widely researched and have not formed a part of the narrative of "mindfulness" prior to Western traditions. For a descendant of Africa and its Diaspora like myself, however, this understanding helps us to see the global footprint of the history of African spiritual technology and allows us to make links between the *orisa* trance of Ifa and *deva* invocation dances of India, the meditational chants of the !Kung and the Twa people, the Buddhist chants of Tibet. Also links between the techniques by which African warriors cultivate *ashe* (spiritual energy), Chinese Chi Gung, the spiritual drumming of Cuban churches, the role of the Nepalese gongs, the sublime music of the Mbira, and modern Western "mindfulness" inductions. In fact, if original and first mean anything, then the assertions of anthropologists that the first humans were African—and the preponderant evidence that so were the first civilizations—could also be interpreted to mean that all the mindfulness traditions of the earth are in fact African!

NOTES

1 "Interview with Dr. Runoko Rashidi," 2012, http://drrunoko.com /african-history/interview-with-dr-runoko-rashidi-2012/.

2 Geral Blanchard, "Mysteries of African Shamanism: What Can't Be Explained Must Be Experienced," *Sacred Fire,* www.ortablu.org /topics/organic/mysteries-of-african-shamanism-what-can't-be -explained-must-be-experienced.

3 Balogun Ojetade, *Ori: The Afrikan Warriors' Mindset* (CreateSpace, 2018).

4 Yaya Diallo and Mitchell Hall, *The Healing Drum: African Wisdom Teachings* (Inner Traditions, 1989), 104.

5 "Mbira Healing," MBIRA, https://mbira.org/what-is-mbira/mbira -music/mbira-healing/.

6 Ayi Kwei Armah, *The Healers: An Historical Novel* (Per Ankh Publishers, 2000).

MINDFULNESS FROM THE
CRADLE OF HUMANITY

by Elizabeth Nyirambonigaba Mpyisi
Former Senior Legal Advisor at the United Nations
High Commissioner for Refugees

IN OUR CULTURE WE DON'T COUNT PEOPLE

When my mother said this I remember exactly where I was aged fifteen. I stopped, I asked for an explanation. After all, we had visitors coming and she was polishing the silver. It's taboo to count people. Whoever comes to our house in peace to eat with us is a blessing; we are one with them.

This epitomizes the spirit of Pan-African philosophy throughout sub-Saharan Africa among Bantu-speaking communities, traced to the pre-colonial mid-fourth century as epitomized in ancient writings in Timbuktu in Mali, to ancient Egypt, down to coastal Lamu, and farther south to Zululand and the Nguni peoples of current-day Zambia, Zimbabwe, Malawi, and South Africa. Bantu people stretch from Ghana in the west (influence of Kwame Nkrumah) to Kenya in the east (influence of Jomo Kenyatta). Central Africa from the Congo to Cameroon in the west have language and ceremonies in common. In Kirundi it's referred to as Ubunu. We call it Ubuntu, a Zulu word, laden with deep cultural significance. Interconnectedness, generosity, humanity, and humanistic philosophy are synonymous with Ubuntu.

Wisdom was handed down from one generation to the next based on communal living and healing fine-tuned into the ceremonies, dances, and rites of passage. Inherited along specific genetic family ties, families of *sangoma* would serve the entire community using herbs, meditation practices, and chants.

It takes a village to raise a child and indeed it does. I recall knowing that any elder had the authority to advise me, to take care of me, to punish me if necessary, to scold me if they found anything I was doing was improper or unethical or against family, clan, tribe, or a nation. Out of my home I represented more than myself. I was part of a greater whole, part of a greater commitment and a very big family. Children in Africa are disciplined by a network of adults who are all your aunties and uncles. This was another concept that I found difficult to understand. I would ask, "Now, is this a real aunty or just one of your friends?" This would provoke laughter and chastisement in equal measure. You have to respect the elders as much as you respect me.

I was African by nature and European by nature, with parents trying to bridge formal school education in a delicate dance with our proud African heritage. As Martin Luther King Jr. said, "Learn to live together as brothers and sisters or perish as fools." One of the family's favorite stories from the Bible was that of the Good Samaritan because it brought my two worlds together. Ubuntu means precisely that, a person, and you become a person, you become a human being, you develop the qualities of humanism. The national philosophy of the territory, formally Northern Rhodesia, and espoused by Kenneth Kaunda, former first president of post-independent Zambia, was that of humanism. "I am because you are." Archbishop Desmond Tutu in 2013, when he was awarded the Templeton Prize, gave the best description I have ever heard. According to this man of the cloth who became famous for storming the white-only beaches of his homeland in Cape Town, Ubuntu is an evolutionary process. I become human through relationship with you. It is through that interconnectedness that we learn to speak, to walk, to empathize, to communicate.

There is a beautiful Zulu saying, "Sawubona," which means I see you. I acknowledge you. I recognize that you and I are the same. I see myself in you.

We have, therefore, a uniqueness as individual human beings, but as a collective we again stand as one. So the concept of Ubuntu is one that is in line with the keeping of Pan-African philosophy, of socialist and communal policy, of governance throughout sub-Saharan Africa, and it came to its fore immediately after independence by several countries in the mid-1960s and one in particular—Tanzania, under the leadership of Mwalimu Julius Nyerere. He created the philosophy of Ujama whereby we lived and cultivated and took care of each other through joint endeavors in agriculture, housing, economy, and barter trade. Nobody can be happy if they see their neighbor unhappy. Variations of the Pan-African theories of philosophy can be found in the words and writings of Thomas Sankara, first president of Burkina Faso, and poet Léopold Sanghor, first president of Senegal and an esteemed member of the Académie Française.

The migratory patterns and the predominant philosophy of assimilation absorbed smaller tribes into larger populations to ensure continuity and stability. Shaka Zulu consolidated power by intermarriage and sharing of cultural norms, in particular the importance of peace and restorative justice.

THE ANCIENT WISDOM OF GOVERNANCE BY CONSENT AND COMPASSION

How is Ubuntu practiced today? In reality, after being devastated by the mass slaughter of almost 800,000 people in a period of about ten days through intertribal warfare galvanized by their former colonial masters who sought to divide and conquer the Tutsi and Hutu peoples, my ancestors, Rwanda restored itself by cleansing the earth of the unholy bloodletting. It revived the Gacaca courts where perpetrators of this genocide were able to come forth to explain, to confess what they had done, and to be questioned. It has often been said that the crowds listened intently while the elders who were leading this investigation would remind the perpetrator of the good things they had done, of their inherent value prior to the genocide. Are you the same person? they would ask. Do you not remember how you helped so-and-so? One by one, villagers would be called upon to recount the wonderful things this person had done. As a result, instead of punishment they were able to build bridges that emphasized the need for rehabilitation of the fabric of the village, of the country, and that community spirit. Rwanda today is one of the most advanced countries that has made the most progress, and where it is now illegal to mention anybody's ethnicity. Everybody is a Rwandese and there is no need to enforce that through punishment because it is understood that never again should we go through that. In neighboring Burundi, Umuntu has the same principle.

When we talk about speaking truth to power, when the concepts of reconciliation are called upon to be made manifest, in front of your neighbors, in front of your people, there is a wonderful healing that takes place. For a supreme example of such a process we turn to South Africa itself: the Truth and Reconciliation Commission. This was spearheaded by Nelson Mandela, who, after being freed in February 1990, a year later was able to talk about how he forgave his jailers. Mandela has been said to have even forgiven the judge who sentenced him to life imprisonment with hard labor on Robben Island. In a letter to his daughter Zindzi, he wrote that the judge is a human being, that judge is a family man who probably has children of his own, but he is part of a system that clouds his innate humanness. His personality, his behaving as a judge and not as a human being, so as a person, from one person to another I forgive him. Mandela used the F word, forgiveness.

FORGIVENESS

The Truth and Reconciliation Commission did not go down so well initially; many people wanted to exact revenge. Western countries could not understand or believe or contemplate that the same rules were going to be meted out between the Black freedom fighters and the whites who had adhered to the policies of apartheid. Anyone wishing to be forgiven for past deeds had to apply to the commission, which was chaired by Desmond Tutu, to be absolved. So instead of facing long-drawn-out trials before the courts, you could obtain, if not absolution, but permission to bring out the truth for your own benefit and for your own salvation. A legally binding amnesty could then be granted if the accuser agreed to use the F word! Honesty was one of the underpinnings of the Truth and Reconciliation Commission. South Africa chose truth over justice, and more than 15,000 people applied to be granted amnesty and could therefore not be prosecuted in any criminal or civil court. They had to pronounce those deeds and tell people what they had done. One of the caveats was that forgiveness must be voluntary. After all, there were some people who could not forgive, such as the mothers whose sons had gone missing. I too recall the Truth and Reconciliation Commission. I recall the white jailers, the men who killed Steve Biko, coming forward and explaining how they used his body as a battering ram, bashing it against the walls of the prison until he died. They wanted to bash his brains out because he refused to recant what he believed in as the leader of the Black Consciousness Movement of Azania (BCMA). His movement led to the Soweto uprising in 1976, where Black children in the schools in apartheid South Africa, refusing to accept Afrikaans as the language of instruction in schools, fled as refugees. The Truth and Reconciliation Commission is a glowing example of the working of compassion in action that is brought about by the philosophy of Ubuntu. There is a very poignant statement that was made by Lulu Thomson when she spoke to one of the Black police officers who had killed many children. He was the only Black officer among the whites. He was responsible for luring a group of Black boys, who were massacred, and then police placed guns beside their bodies as proof of their terrorist intent in blowing up the country. Lulu Thomson cried out, ". . . these other whites I don't blame them because they are doing what they are meant to do, but you, how could you do this? These are your children. They are part of you. How can you do that?" Again this is Ubuntu in action.

In the West there's a culture of revenge and retribution for wrongdoings, resulting in imprisonment, incarceration, and punishment. However, by promoting the Ubuntu philosophy of mindful listening, nonjudgment, and responding rather than reacting, it became possible for a whole nation to heal. Ubuntu teaches us that lowering yourself to the same status as the oppressor is unhealthy for the psyche of the oppressed. Ubuntu seeks peace through a deep spiritual understanding of our inter-connectedness and commonality. Healing through listening bestows rewards on both parties: the person who speaks as well as restoring the respect of the person who has been hurt.

HOW UBUNTU MINDFULNESS SHOULD BE USED TO LIBERATE BIPOC IN THE DIASPORA

Western authors have been able to adapt the Eastern philosophy of mindfulness of breath. Likewise, look to that evolution of these ancient practices and adapt the ancient wisdom of Ubuntu in a mindful way to help our people to liberate themselves from mental slavery.

The basic principles of mindfulness require a stillness of the mind, an understanding and a recognition of the present, moment by moment as we interpret time. Time is infinite. And we can settle in our bodies by recognizing the various sensations and trying to empty our minds as we do in the martial arts of Tai Chi, Chi Gung, and others. The ancient wisdom practices in Africa among the Bantu people are predicated by the use of drums, a capella voices, choirs, singing, chanting—very vocal expressions of our humanity and our interconnectedness. It is suggested that any adaptation of mindfulness that would appeal to Black, Indigenous, and People of Color (BIPOC) in the Dias-pora would need to include drumbeat, percussion, song, and chanting. The drumbeat of Africa is the drumbeat of our hearts. It is suggested that the heartbeat be adapted, as opposed to the gathering of the breath as in Western culture. The drumbeat res-onates like that of the heart, whether it is the Burundi drum or the percussion instruments of West Africa. We are a soulful people. We have that in common for it is deeply embedded in us and finds its expression in soul food, in the way we greet each other, as soul sisters and soul brothers, and through our music, soul music. When we hear the beating as one in community, and with our hands placed firmly on our hearts, we as BIPOC are reaching deep into our souls.

It is proposed that mindfulness practices that pay tribute to the ancestors would include rituals of libation, that we acknowledge those who have gone before us to the spirit, the almighty spirit, our constant companion, our friend, our Savior who gives us the strength to carry on. The book by Jon Kabat-Zinn *Mindfulness: A Practical Guide to Finding Peace in a Frantic World* may well be adapted to "Finding Peace in a Racist World," because this is the reality we have to acknowledge. The reality of the everyday slings and arrows that BIPOC face and have to overcome. We cannot judge those who oppress us. We cannot pray that they will change.

As Martin Luther King Jr. once said, we must accept finite disappointment but never lose infinite hope. The dharma teachings teach us about choice. At the end of the day we have a choice in how we move forward beyond our craving, beyond our suffering, to become awakened like the Buddha himself. Among people of African heritage, we would be looking to overcome our trauma, the communal trauma that has been felt and suffered by the generations that went before. It is not just this present moment, but it is the present time, and what has gone before, and the time that is yet to come. Indigenous peoples in South America, before they make any decision about their community, plan seven generations in advance. The Aborigines in Western Australia and the Native Americans have similar concepts of time. We can adapt our practices to be communal by hand-holding, shaking our feet in the center of a circle of healing, and where we pour the libation. We acknowledge our elders; we place our hands on our hearts, and to the sound of the drum we practice compassion, self-compassion, forgiveness just as we did during post-genocide Rwanda and post-apartheid South Africa. Mahatma Gandhi once said during the time of the Salt March, "Forgiveness is an attribute of the strong." This was a nonviolent march protesting against the British prohibition against local Indians using salt or having access to salt.

Our liberation can only come through our own emancipation and being led as we would be by our elders. We have a brotherhood, a community that is much like the sangha. We may come in different colors, sizes, shades, and hues but what we have in common is that we are nonwhite and any one of us can be subject to a racist remark, a racist look, a racist insult. At any time. There is an African proverb that says rain falls on every roof.

We have a law of humanity that can transcend that suffering. Let us not go down the road of compassion fatigue that says, "We are just tired of fighting these people who will never change." We can change, we can grow strong, and we can look at the broken parts and fit them together. And what makes those parts even more beautiful is that they will be bound by the colors of peace and love, the glue of humanity and Ubuntu that holds us together now and always.

BEING SILENCED, CLAIMING SILENCE

The Practice of Stillness in the Movement for Liberation

by Rima Vesely-Flad

The silence I'm talking about does not happen just on the cushion, and it is not something that you have to leave there. It is not actually damaged by noise. This is not the silence that is the opposite of noise. It is a quality that is intrinsic to us, an inexhaustible energy. It is not dependent on the approval of others, on what happens to us out in the world. It is not an experience that we have now and then. It is inherent fulfillment, which can permeate our lives. We can take it into the world and act from it.

—LARRY ROSENBERG, *Breath by Breath*

AS A PROFESSOR OF SOCIAL justice and critical race theory,
I have taught in elite liberal arts colleges and in maximum security prisons. In both contexts, I am aware of the power of the
pedagogy of silence. One of my former students at Sing Sing
Prison once sent a long letter to me that read, "Soon I hope to
be out of here and I want to do everything I can to help my
people, our people, in their struggles. Maybe one day I can do
for someone what you did for me, teach them how to liberate
and appreciate their minds and spirit." I was deeply moved by
his letter and was reminded as I read it of what it means to teach
and be taught, the quietness of mind and heart that it takes to
learn something new. Such learning is both midwifery and recip-
rocal nurturing, a process of eliciting knowledge that someone
already has stored inside him or her, and also being awakened to
new possibilities. Being able to learn and teach also means not
being consumed in thought or feeling, but rather, cultivating a
spaciousness that is fostered and grown through silence. This is
particularly nuanced for Black people who experience historical
and contemporary trauma: in the experience of people whose
ancestors have been enslaved and segregated, the word "silence"
is often equated with "being silenced." In short, silence is interpreted as oppressive rather than as a practice of liberation. In
this essay, I suggest that silence, reaching a point of inner stillness and breathing quietly into one's heart space, has the power
to heal intergenerational wounds and trauma; it has the power
to teach us something new.

I write from personal experience. I am a Black woman, a
mother and teacher and activist. I am an accomplished professional, and yet the pursuit of accolades and recognition is always
secondary. Rather, if I were to define my lifelong searching, I
would say it is the pursuit of silence. But, perhaps paradoxically,
silence is something that comes to me when I am most attentive
to my breath. The poet Brigitte Frase writes: "As a child exploring

/ a river bank, I turned a grass blade / over and over, discovering / how attention will coax out the strangeness lurking in all things."[1] I think of that line often and am starting, through daily practice and discernment, to do less and pay attention more. I am indebted to the feminist literature that has illuminated the institutions and practices of silencing to oppress socially marginalized people. At the same time, I am engaged in a spiritual practice in which silence is embraced as regenerating, clarifying: an inner space of refuge and ease.

This essay examines two dimensions of silence—oppressive and liberating—through the voices of women of color. In the 1970s and '80s, second-generation feminists extolled the importance of speaking the truths of women's lives. They emphasized speaking to confront patriarchal power that had been used to separate and exploit women's existences; they highlighted the degree to which silence is intimately connected to institutionalized power. As feminist writer Robin Patric Clair notes in her book *Organizing Silence:* "Silence participates in the creation of our lives."[2]

SILENCE AS OPPRESSIVE

In "The Transformation of Silence into Language and Action," an essay published in the 1984 collection *Sister Outsider,* Black feminist poet Audre Lorde stated:

> In becoming forcibly and essentially aware of my mortality, and of what I wished and wanted for my life, however short it might be, priorities and omissions became strongly etched in a merciless light, and what I most regretted were my silences. Of what had I ever been afraid? To question or to speak as I believed could have meant pain, or death. But we all hurt in so many different ways, all the time, and pain will either change or end. Death, on the other hand, is the final silence. And that might be coming quickly, now, without regard for

whether I had ever spoken what needed to be said, or had only betrayed myself into small silences, while I planned someday to speak, or waited for someone else's words. And I began to recognize a source of power within myself that comes from the knowledge that while it is most desirable not to be afraid, learning to put fear into perspective gave me great strength.

I was going to die, if not sooner than later, whether or not I had ever spoken myself. My silences had not protected me. Your silence will not protect you.[3]

Lorde advocates that women communicate across differences, that race, class, and sexual identity be honored despite long-standing historical divisions that have been perpetuated by a dominant culture. Difference is to be embraced rather than feared; in fact, it is difference that must be named and celebrated, for as Lorde says, "There are so many silences to be broken."[4]

In illuminating how women self-silence in order to protect themselves or to avoid naming differences, Lorde rejects a dominant patriarchal culture that perpetuates itself by elevating rational thinking and language. Lorde is among numerous feminist writers who have published critiques of patriarchy, heterosexism, and middle-class normativity.

Audre Lorde noted in numerous essays and public speeches that the term "women," as understood by white women, does not fully extend to the complex social realities encountered by Black, Indigenous, Latinx, Asian, and multiracial women. As white women's critiques of patriarchy and classism gained credence during the second-generation feminist movement, women of color denounced the racism in the white feminist movement. Indeed, it is not only "women," but women with experiences of colonialism, racial segregation after centuries of slavery, immigration, and multilingual communities, who must speak their complicated truths. Gloria Anzaldúa, in her 1987 book *Borderlands: La Frontera,* describes the wounding of the india-Mestiza.

For 300 years she has been a slave, a force of cheap labor, colonized by the Spaniard, the Anglo, by her own people (and in Mesoamerica her lot under the Indian patriarchs was not free of wounding). For 300 years she was invisible, she was not heard. Many times she wished to speak, to act, to protest, to challenge. The odds were heavily against her. She hid her feelings; she hid her truths; she concealed her fire; but she kept stoking the inner flame. She remained faceless and voiceless, but a light shone through her veil of silence.[5]

Anzaldúa describes the multiple ways in which women are expected to adhere to the norms of the dominant culture, including European colonizing culture in which Indian and Spanish languages, as well as brown skin, represent deviance. Yet she also points to her familial "border" culture, in which women's bodies, queer sexuality, and challenges to patriarchy render the feminist writer an outcast. Anzaldúa locates cultural silencing, and therefore visionary writing, at these intersections. To adhere to silencing is to allow white supremacist and patriarchal systems to perpetuate dominance, exploitation, and disproportionate suffering of female-bodied persons. To adhere to one's own inner truth is to speak. Anzaldúa writes: "I will no longer be made to feel ashamed of existing. I will have my voice: Indian, Spanish, white. I will have my serpent's tongue— my woman's voice, my sexual voice, my poet's voice. I will overcome the tradition of silence."[6]

The tradition of silencing to which Alzaldúa refers is found among all colonized cultures. Vietnamese scholar and filmmaker Trinh Minh-ha, trained in the hegemonic discourses of anthropology, describes academic discourse as fundamentally rooted in "othering," in the dichotomies of "us" versus "them." Silencing, then, marginalizes, separates, and alienates. It is perpetuated as a top-down institutionalized practice.

SILENCE AS LIBERATING

Yet Minh-ha also recognizes the regenerating aspects of silence. The first vignette of her 1989 text *Woman, Native, Other* points to the cherished aspects of quietness in the cultivation of wisdom and the bestowing of knowledge by village elders. As women, especially, claim their agency, Minh-ha writes of the power of silence: "Silence as a refusal to partake in the story does sometimes provide us with a means to gain a hearing. It is voice, a mode of uttering, and a response in its own right."[7] Silence, then, can be a tool of resistance, an action that is recognized as powerful in its commitment to speak. Furthermore, Christine Keating writes, it is important to distinguish between different forms of silence: oppressive silences but also silences that are useful—indeed, indispensable—for social change. Keating states: "Another mode of silent resistance might be called 'silent witness.' This form of silence is often—though it doesn't have to be—organized and collective and is used as a marker of respect, or mourning, of protest, and of defiance . . . this form of silence takes on its resistant edge in part because of the alternative sociality that the students create through their action."[8]

As recent scholarship points to a false binary between speech and powerlessness, emerging scholars argue that in asserting the need for women to speak out against their oppression, a tremendous burden is placed on those who are already oppressed in numerous ways.[9] Thus silence can be healing, strategic, and productive. Sheena Malhotra and Aimee Carrillo Rowe, the editors of *Silence, Feminism, Power: Reflections at the Edges of Sound*, write:

> *Silence, Feminism, Power* examines silence as a space of possibility. The authors argue that in entering the stillness of silence we might communicate deeply at the edges of sound. Silence allows us the space to breathe. It allows us the freedom of not

having to exist constantly in reaction to what is said. Standing in silence allows for that breath, for that reflection that can create a space of great healing. We theorize silence as a space of fluidity, non-linearity, and as a sacred, internal space that provides a refuge—especially for nondominant peoples. Silence is a process that allows one to go within before one has to speak or act. This is crucial if our work as activists, writers, and creative artists is to come from a grounded place that connects the spiritual with the political.[10]

These writers root themselves in the feminist traditions of Audre Lorde, Gloria Anzaldúa, and Trinh Minh-ha. And indeed, some of these earlier themes of silence as regenerative can be found in second-wave feminism. Anzaldúa, for example, writes that defiance against the status quo—not being in a constant mode of resisting the oppression that has been given to women— is central for feminist liberation: to pause, to listen, to inquire is to engage in acting (and not reacting): a "new consciousness."[11]

For the "new consciousness" to emerge, recent feminist scholars of color argue, the value of silence must be reimagined and reclaimed. Malhotra and Carrillo Rowe write:

> . . . we consider how feminists (white and of color) deploy, rewrite, and move through silences in multiple and often productive ways. Thus silence is inscribed through diverse tones and textures to reveal how women can be multiply positioned vis-à-vis silence, not always already subjected by it. . . . Here at the edges of sound we might cultivate a host of silent practices: we might dwell within the possibilities of silence; we might use our silences as a weapon; we might rest; we might meet one another; we might encounter our shadow and our light within its expansive embrace.[12]

Using silence for rest, for regeneration, for deeper listening facilitates greater presence, a heightened capacity to be at ease with difference and difficult dynamics. Alexandra Fidyk, writing on a "pedagogy of presence" in classroom teaching, reflects that the deliberate slowing down, cultivated stillness, and resonant silence is a meditative practice that rests on feminist principles:

> Living (teaching, researching, writing) as meditation—a form which silence beckons—involves the mind, but also the heart, the body, the spirit. . . . When one is no longer externally direct (valuing power, control, and predictable outcomes) and attunes to a deeper, inner resonance, the ego grows quiet and there arises an energy greater than itself. Here "living in tensionality" is not a case of either-or [but] rather both-and, marked "with limitations and with openness."[13]

For recent scholars, then, silence is not only oppressive; rather it is being claimed in the broader movement for liberation. Silence and stillness allow for a different kind of collective resistance to the status quo. My own experience with meditation and cultivating internal silence verifies this claim. I suggest that there can be tremendous shifts within the cultures of activist communities when silence as a practice is embraced: silence allows for the ego to subside, so that difference can flourish, presence can be cultivated, and healing can take place. In essence, silence can facilitate an extraordinary interior strength, envisioned by feminist writers and dharma practitioners, in the movement for liberation.

NOTES

1 Brigitte Frase, "Homegoing," in *Looking for Moe: Women Writing about Exile,* eds. Deborah Keenan and Roseann Lloyd (Minneapolis, MN: Milkweed Editions, 1990), 107.

2 Robin Patric Clair, *Organizing Silence: A World of Possibilities* (Albany, NY: State University of New York Press, 1998), 187.

3 Audre Lorde, "The Transformation of Silence into Language and Action" (1977), in *Sister Outsider* (New York: Ten Speed Press, 2007 [1984]), 40–41.

4 Ibid., 44. Audre Lorde was a contemporary of the poet Adrienne Rich, whose 1979 book *On Lies, Secrets, and Silence* was pivotal for highlighting the dimensions on which women are silenced. Rich writes that women are told they cannot take up space, and therefore women must assert themselves in order to take charge of their lives.
5 Gloria Anzaldúa, *Borderlands: La Frontera* (San Francisco, CA: Aunt Lute Books, 2012 [1987]), 44–45.
6 Ibid., 81.
7 Trinh T. Minh-ha, *Woman, Native, Other* (Bloomington, IN: Indiana University Press, 1989), 83.
8 Christine Keating, "Resistant Silences," in *Silence, Feminism, Power: Reflections at the Edges of Sound,* eds. Sheena Malhotra and Aimee Carrillo Rowe (London: Palgrave Macmillan, 2013), 26.
9 Aimee Carrillo Rowe and Sheena Malhotra, "Still the Silence," in *Silence, Feminism, Power,* 1.
10 Ibid., 2.
11 Anzaldúa, 100.
12 Malhotra and Carrillo Rowe, 15.
13 Alexandra Fidyk, "Attuned to Silence: A Pedagogy of Presence," in *Silence, Feminism, Power,* 126.

KEMETIC YOGA, AN ANCIENT EGYPTIAN SPIRITUALITY

by Yirser Ra Hotep (Elvrid Lawrence), AM/MSW, E-RYT,
Master Kemetic Yoga Instructor

THE RE-MEMBERING OF AUSAR: AN ALLEGORICAL PARABLE OF KEMETIC YOGA

One of the ideas we hear associated with Yoga a lot is the concept of union. People appear to view this idea of union as relating to the merging of one's consciousness with that of the divine source of the All. In the spiritual science that emerges from Kemet (ancient Egypt/pre-European-Arab invasion Egypt), we find many aspects of Yogic spirituality and psychology being examined.

One of the most well-known and ubiquitous stories from ancient Egypt is the legend of the resurrection of Ausar. Ausar, who is commonly known by the Greek pronunciation of his name, Osiris, is the Kemetic/African manifestation of the concept of resurrection and rebirth. His story is the root of the Western idea of becoming born again. Rebirth is related to the ideas of salvation and atonement that form the fundamental pillars of Western religious, spiritual, and subconscious psychology. The story of the resurrection of Christ (a word that originates from the Kemetic word KRST, another form of mummy or the everlasting merging of the human with the Divine All called Neter) has its origins from the story of Ausar and his resurrection after being ritually murdered by his brother Set. Ausar, who is the husband of Auset, is also the father of Heru, who in the same story was born via a virgin birth after his father's death in order to restore the natural order of the universe, which was called Ma'at by the Kemites.

According to the Kemetic sages, Ausar was the king of Kemet and father of their civilization. When he descended to the earth, he taught them the arts and science of how to live a spiritual and civilized life under the Principles of Ma'at, which are Order, Balance, Justice, Reciprocity, and Harmony. These five principles were viewed as governing principles of the universe, and each person was committed to live in conformity with them in order to achieve the highest level of spiritual insight, self-mastery, self-realization, and self-actualization. Every king after Ausar vowed to maintain Ma'at and to restore it if it ever was absent due to foreign invasion or social disruption because every aspect of inner spiritual life and outer mundane life was governed by it. The Five Pillars of Ma'at were accompanied by 42 Laws (ten of which were copied by the Israelites and Christians as the Ten Commandments). These 42 Laws provided specific guideposts to supplement the philosophical and spiritual precepts of the five Ma'at Pillars.

One was expected to achieve Ma'at through the practice of what is commonly called Yoga today. In Kemet their "Yoga" was characterized by meditation, postures and movements, prayer/chanting, ancestral connection, the acquisition of divine and scientific knowledge, being of service, humility, ritual, and merging consciousness with the divine by achieving Amen-Ta. Amen-Ta or Amenta is often distorted by the Western scholars who study Kemet as something called "heaven." In actuality Amen-Ta is the abode of Ausar or the hidden land (Amen = hidden, Ta = land/place), a place within the divine consciousness that one reaches as a consequence of practicing and living Ma'at.

In the allegorical story of transition to Amenta commonly called The Judgment, the heart (consciousness) of a deceased person is weighed against the feather (a representation of Ma'at) on the Scale of Ma'at (the original scales of justice). The person's heart, which is the portal through which consciousness and awareness flow to the self initially as one experiences the steady stream of life, contains the accumulation of life's experiences. In this allegory the heart must be lighter or as light as the feather of Ma'at in order for the deceased person (a metaphor for a spiritual aspirant) to enter into Amen-Ta and to reside with Ausar. In this context Ausar is a metaphor for supreme divine consciousness that each of us is tasked with manifesting as we move through the flow of consciousness called existence.

In the story of Ausar, he was murdered, and his body dismembered, cut into fourteen pieces. Each one of the fourteen parts of his body were spread to different regions of the world by his "enemies" in order that he become forgotten and outside of consciousness. All of mythology is metaphor for larger truths and is often based upon actual events that took place in some form or another in the mist of forgotten time. Ausar's body parts were reassembled by his female counterpart (sacred feminine) Auset. In one of the greatest acts of sacred feminine achievement, Auset gathers the body parts, reassembles them, reanimates Ausar, and causes herself to become pregnant with their son Heru, who brings Set back into his proper place and in the end restores Ma'at or the Divine Order.

When Ausar awakens, he realizes that the disparate parts of his self have been reassembled or re-membered. He also realizes that his true nature is not to exist on the terrestrial plane of existence but to simultaneously remain in the Amen-Ta or spirit world to which he had gone when he was without the body. He is therefore in the physical realm and spirit realm at the same time. "In the world but not of the world." In Kemetic spiritual science, this state of being is known as RSWT QWED, a meditative state where one achieves a consciousness similar to lucid dreaming where you are awake and conscious within your sleep simultaneously. The hieroglyphic symbol for this state is an open eye resting on a bed. The priests of Kemet used this technique to heal those suffering from trauma when they came to the Per Ankh (House of Life/Temple) for healing.

The practice of engaging in movements, postures, breathing, meditation, and everything that is called Yoga today were all meant to lead the spiritual aspirant back to Ausar (self in the awakened divine form) or a form of remembering your true nature as a divine being.

THE AFRICAN SYSTEM: KEMETIC YOGA

There are two basic aspects to my practice of Yoga. One is what I call the YogaSkills Method or YSM. The other is Kemetic Yoga, which originates from Egypt. This African system of Yoga is a wisdom that combines self-development, self-discovery, and the transformation of mind, body, and spirit. Through deep breathing and meditation one can connect to the higher self.

YogaSkills Method is my understanding of the nature, purpose, and way of Yoga philosophy, theory, and practice. I believe that YSM encompasses the best of what Yoga has to offer and is based upon the ancient intent of Yoga as a system of spiritual transcendence. Transcendence simply means becoming aware of your true nature and achieving your true potential as a spiritual being. This same concept is at the heart of Kemetic (ancient Egyptian) spiritual science that was at the core of their ancient culture that allowed them to create a civilization that is unsurpassed today in many ways.

YogaSkills Method has ten basic components in relationship to the practice of Yoga. They are:

1. The purpose of Yoga movements and postures is not primarily for the body but to benefit the development of the mind.

2. Yoga movements and postures place primary emphasis on the control of the breath in order to move and circulate life force.

3. In the same way that we have a physical body that has a specific anatomy and physiology and that operates in a specific manner, we also have a spiritual or energetic body that has a specific anatomy and physiology and operates on the circulation of life force. This life force is something we are born with and is replenished from a substance in the air that the Indians call *prana* and the sages of ancient Kemet (Egypt) called *ankh*. This substance is the force called *vital* in Latin and that God breathed into the clay after forming it into the shape of a human being. The Chinese call this substance *chi*. In Japan it is called *ki*.

4. The physical body has a corresponding subtle body or bioenergetic body (nonphysical, invisible, and energy

based). The major energy structures in the physical body—i.e., the nerve plexuses and endocrine glands—correspond to the major energy structures in the bio-energetic body, commonly called the *chakras* in India or *karkars* (energy circles) in the Kemetic language. In the same way that the physical body operates due to the operation of organs, circulation of blood through blood vessels, nerve impulses through nerve endings, and chemical messages via the endocrine system, the bioenergetic body operates through the generation and movement of energy via the *chakras/karkars* and the numerous energy vessels or channels.

5. In the same way that Yoga postures are supposed to be done in a manner that is in harmony with the physical anatomy and physiology of the body, YSM demands that they also be performed in such a manner as to be in harmony with the exact way that energy moves and operates in the bioenergetic body.

6. Therefore, YogaSkills Method recognizes that each inhalation of the breath should cause energy to rise up the energy channel that corresponds to the spine and connects to the energy center (*chakra/karkar*) at the crown of the head. Each exhalation should send energy through the energy channels that correspond to the arms and legs into the hands and feet. In this manner the entire being is inundated (flooded) with life force in the same way that the land of Kemet (Egypt) was inundated annually with the floodwaters of the Nile River (properly called Hapi) that deposited fertile soil from the deepest heart of Africa.

7. Under YSM we utilize a technique called Rule of Four Breathing and Geometric Progression. This means

that four steps characterize each breath: inhale, pause, exhale, and pause. Each pose is divided into steps that correspond with this breathing pattern.

8. By performing our Yoga postures in this manner we are developing specific mental skills that should transfer into our everyday life and provide us with the ability to manifest what we seek to accomplish in life.

9. Some of the mental skills we develop are concentration, focus, patience, self-love, critical thinking, discrimination, independence, withdrawal, etc.

10. We also develop our psychic abilities such as precognition, telepathy, and clairvoyance.

Kemetic Yoga refers to the entire spiritual system of self-development created by the sages of ancient Egypt. It is a worldview that recognizes the nature of reality and our place in the universe. Kemetic Yoga is the understanding of our connection to the spirits of our ancestors and the true nature of Divine Universal Forces (deities properly called Neteru). From this perspective we recognize that there is an omnipotent and unknowable creative mind called Neter from which all in the universe comes from. Religious minds attempt to call this unknowable Mind a being (named God) and give it a human personality (based upon a European male).

Our ancestors in ancient Kemet simply accepted that this force is beyond our human ability to fully grasp and were content with this acknowledgment of human limitation. At the same time they recognized that this universal force manifested itself in a myriad of ways. These manifestations of Neter (where we get the word nature) are the forces of nature. These are galaxies, constellations, stars, planets, and the elements of Earth, Air, Fire, and Water. They are those ascended spiritual beings that lived in physical form thousands or even millions of years ago in epochs when the possibility of human potential was much greater and they were able to reach tremendous heights of spiritual consciousness and power far beyond our current ability to comprehend.

These are the Neteru (Divine Forces). Allegorical stories were created to convey the underlying truths that these forces represent, and these allegories gave rise to myths and legends. Ausar, Auset, Heru, Tehuti, Set, Sekhmet, Selkhet, Min, Ra, Shu, Geb, Nut, Nebthet, Hetheru, Imhotep, etc., are legendary beings that became the archetypical examples of how we should pattern our lives.

Kemetic Yoga emerges from this cosmological foundation and an understanding of the Seven Laws of Ancient Kemet as enunciated by the Great Sage Tehuti or Thoth. These principles were enunciated by Wayne B. Chandler in the book *Ancient Future*:

1. The Principle of Mentalism: The All is Mind. (Everything that comes into being is a result of a mental state that precedes it.)

2. The Principle of Correspondence: As Above, So Below.

3. The Principle of Vibration: All things vibrate and are in motion.

4. The Principle of Polarity: Differences are illusions and only a matter of degree.

5. The Principle of Gender: Everything has its masculine and feminine aspects.

6. The Principle of Rhythm: All things rise and all things fall.

7. The Principle of Causation: All things have a cause, and all causes have an effect.

Upon the foundation of this understanding an entire civilization with all of its scientific and psychospiritual content was built. It is from this framework that Kemetic Yoga is based. In fact this framework is the foundation of the original philosophy of all Yoga prior to its distortion and ultimate descent into its current commercial state as simply a physical exercise used primarily for fitness.

ANCESTRALIZATION

by Cosmore Marriott, Dagara Elder

ANCESTRALIZATION WAS ALWAYS PART OF the African culture; it was part of our wisdom teachings. Many of us who were taken from our Indigenous lands lost this important connection to our ancestors. It is my belief, the belief of the Dagara people (from Burkina Faso), as well as that of most Indigenous cultures that everyone is born with a purpose. When an individual is observed, accepted without the need to be molded, and is nurtured based on what is observed naturally, there is a greater chance that their life's purpose will be brought to fruition without inertia. Unfortunately, that is rarely the case. It is my understanding that we are sent here from the realm of the ancestors with a clear purpose. In addition, our ancestors are there to support us in fulfilling our purposes.

According to the *Cambridge Dictionary,* purpose is defined as "an intention or aim; a reason for doing something or allowing something to happen." In an ideal world, everyone would be born, their purpose realized, and then it is brought to fruition. Typically, this does not happen. "I need to find my purpose" is a common phrase often uttered by many adults who find themselves in a spiritual crisis. This usually manifests as a state of unrest and a constant searching.

So how do we get to this state of unrest where we find ourselves searching for our purpose? There are numerous reasons for such a phenomenon to exist. In his book *Let Your Life Speak,* sociologist Parker Palmer wrote about how the purpose or the essence of an individual is observable around the age of four. When the parents or primary caregivers ignore what is obvious and choose to nurture their children according to their own desires, this will result in the diminishing of the child's true nature. Some of these children will eventually reach a point in life when they begin to experience this unrest. If they are courageous, they will then choose to take on the task of the journey home to their authentic self. On the other hand, some will never experience this unrest and accept a life possibly because they have never developed an awareness of self or they are not courageous enough to move beyond a limited state of being.

Some individuals experience trauma, which causes them to constrict in order to avoid any recollection of any emotional or physical pain. This also results in the inability of such individuals to function at their full potential. Transgenerational trauma also has a negative effect on one's ability to live at their full potential.

A lot of what we learn and how we show up in the world is modeled from one generation to the next. Moreover, this is typically not intentional. Most of the patterns that we adapt to were originally started by previous generations as a way of survival. Some of these patterns served our ancestors well and eventually are beneficial to us today. Other patterns were the result of mal-adaptive coping skills that might have served our ancestors to give them a sense of safety. Without the awareness that these skills no longer served them, they eventually became a way of life and were passed down to the next generation. According to Native American tradition, it takes three generations for a pattern to become fixed within a lineage. This tradition also believes that it takes seven generations until it is realized that the pattern of living or behavior is an obstacle that has been preventing each generation from realizing their full potential and living their purposes.

Today, when an individual realizes that they are exhibiting dysfunctional thoughts and behaviors that are getting in the way of their relationships, their work, and even their state of well-being, they typically seek help in the form of psychotherapy in order to find some relief from their situation. The technique usually employed is Cognitive Behavioral therapy (CBT). The process of CBT will guide the individual to take a look at their core beliefs and their values, which are often limited to the individual's recollection of their life events. They might remember that some core beliefs and values are passed on or they might also recall why they created them as a way of coping. CBT is recognized as a very effective technique for changing an individual's thought and behavioral patterns.

Ancestralization is a way of correcting these patterns at a very deep level. The process of Ancestralization involves a very deep and long ritual aimed at raising the frequency of a particular ancestor to their divine blueprint. Just as we find that we have endured hardship in realizing our divine potential, so did our ancestors. But we must remember that some of these core beliefs and values that we have been living by were started by our ancestors all in the name of survival.

Now imagine that you have been standing on the shoulders of ancestors who have been supporting you from a limited reality of self. This is what resulted in some of the maladaptive coping skills that have been passed on and rendered us feeling unfulfilled. Although a particular ancestor might not have fulfilled their purpose, through the process of Ancestralization, they are given an opportunity to remember what it is like to be fully alive; to be in the frequency of their divine blueprint. From that place, they are able to better support us in reaching our fullest potential. This is, however, not automatic. It is necessary that we deliberately engage these ancestors in our endeavors to aid us in remembering who we really are. That is liberation!

In order to do this, we must establish and maintain relationships with them. Imagine running into a relative you have never met but have heard of, and you immediately begin to ask them for favors. How do you feel that would go over? Just like you've been always connected to this relative, you are also always connected to your ancestors. Yes, it is true that they are with us all the time; however, they have to be called upon in order to help us. When they are intentionally invoked and a specific request is made, the outcome seems fortuitous. In the Judeo-Christian world this would be referred to as grace. This means that they are doing an immense amount of work on our behalf from the nonphysical realm, the ancestral realm.

Ancestors who have been ancestralized and to some degree those who were not are also capable of doing work for other family members and not only for the individual who engaged the Ancestralization process. Very recently I engaged in an ancestral ritual to address a transgenerational issue that has been showing up in the family and has seriously affected one of my sisters. Ancestors who have been ancestralized, along with others who exhibited behavior that has perpetuated this pattern, were invoked and tasked with correcting the issue. They were also asked to show me a sign that they have heard my request and to show me a sign that they are addressing the issue. By the next morning, my sister demonstrated a sign that the work had started.

Having a relationship with our ancestors was a way of life for our forefathers. Through colonialization and the need to survive, many ancestors from the African Diaspora were forced to relinquish this part of their culture and had to take on the ways of the dominant culture. My observation now is that individuals are seeking the ways of our ancestors as a way of healing and finding one's way in life. I've also noticed that the numbers of persons of the African Diaspora who are engaging in ancestral work are increasing. With this movement there is a great potential for the liberation of the race.

RESOURCES

Parker Palmer, *Let Your Life Speak: Listening for the Voice of Vocation*, Jossey-Bass, 2000.

Malidoma Patrice Somé, *The Healing Wisdom of Africa: Finding Life Purpose through Nature, Ritual, and Community*, Jeremy P. Tarcher/ Putnam, 1999.

Malidoma Patrice Somé, *Of Water and the Spirit: Ritual, Magic, and Initiation in the Life of an African Shaman*, Penguin, 1995.

WHY DID JESUS TURN WATER INTO WINE?

by Biko Agozino

CHRONIC ALCOHOLISM WAS INTRODUCED TO Africa during the raids to kidnap millions of Africans to be enslaved for more than 400 years. The European human traffickers used to arm the African kidnappers with rum and brandy to give them Dutch courage. Since then, the consumption of what American Indian Natives derogate as firewater by Africans remains incredibly high. In order to create a monopoly for imported gin during colonialism, the British banned the local moonshine for supposedly health reasons. However, the brewing of local gin from palm wine and its sale remained high enough for Isaac Adaka Boro to claim that his band of "twelve day revolutionaries" arrested an Igbo woman who had gone to Port Harcourt to purchase the gin for sale in Onitsha.[1] They claimed that the local gin was part of their resources and they detained the woman for two days while drinking all her gin but she escaped probably while they were drunk and asleep. It is reported that South Africans now lead in the consumption of alcohol in Africa with Nigeria coming second and this might be an explanation for the high rates of violent crimes and chronic diseases in both countries.[2]

To critique such high levels of alcoholism in Africa, Professor El Anatsui of the University of Nigeria makes most of his sculptures and installations from the aluminum tops of liquor bottles consumed in Africa.[3] The double entendre here is that wine traditionally came in pots among Africans and so using the bottle tops of intoxicating liquor to sculpt the folktale about the breaking of the pot of wisdom is a riddle intended to refer to the need to break the habit of consuming pots of wine in order to develop wisdom in Africa. As the folktale goes among the Igbo of Nigeria and among the Ashanti of Ghana, the tortoise or *mbe* and the spider or *ananse,* respectively, being physically weak in the animal kingdom, had to rely on their wisdom to survive. To ensure their survival in a world where might was right, they decided to collect all the wisdom in the world and hide it up an iroko tree where no one could reach it but themselves. However, while they were climbing the tree with the pot of wisdom, along came the goat who was known to lack wisdom and so was not asked to contribute to the pot of wisdom. The goat looked up and said to the wise guys climbing with a heavy pot, "Why are you climbing that tree so clumsily with that pot when everyone knows that the tortoise does not know how to climb and the spider is not strong enough to carry such a heavy pot?" This revealed that even the goat had some wisdom that needed to be added to the global pot of wisdom. The climbers decided to go down and ask the goat to add his wisdom to the pot but slipped and the pot fell down and smashed to pieces with the result that wisdom spread all over the world for everyone to access. In other words, the colonizers did not have any monopoly over wisdom, contrary to the assumption of Orientalism and the Western Enlightenment.[4]

Indigenous Igbo worldview frowns upon habitual drunkenness just like Baptist doctrines that teach against the ills of alcoholism. The Igbo are mainly agricultural, commercial, or educational in occupation and these are not the kinds of professions that could mix easily with alcoholism. Going to the farm drunk is unheard of and going to the market drunk is a recipe for disaster. No serious student or teacher would dream of going to school drunk either. Yet the Igbo do not completely ban the consumption of wine and, indeed, they require wine for many religious and communal rituals. Interestingly, the palm wine required is often in small quantities and the first drinks are always to be poured on the ground as libations to mother earth before the rest is shared by all the men gathered for the ritual in such a way that there was no risk of anyone getting drunk and the libations are not big enough to get the ancestors drunk either.[5]

Only an entertainer like Unoka, the father of Okonkwo in Achebe's *Things Fall Apart,* was tolerated as a drunk but even he was a talented musician who performed without charging a fee.[6] Achebe used his character to encourage the Igbo to address alcoholism as a public health issue instead of blaming Unoka as a lazy man who died of malnutrition when it could have been alcoholism that caused the malnourishment. Hence, the parable of the creditor being told by Unoka to read the writings on his wall and realize that his debt was a small one compared to the bigger ones may have been an admonition by Achebe to the materialist Igbo to avoid regarding intellectuals and poets as lazy, because the society owed them much more than they may owe society. The writings on the wall by Unoka, the talented

musician who charged no fee for his performances, could have
been what his society owed him.

After the Women's War of 1929 against colonialism in Igboland, an Oxford University–trained theologian, C. K. Meek, was
dispatched as a colonial anthropologist to find out if the Igbo
women and their Ibibio neighbors were drunk on something to
make them resist colonization. To his surprise, he found that wine
sharing was almost always ceremonial and that the wine was
always offered to Chukwu, the great God, or to Ani, the earth
Goddess, or to Anyanwu, the Sun spirit before the remnants were
shared equally by the men present. In the case of Chukwu, the
preferred offering was water. There was no reference to women
sharing wine among themselves though they could be given some
drinks by the men, not a lot, and so, by implication, the women
who waged the Women's War were not drunk.[7]

The Yoruba neighbors of the Igbo have a different view of
alcoholism even though most of the palm-wine tappers among
the Yoruba were of Igbo origin. Wole Soyinka, the 1986 Nobel
Prize in Literature laureate, highlights the danger of alcoholism and the blind worship of authority in his poem "Idanre,"
in which the Yoruba war and iron deity, Ogun, got drunk and
slaughtered his own followers in the battlefield.[8] The poem was
published in 1969 while Soyinka was in solitary confinement
for opposing the genocidal war against the Igbo with the support of Yoruba elites who were apparently drunk on power but
remained the idols of their followers despite their complicity in
the killing of millions of their Igbo brothers and sisters in Biafra.

Amos Tutuola caricatured the culture of binge drinking in
The Palm-Wine Drinkard by presenting the hero as someone who
consumed hundreds of kegs of palm wine in the morning before
going to the farm and then consumed dozens more kegs in the
evening when he got back from the farm.[9] That obvious exag-
geration on the insatiable appetite for wine among the Yoruba

is missed by most readers of the book but Achebe alluded to it in his lecture at the University of Ife (now Obafemi Awolowo University, Ife) where he talked about the truth of fiction.[10] According to him, anyone who lusted after power risked being power-drunk just like the palm-wine drunkards of Tutuola. Such power-drunkenness was evident in the fact that highly educated Yoruba elites shamelessly supported the genocide against the Igbo in Biafra and claimed that "all is fair in warfare" and that "starvation is a legitimate weapon of war." Were they drunk?

The Southern Baptist Convention teaches that there are two kinds of wine referred to in the Bible—alcoholic wine and non-alcoholic wine. When the reference is positive, they believe that it is a reference to nonalcoholic wine.[11] I did not know this when I traveled and my neighbor who was a pastor in the SBC helped me to receive some furniture that I ordered. I bought him a bottle of wine on my return and he said that his doctrine was against alcohol. I asked him why Jesus changed water into wine. He said that he wished that he would change it back to water. I laughed and told him that it was still water because the Bible said that he asked the servants to fill the six stone water jugs that held 20–30 gallons each with water (John 2:6). He blessed it and asked the servants to serve it to the wedding guests. They loved it and said to the bridegroom, you saved the best drink for last (John 2:9–10). Jesus must have laughed and said to himself, that is right, water is the best drink, drink it and enjoy it like you enjoy wine. I keep having this discussion with pastors in Africa and with students in the United States, and they keep insisting that the water became wine, but I keep wondering if Jesus, the healer, would support alcoholism? It is true that Jesus was always giving the good wine to his followers, especially at the Last Supper where he turned the wine into his blood and asked them to drink it in his memory, but seventy-two disciples were shocked by such a ritual and deserted him earlier when he preached that whoever eats of his flesh and drinks of his blood remains in him and he in them (John 6:56–66). The only follower of Jesus who apparently got drunk was Judas after collecting the thirty pieces of silver and before ending his own life in regret over the betrayal. Lot got drunk and his daughters knew him, whereas Noah got drunk and cursed his son for laughing at his nakedness.

In 1995, South African political leaders gathered to celebrate 100 years of the South African Breweries. Nelson Mandela was reported as noting that the brewery was part of the oppressive structures designed to control the labor of Africans under white minority rule. Africans were not allowed to be served in bars that were for whites only, some workers were paid parts of their wages in alcohol, and African women who brewed illicit drinks and served in the shebeens were regularly raided and arrested with their customers to ensure a monopoly over alcohol sales for the white-owned breweries. The shebeens became symbolic as the space for the resistance against apartheid but the alcoholism also served to worsen the violence and public health crises facing Black South Africans.[12] Though a nondrinker who avoided the shebeens, Mandela recognized the rights of adults to freely choose to drink in moderation as a form of "innocent pleasure."

I am happy to note that the residents of my village were the ones who made a rule to ban the drinking of moonshine or *ogogoro* during community events like weddings and funerals in the village. They had seen too many villagers die from addiction to the push-me-I-push-you drink and so they could not tolerate it anymore as a public ritual. I commended them and asked them to share the ban with neighboring villages and also teach that our women have always been wise enough to avoid alcoholism with hardly any women being found to be a habitual drunk in the villages. We should learn from the women to avoid binge drinking.

The teaching against alcoholism among people of African descent is also found among Rastafarians who shun the firewater and prefer the natural herb that heals the nation. Also, Muslims proscribe alcohol as *haram*, but they differ from the traditional Igbo democratic republicanism that allows individuals to consume what they prefer privately while using education and public health campaigns to get people to say no to alcoholism. Education works better than prohibition as a public health measure given the failed experience of the United States with Prohibition, during which African Americans were racially profiled as posing a threat to (white) women whenever the men drank in segregated saloons that were for "Negroes Only."[13]

NOTES

1 Boro, Isaac Adaka. (1982). "My Early Life," chapter 1 of *The Twelve-Day Revolution,* https://web.archive.org/web /20150420192128/http://www.adakaboro.org/the12dayrev /chap-1-my-early-life.

2 Ngugi, Fredrick. (2016). "Why Alcoholism Is on the Rise in Africa," *Face2faceAfrica,* https://face2faceafrica.com/article/alcoholism -rise-africa.

3 Agozino, Biko. (2014). "The Broken Pot of Wisdom," http:// massliteracy.blogspot.com/2014/04/the-broken-pot-of-wisdom.html.

4 Said, Edward. (1978). *Orientalism.* New York: Penguin.

5 Nehusi, Kimani. (2015). *Libation: An Afrikan Ritual of Heritage in the Circle of Life.* Lanham, MD: University Press of America.

6 Achebe, Chinua. (2010). *The African Trilogy.* London: Everyman's Library. Edited with an introduction by Chimamanda Ngozi Adichie. The book collects *Things Fall Apart, No Longer at Ease,* and *Arrow of God* in one volume.

7 Meek, C. K. (1931). *Law and Authority among a Nigerian Tribe: A Study of Indirect Rule.* Oxford: Oxford University Press.

8 Soyinka, Wole. (1969). *Idanre and Other Poems.* London: Methuen.

9 Tutuola, Amos. (1952). *The Palm-Wine Drunkard.* London: Faber and Faber.

10 Achebe, Chinua. (1989). "The Truth of Fiction" in his *Hopes and Impediments: Selected Essays.* London: Doubleday.

11 Roach, David. (2018). "Baptists & Alcohol: Is the Consensus Shift-
     ing?" *BaptistPress,* www.bpnews.net/51897/baptists-and-alcohol-is
     -the-consensus-shifting.
12 Ambler, C. (2014). "The Drug Empire: Control of Drugs in Africa, a
     Global Perspective." In Klantschnig, G., Carrier, N., and Ambler, C.
     (eds.), *Drugs in Africa.* New York: Palgrave Macmillan.
13 McGirr, Lisa. (2016, January 1). "You'll Never Drink Again: Sex,
     Race, Science and the Real Story of Prohibition," *Salon,* www.salon
     .com/2016/01/01/youll_never_drink_again_sex_race_science_and
     _the_real_story_of_prohibition/.

WHEN WILL WE SING, DANCE, TELL OUR STORIES, DWELL IN SILENCE, AND BEGIN BREATHING AGAIN?

by Valerie Mason-John (Vimalasara)

IN MANY BUDDHIST TRADITIONS, THERE is the devotional practice of *puja,* a recitation to help purify body, speech, and mind. It is another form of mindfulness unifying the breath, voice, and body, which helps to soothe the heartmind. Sometimes people chant the text together. And sometimes it's done in call-and-response.

Call-and-response has a long history in the African tradition. It has been used in public gatherings, in music, and in religious rituals as a way of focusing and stilling the mind. Our ancestors also taught us mindfulness from the juju of the drums, the stomp of our feet, and through the resounding and healing a capella voices.

The transatlantic theft of African people, the Maafa, African Holocaust and the Holocaust of Enslavement, took away our song, our dance, our stories, our silence, our breath. We couldn't even beg for our breath, our life force lynched from the moment the white colonizer came and conducted such atrocities and genocide on the continent of Africa.

The origins of mental illness among Black Africans can go back to 1526 when the Portuguese first came to West Africa and took many of us to Brazil. If there was mental illness before, at least there were the close-knit families to take care of it.

In Africa when someone is spiritually, mentally, and/or physically sick, it is said that the healers will ask four questions. These questions were popularized by the late Angeles Arrien, who was a Basque American anthropologist. It's not certain where these first questions originated from.

- When did you stop singing?
- When did you stop dancing?
- When did you stop being enchanted by your own stories?
- When did you stop dwelling in the sweet territory of silence?

Spiritually, physically, and mentally all of this was taken away from us when we were ripped from the womb of mother earth. I add the final question to this list.

- When did you stop breathing?

These five questions are a mindfulness practice expressed through the body, speech, and mind. The breath is in every action, in every word, in every thought and feeling. It was through ritual, through dance, through the drums that we begin to taste the sweetness of the breath, and begin this reclamation of the spiritual, physical, and mental well-being. And many of us still cannot sing, dance, connect to our stories, be in the silence, and breathe, due to the systemic racism that continues to oppress us.

It's through devotional acts and ritual that we can tell our stories, renounce our stories, and find our voice, our play, our stories, our silence, and our breath again. *Pujas* in Buddhism are devotional acts of worship. The words often recited point us in the direction of wisdom. The words are the fingers pointing to the moon. The practice is to surrender to the text, by not getting caught up in what is said, and whether you believe it or not. If we surrender to the practice we will enter into the unknown.

I invite you to begin singing again, dancing again, be enchanted with your new stories, and allow yourself to enter into the sweet territory of silence when you can begin breathing again.

A DEVOTIONAL TEXT DONE IN CALL-AND-RESPONSE (IT CAN BE DONE IN UNISON IF PREFERRED)

- One person leads the text by saying a line, and everyone repeats together.

- The heading of each section is said only by the person leading, and then the rest of the section is done in call-and-response.

- The person leading invites the participants to reflect for 5 minutes at the end of each section.

- The word Buddha is used, and you can transpose it with the word God, Allah, Guides, or whatever is appropriate for your community.

- The word Dharma can be transposed with the word Teachings, Truth, or whatever is appropriate for the community.

- The word Sangha can be transposed with the word Community, Communities, or whatever is appropriate.

- The three lines referring to the Buddha, Dharma, Sangha are taken from a traditional dedication text written by my teacher, the late Venerable Sangharakshita.

The teacher/leader rings the gong/bell three times—and then says:

Repetition is the mother of knowledge.

(AFRICAN PROVERB)

OPENING REVERENCE

Done in call-and-response (the teacher/leader says a line and everyone together responds):

We reverence the earth, and give thanks for its food, shelter, and solidity in our bodies.

We reverence the water, and give thanks for its rain, its moisture, its fluidity in our bodies.

We reverence the fire, and give thanks for the sun, the heat, and the warmth in our bodies.

We reverence the wind, and give thanks for the air, the inhale and the exhale in our bodies.

We reverence space and give thanks for the space within us and surrounding our bodies.

We reverence consciousness and give thanks for it's awareness within and outside our bodies.

We reverence the Buddha, the perfectly enlightened one, the shower of the way.

We reverence the Dharma, the teaching of our Guides, which leads from darkness to light.

We reverence the Sangha, the fellowship of all our communities, that inspires and guides.

(THE LAST THREE LINES ARE ATTRIBUTED
TO THE VENERABLE SANGHARAKSHITA)

Reflection—the teacher/leader rings the gong/bell and says:

> Pause and reflect. What are you reverencing in your life? For example, what are your thoughts filled with?

The teacher/leader rings the gong/bell three times—and then says:

> Even the best dancer on the stage must retire sometime.
>
> (AFRICAN PROVERB)

OUR PRECIOUS OPPORTUNITY

Done in call-and-response (the teacher/leader says a line and everyone together responds):

> Our human birth
> ordinary and extraordinary
> Our human birth
> joyful and painful
> Our human birth
> healthy and unhealthy
> Our human birth
> longevity and fleeting
> Our human birth
> precious and worthless
> Don't let our birth be worthless.
> Let's embrace this precious opportunity.

Reflection—the teacher/leader rings the gong/bell and says:

> Pause and reflect on: How am I making the most of this precious life?

The teacher/leader rings the gong/bell three times—and then says:

> Life is the beginning of death.
> When an elder dies, a library burns to the ground.
>
> (AFRICAN PROVERB)

IMPERMANENCE

Done in call-and-response (the teacher/leader says a line and everyone together responds):

I love you and one day you and I will die.
We cannot escape it.
Death comes to everyone.

Death is unavoidable.
It will come to all of us,
today, tomorrow, next month, next year.

Death is unavoidable.
Even I will die.
Even you will die.
Everyone we know will die.

Death is unavoidable.
We may die before our parents.
We may die before our children.
We may die before our friends.
We may die before our loved ones.
We may die after our loved ones.

Death is unavoidable.
This is one of the few things we can guarantee in life.
During this next year someone we know will die.
Or we will know of someone who knows someone who has
    died.
In five years some of us may have even died.

Dying of old age, sickness, and disease is not a tragedy.
All compounded things are subject to death.
Denial of this kind of death is a tragedy.
Blame is a tragedy.
Saying it's not fair is a tragedy.

How we respond to these types of passing away can be a
   tragedy.

Somehow, some way we will have to face the death of
   ourselves,
The death of loved ones,
The death of family, the death of friends.

Dying from murder, fatal accidents, natural disasters is a
   tragedy.
And this kind of death can come to any one of us.
There is no guarantee that our life will come to an end due to
   the decaying body, the diseased body.

We must still learn to make peace with the death of a loved
   one, no matter how tragically they die.

As soon as we are born we are old enough to die.
The fragility of life will either haunt us, or liberate us.
Make peace with this unwanted friend,
They will point you in the direction of freedom.
Death will come to us all.
The fact is we just do not know when.
The resistance to this uncertainty will cause us suffering.
The clinging to the past will cause us misery.
Yes, Mourn, Wail, Rejoice, Celebrate, Commemorate.
Remember there is not a household who does not know
   death.
Buddha died, Jesus died, Allah died, Muhammad died.
Haile Selassie, Nelson Mandela, Toni Morrison, Martin
   Luther King Jr., Malcolm X, Harriet Tubman, Stephen
   Biko, Viola Desmond, Maya Angelou, Muhammad Ali,
   Rosa Parks, Mary Seacole, James Baldwin, Bob Marley,
   Marcus Garvey, William Cuffay, Sojourner Truth, C. L. R.
   James, and many more have died.

The longer we live, the more we will witness death.

In twenty years more of us will have died,
And in sixty years most of us will have died.

Never be too overjoyed when someone arrives.
Never be too saddened when someone leaves.
This can be a mini rehearsal for facing the inevitable.
An end of a beautiful meal, an end of a beautiful holiday, an
    end of a retreat,
An end of a relationship are mini rehearsals for death.

The wise mourn and move on.

Always hold lightly in your heart that this may be the last
    time you see the people you are with now.

If you can live like this, only loving-kindness, compassion,
    sympathetic joy, and equanimity will flow from your
    heart.

Death is unavoidable and it will come to all of us.

Reflection—the teacher/leader rings the gong/bell and says:

Pause and reflect. There is birth and there is death. How are
    you making the most of the in-between where life can
    flourish? (5 minutes)

The teacher/leader rings the gong/bell three times—and then
says:

No elephant ever complained about the weight of its trunk.

(AFRICAN PROVERB)

SPIRITUAL DEATH

Done in call-and-response (the teacher/leader says a line and
everyone together responds):

What perfect conditions I've had today
to help me make peace with the weight of my negative
    mental states, strong views, and aspects of self that keep
    me imprisoned in the mind.

Today is a good day to die because I have faith.
Today is a good day to die because I have energy.
Today is a good day to die because I have mindfulness.
Today is a good day to die because I have concentration.
Today is a good day to die because I have wisdom.
Today is a good day to die.

Reflection—the teacher/leader rings the gong/bell and says:

Pause and reflect. What are some of the conversations you
    still need to have? What do you need to let go of?

The teacher/leader rings the gong/bell three times—and then says:

Know the world in yourself. Never look for yourself in the
    world, for this would be to project your illusion.

(AFRICAN PROVERB)

SPIRITUAL REBIRTH

Done in call-and-response (the teacher/leader says a line and everyone together responds):

In this present moment I emerge without name.
In this present moment I emerge without gender.
In this present moment I emerge without sexuality.
In this present moment I emerge without race.
In this present moment I emerge without class.
In this present moment I emerge without disabilities.
In this present moment I emerge without color.
All that is left is a clear bright mind

Without fears, doubt, low self-esteem, self-hatred.
Just a loving mind toward the body I inhabit in this life.
It is empty of all thoughts, put-downs, and insecurities.

I can now move into the next moment with a lighter load.
I can now see how every thought
Is a rebirth of the one before.
I vow to keep on spiritually dying
Until my thoughts become dateless
Until my thoughts become emptiness
Until my thoughts become trackless.

I have confidence and trust because many African peoples for
     thousands of years have gained wisdom
And many more will continue to do so.
They have by letting go of their mental conditioning
Of being described as primitive, as savage, sambo, coon,
     wog, nigger, black, mugger, as athlete, as dancer, as per-
     former, as a failure, as unable to attain enlightenment.
All their conditionings they have destroyed. And I can
     destroy them too.

As I enter the stream of compassion,
Awake with Buddha mind
Awake with Dharma thoughts
Awake with Sangha communication

I will harken to the cries of the suffering in the world
And work tirelessly to save African Diaspora people
Roaming in the hell realms of police brutality
Abandoned in the hell realms of white supremacy
Chasing their tails in the hell realms of poverty
Living in the hell realms of their own tortured minds
I will not rest until the people living in the African Diaspora
Are Liberated, Free, and Black Lives Matter

In unison everyone says as loud as they can these three words, which mean well done, well done, well done:

Sadhu Sadhu Sadhu

The mantra can be sung as a lullaby or chanted, in a round, or as a harmony—find your own rhythm. The teacher/leader begins it and everyone joins in.

Move your voice, Move your body, Move your stories, Move your silence, and Move your breath.
Sabbe Satta Sukhi Hontu

(It means may all beings be happy, may all beings be well.)

PART FIVE

The Personal Is Political

IN SEARCH OF HYPOLITES

Making Sense of My African and Native American Ancestry

by Kabir Hypolite

WHERE TO BEGIN WHEN THE beginning is lost? The land-grab that drove Europeans to enslave, remove, and exterminate Native Americans also inspired them to capture and enslave millions of Africans from across the Atlantic. In the name of Christianity, racial superiority, and capitalism, Europeans distorted the realities of chattel slavery and Native genocide, deemphasizing their horrors and rationalizing their own behavior. The ensuing seesaw of military invasions, human trafficking, wholescale religious conversions, and spiritual demonization produced a kaleidoscope of social collapses, miscegenation, linguistic erasures, cultural amalgamations, and blurry color-based racial caste systems. Amid the passage of time and bloody conquests, Mobile and New Orleans became American cities. African slave trading and Native American genocides continued as individual personal traumas were continually minimized, normalized, rationalized, buried, and erased. Trying to identify ancestral connections in this mishmash is akin to finding multicolored needles in jumbled haystacks.

For me, the rural cotton bales and sugarcane barrels that eventually floated down the Mississippi and Alabama rivers to New Orleans and Mobile symbolize tragedies drowned in colonial silence. Like millions of Black and brown people today, I cannot identify my ancestors with confidence. Despite this white-washed history, my physical existence bears stubborn witness to the Caucasian, African, Asian, and Native American ancestry running through my veins. Mixed blood. Here am I.

My parents, Stella Mae MacCaskill (deceased) and Oscar Joseph Hypolite Jr., are two Deep South Creoles from Mobile, Alabama, and New Orleans, Louisiana. Originally, these cities were French colonial outposts seized from Native American lands along the Gulf's northern shores. Cherokee, Creek, Choctaw, Houma, Natchez, Chitimacha, Alibama, Coushatta, Hitchiti, and Chickasaw populated the areas that surrounded these frontier French fortress towns in the early 1700s. British, Spanish, and French colonials all traded control of these colonies before they ultimately became American cities in 1803 (New Orleans) and 1813 (Mobile).

New Orleans, from whence my father would flee in 1949, became a slave trading hub under France, Spain, and the United States. Africans originating from fifty-plus tribal kingdoms from West Africa, Mali, Nigeria, the Congo, and beyond found themselves in slavery's grip in New Orleans and surrounding plantations. I have repeatedly returned to New Orleans to make sense of the historical, cultural, and spiritual vortex that produced and expelled him.

Before the Catholic Church began systematically recording frontier births, European invaders (explorers, missionaries, settlers, etc.) mixed sexually with enslaved female Natives and Africans. Liberated and escaped Africans also integrated into Native tribes in the coastal and rivers areas surrounding New Orleans and Mobile (e.g., Maroons). They often raised families with the local peoples.

The slave trade Diaspora and Native American genocides spawned race-based oppressions for more than 400 years. Its legacy still swirls and collides even as its heirs try to identify, honor, or forget those who struggled to survive. My family's individual stories of unimaginable sufferings, deep losses, and triumphs are literally erased and distorted by historians, minimized and sanitized by educators, and paved over by industrialists. I've been transformed by these assaults. "Who am I?" "Where do my people come from?" "To which tribes do I belong?" "How do I meaningfully embrace my Native American ancestry?" "What European ancestry runs through my veins?" "How do I hold the answers to these questions even if I cannot find them all?" I share their pain.

Multiracial identity is a stubborn fact that demands a truth-telling, that lifts the historical bloody carpet and examines its threads: centuries of European domination and African and Native American resistance in as many forms as there were oppressive tactics heaped upon them. In order to survive America's cauldron, some ancestors became complicit in their own oppression. Tangled lineages, poor record keeping, altered names, destroyed archives, passing tactics all conspire and obscure my identity. Still, some mesmerizing stories and hints have emerged.

In 1982, during a weekend visit to Mobile, I established a connection with my Aunt Dot and my cousins on Mom's side.

At last, I had faces and names together with stories Mom had sketched for me as a child. It was a short but transformative weekend—during which I could not help but notice that we looked absolutely nothing alike. I would not return to Mobile again until 1987 when Aunt Dot passed away. This time my mother, sister, brother, and I traveled together to her funeral. It would be our only time visiting Mobile together. Mom had not been home in decades, so she was eager to introduce us to extended family. None of us expected that the curtains hiding our "mystery relatives" were about to fall away.

As Aunt Dot's funeral ended, my first "mystery relative" showed up. Two older Black women whispered and pointed at us. I shrugged and invited them over, at which point they asked to speak to Mom privately. No more was said to me at the time, but I pressed my mother later, and she told me they claimed one was her half-sister. Mom declined to discuss the matter further, and I knew I'd touched a nerve. Twelve years passed without another word. In 1999, Mom died of cancer. Four days later I received a call from one of the two women at Aunt Dot's funeral. "Hello, this is Hattie Mae Abrams from Mobile, Alabama, and you don't know me, but I just want to know who you are." With that the floodgates opened to a mysterious story and a photograph of a Black Indian woman who "came from across the Alabama River" to Peach Tree, Alabama, and married into the family in the 1800s. Peach Tree sits along the Alabama River where Creek, Cherokee, Choctaw, and Chickasaw territories converged. Which tribe might she have come from?

France's Code Noir, enacted in 1685, created a Creole caste to regulate slavery, free People of Color, and Native Americans. It remained in place for 163 years. Spanish colonialists who held Mobile until 1813 and New Orleans from 1763 to 1802 followed a similar Mulatto classification system, the Código Negro. After 1776, American southern states began to abolish

Native Americans' enslavement in favor of temporary military alliances with them against Britain and Spain. Cherokee, Choctaw, Creek, and Chickasaw tribes all enslaved Africans while the Seminoles gave Africans sanctuary. Over time, Creoles enslaved people and were also enslaved themselves. As social and legal notions of racial status shifted around patriarchal and matrilineal lineage and skin color, African Americans alternately maintained, embraced, rejected, and reclaimed African heritage. Their connections to Native Americans remained equally complex.

So, I am the product of oppressed and oppressor. My liberation is not simple. Sometimes, Black people who claim Native American blood are ridiculed or accused of "putting on airs" because they are ashamed to be of African descent. Some Native Americans not only enslaved people, they shunned Black Indians from their ranks. Yet, African and Native American spirituality share deep reverence for nature, and both honored a pantheon of spirits.

In 2017, I placed Native American icons on my altar, and I practiced the Native American flute even as I took up djembe drumming. I attended a Choctaw Pow Wow ceremony just north of Mobile where several Black Choctaw wore ceremonial dress, called upon Great Spirit, and included Christian prayer. These small steps were not only significant acknowledgments of two Indigenous aspects of my multifaceted heritage, they were offerings and affirmative steps toward healing my ancestry.

That year, I also shared my research with my father, then eighty-seven. For the first time, he told me with palpable contempt that my grandmother and my great-grandmother "considered themselves to be Creole." I have never seen my grandfather's photograph, but he was a dark-skinned Black man. In 1930 New Orleans Creole society, black skin was socially undesirable. Whether my grandmother and great-grandmother claimed Native American ancestry remains a mystery, but Ancestry.com's

DNA story map indicates they had Native blood. There are also indicators from Colombia, Venezuela, and the Carolinas. I sit with these clues.

In 1982, I sought to identify my paternal grandfather, Oscar Joseph Hypolite Sr. I was twenty-two with many questions, so I visited my grandmother, Lydia, in her New Orleans home. Lydia gave birth to my dad in the Ninth Ward in 1930, the Great Depression. What little I knew of my grandfather came from my mother. She said that when my father was a young boy, Lydia sent him across town to beg my grandfather for money. He often came home empty-handed. Oscar Sr. did not help raise my father, his son. Confused, I wanted to know more about Oscar Sr. Did he have another family? Do I have cousins on my father's side? My father didn't know, and, to my great disappointment, Lydia offered no information. Instead, she secretly arranged a call from Oscar Sr., but he never introduced himself when he called. Instead, he spoke in an animated, accented voice that was very difficult to understand. Confused to have this strange voice speaking to me in such a manner, I was speechless. About the time I realized the voice was my grandfather's, he said, "Well, I'll see you later," and hung up! Sadly, that was our only contact.

Lydia's reasons for reticence escaped me. Mom had warned me that Lydia had an oddly suspicious personality. Looking back, my father's near complete silence before my trip was also strange. He only commented when he picked me up at the airport. As I plopped wearily down on the passenger seat beside him, he wryly asked, "So, what did you think of your grandmother?" I don't remember what I replied, but I do remember that we drove home in silence, a swirl of disappointment and fatigue filling my mind. Frustrated, I let go of my curiosity, and nine years later Momma told me Grandpa had died.

Lydia had pointedly avoided her personal history. Not having grown up in a poor Black community, I misunderstood my family's secrecy for years. I failed to recognize their shared reluctance is widespread in dysfunctional domestic and violently racist settings. Later I would appreciate how the silent wounds within our community contribute to the painful ways we act out and compound our oppression one generation to the next. This was certainly true in Lydia's house, where my father experienced abandonment, physical abuse, and witnessed two alcoholic step-fathers before he turned fifteen.

By the time I visited, Lydia was a pious old woman. Catholics dominated New Orleans society, and she'd raised my father in the Church. Perhaps because of her age we did not attend Mass. Yet, as I watched one evening, she peacefully rocked in her simple chair and adored Rev. Billy Graham on a tiny black-and-white TV. Never mind that he was Protestant.

Though I turned my attention to education and career, I was still haunted by the mystery of my grandfather and my secretive family tree. My inability to name relatives and ancestors, to claim a people, a place of origin, a country name, a mother tongue, and an Indigenous culture often felt like amnesia.

This year, my brother shared his Ancestry.com results. DNA evidence confirms our racially mixed ancestry. I am 73 percent "African," 24 percent European, 2 percent Southeast Asian/Filipino, and there are three areas of less than 1 percent in the Americas. They include blue, orange, and green spots hovering over Gulf Shores, North Carolina, and Colombia/Venezuela. These spots are illuminating but also as deeply unsatisfying as Ancestry.com's DNA stats that say we are 43 percent Nigerian, 13 percent Malian, 9 percent Beninese, 7 percent Congolese and Bantu, and 1 percent Senegalese. What Nigerian tribe can I claim? Igbo? Hausa? Yoruba? Fulani? There are nearly 400 ethnic tribes in modern Nigeria! Am I Malian? Congolese? Bantu? Could my distant Native American ancestry be Chitimacha, Atakapa, Caddo, Choctaw, Houma, Natchez, or Tunica? All lived in that blue spot covering the New Orleans area when the French and Spanish arrived. Perhaps I am a Maroon descendant?

Who were the people? What pieces of the stories of "me" do any of them hold? To which spirits did they pray? What prayer songs did they sing? What did they endure and to what end? My identity search is more than a spot on a DNA map. The search is for my birthright. A way of divine connection. And it feels lost like a severed hand.

From 1791 to 1804, more Africans, predominantly originating from Congo, were brought to New Orleans from Saint-Domingue by French colonials fleeing the Haitian Revolution. Enslaved Congolese and West Africans included warrior tribes inspired by dreams of a free African/African American territory. Yoruba deities and Congolese spiritual practices emerged strongly in New Orleans. On January 8, 1811, some 500 Africans, African Americans, and Maroons risked certain death in the "German Coast" slave revolt, the largest in American history. Terrorized Frenchmen and American authorities brutally massacred the insurgents.

I learned of this brutal episode in 2017, when I renewed my efforts to discover my grandfather and to heal my ancestry. I made a pilgrimage to an African American spiritual retreat in Mississippi. The organizers took me to the Whitney Slave Plantation north of New Orleans. I was shocked to discover a "heads on pikes" monument to the slave revolt, but I was absolutely stunned that an enslaved African named "Hippolite" was a key insurgent leader. Hypolite is my surname!

Speechless, I stood there as Black people wept around me. Our sense of loss, despair, and outrage was palpable. Curiosity and anger flooded through me. How did I not know of the uprising? Then my spirit swelled with pride and inspiration by the insurgents' courage and Hippolite's valor! They fought for freedom! What a price they paid!

Might this Hippolite be a relative? Riding horseback, he flashed a saber and shouted, "Onward to New Orleans!" He led the insurgents' charge against American troops and French plantation owners. They were no match for American military cannons and French muskets, but Hippolite survived the ensuing massacre. According to tribunal records Hippolite was captured, tortured, and tried, but he did not betray his fellow insurgents. He remained defiantly loyal to the bitter end. His decapitated body was left exposed along with the others, and his head posted on the grounds of the Etienne Trepanier plantation where he had liberated himself. American authorities tried to erase the insurgency, but their spirits live on.

Later I learned of eleven more brave Hypolites, likely Catholic Creoles, who fought in the Union Army during the Civil War (1861–1865). One, Oscar Joseph Hypolite, served in the only African American artillery unit. He shares my father's and grandfather's exact name. Might his Catholicism have been infused with African or Native spiritual practices?

Despite my limited Native American blood ancestry, I know Africans and Native Americans share a socially complex history from the dawn of colonialism to the present day. This relationship informs my family history, lineage, and culture today. I continue to write about my family history, to play djembe and Native American flute as a means of fostering a greater sense of connection. I continue to explore and document my lineage, to understand the ways in which African, Native American, Creole, and African American cultural practices and survival strategies, as well as white supremacy, have all shaped my ancestors and my evolving identity. In recent years my attempts to make sense of my ancestry have borne significant fruit. In the spring of 2020, my brother accidentally discovered a small trove of my grandfather's personal documents, including his March 29, 1943, army discharge papers, his 1982 Louisiana driver's license. On a Sunday morning in spring my brother texted me photocopies with one word: "Grandpa" as I lay in bed snoozing. When I saw his message and the photo contents, I caught my breath and whispered, "Grandpa." It is impossible to find words to describe the ways in which this revelation—I had been lost for the sixty years I had been living on this planet—moved my spirit that morning, but I felt it shift like an earthquake shifts a continental plate along a fault line.

Healing ancestral wounds for me has necessitated an investigation of the specific nature of those wounds. I do not believe I can accomplish this work with any degree of success without first gaining an understanding, no matter how painful or incomplete, of the historical events, sociopolitical contexts, and cultural and spiritual influences that precede me. All this, together with their erasure and reconstruction, give rise to the man that I am.

TURNING, TURNING, TURNING

by Dr. g

I HAVE SPENT A SIGNIFICANT portion of my life being afraid to see myself fully because it came with the potential risk of punishment, abandonment, rejection. Being able to risk being alone for the sole liberation of being fully you is a daunting task, but choiceless. As I engaged deeper and deeper into dharma practice, layer upon layer slid off.

When I was seven years old in Staten Island, New York, I was introduced to Buddhism. In one of the three homes where I was permitted to sleep over, I was intrigued by various iconography ranging from Jesus and the saints to the Buddha and distorted images I couldn't make sense of. I was fascinated by all those small people in the *thangkas* doing seemingly mundane things. I had a million questions. I remember Pop, as I began to call my friend's father, deeply respecting the faith I was raised within, said if it was of interest, when I was older, my questions would be answered. Some twenty years later, I returned home to see Pop. I said, "Guess what, Pop? I'm Buddhist!" "Of course you are," he chuckled. Proof. It was my path.

What follows are some of those sheddings, the process, and how the dharma, repeatedly, showed me the truth of my Being.

OCTOBER 6, 2008: TAKING REFUGE (EXCERPT)

. . . I believe in this path because of when I chose to enter it; namely, I began the path when I was being honest with who I was, where I wanted to go, and moving toward things that helped me reach my potential, versus wallowing in a path of blaming the past and numbing. I engaged in this path, in this spiritual journey, in this relationship because I was tired of being numb.

. . . I realized that my hold on Catholicism was the fear that if I were to linger too far from the path that was drawn for me, that I would lose attachments. Attachments. Defining oneself by the attachments I have. More and more, the loss of those attachments seems not only inevitable, but also necessary. So, if I want to engage and engage fully in this life and on many levels, that means being open and willing to feel it *all*. I hope that in my openness to experiencing this life that I may model that fearlessness to others.

> I take refuge in the Buddha.
> I take refuge in the dharma.
> I take refuge in the sangha.

THE FIRST TURNING

First-generation. Only. Daughter. I can feel the weight of each word. Oh, Black. And not just any kind of Black. My mother was from Trinidad and my father, with his fleeting presence, from Haiti; in sum, a heavy influence in West Indian culture. Growing up, it didn't feel like I was American. It was also made apparent that we were different from the Blacks in this country. We were a liberated people who were "not still enslaved." I didn't question it when I was younger and it became quite solid. It was generally assumed that there was some superiority between myself and other Black-skinned folks. It was even inferred that my skin may not be noticed, even passable, despite its mocha hues, as white. I saw roles were not gender defined, that the dominance of the female bodies that surrounded me blazed with masculine energy. The women in my home were the breadwinners and caretakers, the mechanics and nurses. There really wasn't anything they couldn't do, no boundary of gender to bar their way, that was clear. I was constantly reminded of who I was. I felt encouraged away from other Black kids, and even with the three others in my school, it felt apparent I was not like them, I wasn't cool, couldn't double-Dutch, had no rhythm, but most, I had an undercurrent of rejection of them and perhaps was simply unaware of my Blackness.

As I grew older, I didn't find substance to this stance and questioned it. One thing was clear: the rest of the community didn't view me as anything other than Black, whether I acknowledged it or not. To others, there was no differentiation between nation of origin; Black was Black was Black. I began to see that my reality wasn't reflected in the spaces I sought refuge. It seemed like I had a yoke on my back constantly and no one else saw it. It wasn't a yoke I picked up, but somehow my body and its frame made it out of that uterus together. Somehow my shoulders always hunched with the weight: the truth of suffering—that no matter how many letters I have behind my name, I am still viewed as less than, killed without punishment, given a third of a dollar, disregarded, attacked, jailed, deported, feared, expected to accommodate, and always with the plight to do more. I began to see that the cause of this suffering was reliance on the definitions of the System, and that is temporary, and knowing that it is temporary allowed me to connect with my true nature and to keep practicing to foster clarity for myself and others of how to move through.

When I finally began identifying with the internalized racism toward other Blacks, I felt both pain and peace. Tantra practice opened the doors to the magic of my lineage through Voodoo, the *orisas,* and our inseparability with Nature. It reconnected me to the strength of why we Black people thrive—the cessation of suffering. Something released. My Afrikan siblings seemed to see and know my yoke because they too were swinging theirs around. There was a natural rhythm that occurred because we somehow knew the truth of suffering in this Black body; it was a truth to consider wherever we moved.

The dharma allowed space for me to deeply feel the suffering of this Black human existence, but it also offered a path out of it. I began to practice like my hair was on fire. The practice of being still with what is with awareness, Samatha-Vipassana, allowed various parts of my experience to surface, be felt, and dissolve, each time with bigger and bigger gaps between generation of another image of self. In those gaps, I found the construct of me was illusory and penetrable; less my definition. Most importantly, it seemed this was a currency that valued my being as a person rather than a price tag or a stereotype. Being with the truth of suffering allowed me to connect to others more deeply, and even though the yoke still found its home on my shoulders, it was hollow; it was hollow as long as I could find my breath and know the truth of who I was, which was not, thankfully, this sinful Being I once felt damned to be.

THE SECOND TURNING

Worldwide, there was a co-emergent arising of Beings of blood and bone, just like myself, who accessed a clarity of life; a kind of freedom beyond the constructs of this System. Beings like Jesus, Mohammad, Buddha, or contemporary Beings like Amma and the collective awakened consciousness.

Initially, I was a devout Roman Catholic on my way to being a priest. I found liberation in the seeming consistency of the outer form after spending eighteen years of my life in uniform. To think, even in this religious path, even though Jesus himself wore androgynous wear daily, I would be locked down in a habit and frock. And to boot, I couldn't serve Mass, and thus, I couldn't fully receive the teachings of Jesus. I was deeply discouraged. Then I was given *The Seven Storey Mountain* by Thomas Merton and found myself trapped to embrace many paths of spirituality—that I could taste the truths of all because although there are apparent differences, Truth is of one taste, there was nothing to reject. And even though these gendered barriers also exist in Buddhism of the West, I found the Heart Sutra imperative to allow space.

"Form is emptiness, emptiness also is form; emptiness is no other than form, form is no other than emptiness." This phrase is from the Heart Sutra, the heart of the Mahayana teachings, the pith of the Prajnaparamita Sutra. The Buddha really punctured concept with these lines! This was the first time my mind stopped. The Heart Sutra was the first piece of Buddha-dharma that I devoured; I even memorized it because I didn't want to be without it because it was both frightening and freeing. To think, all this, all this experience and solidity that we place as we move through this world, all of it is both solid and effervescent. It was the first piece of dharma I encountered that spoke to the nature of my fluid being. I just happened to be born of this female body and it is not fixed. I felt, once again, the dharma gave me the practice opportunity to view how my form emerges and dissolves in every moment. And as frightening as that was initially, I gradually practiced to remember that it wasn't a dissolve into nothing, but an emptiness so vast it accommodates everything. This was tested on two very important periods in my life.

For most of my life, I hated who I saw in the mirror: plastered in scars, acne, and a disfigured body that was perpetually prepubescent. As I approached any mirror, echoes of abusive taunts would ripple at me, so I hung mirrors below the neck or didn't look at them at all. During a monthlong silent meditation program, a *dathün,* I decided to spend time with my reflection and realized my worst fears erupted in taunting thoughts, then dissipated. Another wave, of different insult and content, arose and dissipated. I actually didn't know who that reflection was. So I got curious. I asked it. I began to notice the faces of several family members and of no one at all. This shifted something for me. Perhaps I wasn't who I thought I was.

My mother was diagnosed with early-onset Alzheimer's and I returned home to care for her. During that year and a half, I moved from only daughter to whomever she decided in the moment. Initially, I was not only sad, but irritated that she would forget my name, of all people. In that moment, the clutch onto my existence and identity became persona. I felt my I disappearing. I would constantly correct her, quiz her, show photographic evidence, all for her to remember. After a few times of losing my patience, praying to the *dralas* for clarity did note the impact of my righteousness. My mother would grow more irritable or worse, sad, as she momentarily realized I was correct and, even more stunning, that she forgot and would continue to forget. When I took in her pain, when I felt how out of control it must feel to, for any given amount of time, have no reference point, I was grateful for the ingenuity of mind to pull some memory and place it in the present. It was then these teachings became more salient. I began to be less uptight of my identity and more focused on the energy of the interaction. I was able to feel all the love my mother had for me, all the while calling me her sister, or friend, or mother. There was a knowing, an is-ness that was beyond any conceptual picture of who I thought I was, who I knew myself to be, who I thought I was to her. That is-ness was made of goodness and love. It eased her nerves, and more play was invited because there was space.

One of the last sentences I heard my mother speak was, "I love how you make me feel." It was then I saw the dharma in action, that the energy of our being is what is felt by others. So, even regarding my gender, I found tremendous freedom to manifest as whoever emerged in that moment. For me, this is the invitation of being nonbinary: the concepts of either male or female are not fixed ways of being but rather a flow, free to rise spontaneously and then subside.

But those questions . . . How does one differentiate "waking" life from the "sleeping" world?

I was, and still am, a rather lucid dreamer and privy to numerous occurrences of déjà vu. The life I led in my dream-world wasn't all that different from the one I was in: grown-ups did mundane things, people moved to and fro, people aged, got ill, celebrated, mourned, slept, and had a conversation. Count-less times, I feebly tried to "wake" from that world and found myself repeatedly thrust back—dreams within dreams within dreams. When I "woke," I would ask my mother questions: What made that world less legit than this? How did we come to believe this waking is real? Can we control what we do in that space? Do people exist in both spaces? Most times she diverted the questions and became fascinated with my dreams, asking me to repeat them as she fervently shuffled through the pages of *The Lucky Red Devil Combination Dream Book and Numerology*

Guide for that year, asking, "Do you remember any numbers?"
My dreams were her gamble if they were good dreams; but if
they were "bad," if I found myself being bitten by a snake and
waking with bite marks, or had a mysterious premonition of
someone dying, she would quickly urge, "Claudelle, did you say
your prayers?" "Yes, Mom." "Well, it's OK. So-and-so is OK."
And I could bet 769 would get played in the lottery, no sifting
through the book required. It was the number for death, and
slowly I began to trust someone was not well. I never let go
of a question when it arises, so, when I entered the Buddhist
path, I asked the same questions. I am still asking the same questions. What the path opened was the wisdom of the dream-like
nature of life itself, no matter the stage of consciousness. What
I dreamed of was an enlightened world and what benefit could
come if I could practice in my "dreams" what a full use of this
life was. All this made me more intentional in my practice, both
sleeping and waking, to connect with that space of freedom.

JESUS AND BUDDHA POINTING TO BLACK LIBERATION

by Thomas Davis IV

Enlightenment (personal): a full comprehension of a situation

Freedom: the power or right to act, speak, or think as one wants without hindrance or restraint

Liberation (relational): the act of setting someone free from imprisonment, slavery, or oppression; release

MY PRESENT QUEST FOR THE experience of liberation is governed by personal questions and a commitment to the practice of meditation as a means to see clearly. There are a few questions that I can share with you.

- What is enlightenment? What is liberation? What is freedom?

- Are these permanent states of existence or temporal experiences that we can have every now and then?

- How do I know if I have experienced them?

- Is enlightenment the same for everyone?

- What conditions do not change if and when enlightenment is realized?

- Does my experience of liberation require any outside validation or confirmation?

These questions were formed by my research of the basic definitions of liberation, enlightenment, and freedom. These basic definitions, I feel, should be included within the context of spiritual traditions because they are valid in and of themselves.

My experiences with the idea of enlightenment have been informed through years of cumulative experiences through various spiritual traditions. I was first informed of the idea of enlightenment through the Judeo-Christian faith, through a predominantly Hispanic Pentecostal church. Although the term "enlightenment" was not officially used in this community, the tenets of the faith still carried the promise and possibility of an end to my experience of suffering in this present life, by following the examples set forth by Jesus.

Approximately eight years into my initial Christian experience, my awareness had evolved, and I began to seek out another church wherein I could continue to learn and practice in community. I began visiting a church in West Oakland, California, called Olivet Institutional Missionary Baptist Church. This faith community was located right in the middle of a neighborhood where prostitution, drug sales, gang activity, houselessness, schools, and families all co-existed. These peripheral elements imbued the congregation with a felt sense of urgency, and fervency to the weekly worship. What was so markedly different from my previous Christian experiences was that oftentimes the gang member, prostitute, or houseless person visiting the congregation was welcomed! There was a sense that there was a common struggle and we identified with each other that way, while also not condoning violence or methods that create harm. What contributed to this inclusive community attitude was that the standard Christian teachings were integrated with Black Liberation theology, of which I had no prior exposure to in my prior learnings. So in essence, a veil was being lifted from my consciousness on this figure of Jesus who symbolized the liberation that I had previously given my whole heart to. Black Liberation theology illuminated my understanding of who I was and brought context to why my life experience had been so arduous. At this juncture, I was able to distinguish a difference between what I referred to as a White Jesus and a Black Jesus. The historical Jesus was born in Palestine, which is a geography historically inhabited by People of Color. Palestine was occupied or colonized by the Romans, who had conquered and colonized much of the world in that time. The elements that cause me to make a racial distinction between a Black Jesus and a White Jesus have to do with the systemic oppression that existed in Jesus's time that created a social climate of injustice and inequality. Very much the same conditions that I have known, except that my previous Christian learning experiences were silent on these issues. So, this leads me to see my Christian experiences as being influenced by a White Jesus and a Black Jesus.

Twelve years later in 2010, after serving in the Christian community as an associate minister and a teacher, my curiosity, and my need to know more intimately about who I was, created a new sense of pain and restlessness within, which I had tried to ignore for several years. So, I decided to depart from the

Christian community with an intention to figure out what my next move was. I ended up relocating to a neighboring city of Oakland while unemployed, spending my days exercising, reading, and praying for clarity. During the course of a year, I had come to understand that although I was not active in a church community, that Jesus was in fact very much active in my life. This led me to accept my own divinity and accept that I embody all the wisdom, love, and compassion that God represents.

It was in January of 2012, after accepting my intuitive sense of presence within, that I decided to try meditation practice as it seemed to offer the best orientation to see oneself introspectively. I joined a community called the East Bay Meditation Center and took to this practice without any complications. What was interesting was that I was not as enamored by meditation as I was by the Buddhist philosophy called the dharma. The dharma is the philosophy and teaching of the historical Buddha and offers a direct path to liberation! This seemed like a much more direct and concise path to follow compared to the Bible. However, as I became a student of the dharma, I began to see that the Buddha and Jesus were on the same page from a philosophical standpoint. Cultural context and practical applications being different, I discovered that Jesus and the Buddha were both internally oriented, were not invested in worldly values, and actually insisted on lives marked by simplicity and nonaccumulation. Jesus opposed the hypocrisy of the extreme sects (Pharisaism) of his culture, and Buddha Gautama renounced the Brahmin caste system within his culture. Today, I am still practicing and teaching in the Buddhist tradition, and the innate aspects of my Christian experience are flourishing at the same time. My present understanding of liberation is continuing to be shaped by personal experience and insight. I want to share a couple of examples for your consideration.

Merriam-Webster's definition of enlightenment is: "a full comprehension of a situation." This suggests to me that anyone can be enlightened without subscribing to a particular spiritual tradition.

Freedom is: "the power or right to act, speak, or think as one wants without hindrance or restraint." If we add the word Black to liberation, we will have the following result: the power or right for Black people to act, speak, or think as we want without hindrance or restraint.

Liberation: "the act of setting someone free from imprisonment, slavery, or oppression; release." The most basic interpretation of liberation in the English language suggests that "someone else" must be willing to relinquish their power in order for another to be considered free.

In my experience as a student of Buddhist philosophy, the terms enlightenment, freedom, and liberation have been presented and used interchangeably. The Buddhist interpretation will say that the eradication of an individual's propensities for greed, hatred, and delusion are synonymous with enlightenment, freedom, and liberation. There's nothing wrong with this interpretation; however, one can be a Black practitioner and still have relational obligations to people, places, and things that suppress one's speech, actions, and ideas. So, for the Black practitioner it becomes a little more complicated to deepen one's own practice with the built-in systemic oppressions that are perpetuated within our society.

I'm allowing more space for my views of full liberation to evolve as I grow and change, as I believe that a true and full liberation must occur on multiple levels of one's experience. It's no longer solely held as something that I attain for my own benefit or convenience. My perspective of true liberation must impact the psychological, relational, and social planes of existence. In order for this experience to be sustainable it must be attainable by others. The Buddha had many in his community who attained full liberation, and therefore they could uphold and sustain new values that would create an equal and balanced community. Jesus, also, before his death and post-resurrection attained a community of followers who impacted their societies with new values for a time. As proud as I am of being Black and, by extension, a tradition-holder of a great and powerful heritage, I am also becoming more accountable for my own racial conditioning. Freedom must begin with my lens of myself and my relationships with others; or else I can easily fall into a slumber of thinking I'm doing good if I meditate daily and listen to dharma talks regularly. Furthermore, I am enthused with the prospect of exploration and "dis-cover-y" of truths that lend both a sense of balance and agency for me to exercise my life in this society. I hold a deep amount of respect and gratitude for the spiritual traditions and teachers that I have had; and I cannot ignore the blind-spots of history that the content of traditional texts could not predict, and the perspectives of teachers who are sympathetic to, but do not share, my experiences.

I hope that you will find the unrest within yourself, to find the wherewithal to question your experience as a human being.

Thank you!

HEALING MY
BROKEN HEART

by Angela Dews

I'M A BLACK BUDDHIST WHO was working in Harlem to get a candidate elected. They were committed to protecting the homes and jobs and health of the dominant Black and Latino populations who were already there against the greedy opportunists, who were not always white and not always outsiders.

When I brought my broken heart to Venerable Thich Nhat Hanh (Thay), my first teacher, he said: Harmony is possible. Your way of life is your message. Don't think because you are poor you are helpless. Anger is not the only source of energy. Compassion is a verb. Mindful consumption is essential for community building.

MINDFUL CONSUMPTION

Many Buddhists believe in ghost beings who exist in realms after they die because of their actions. One is the realm of the hungry ghost. The hungry ghost has a mouth the size of a needle's eye and a huge stomach and suffers in a desire realm where it can never be satisfied. The realm of the hungry ghost is between the animal realm and the hell realm.

I got that. And I don't have to believe in things that I don't directly know to learn from this teaching. I state this for a few reasons.

First, the hungry ghost realm is not necessarily literally a place to be reborn but it is a quality of mind. It is suffering that arises due to unmet needs for acceptance and safety and the substitute gratifications that we make into obsessions and habits. Once I know its name, I can recognize the hungry ghost sitting on the cushion with me, walking with me, being the third person in an intimate relationship.

Second, the hungry ghost is suffering that arises due to cravings. Addiction is exactly what is personified in the hungry ghost. The addiction that got my attention was to a substance. But I am addicted to many things. They all keep me dependent. When I first got high we were listening to music, meeting new friends, and planning the revolution. Many of my people went on to put down the substances so they could get on with their lives. By the time I did that, many things had slipped away. One was a career forged out of being on hand for the breaking news of the student and community unrest. People also slipped away. But if I judge myself, the hungry ghost hates itself and I hate me.

Third, I have learned from this practice that the suffering can be ancestral. There are festivals throughout Asia where people offer food and celebration to hungry ghosts who are ancestors who are suffering. Once, at a retreat of Buddhists of the African

Diaspora, writer and activist Alice Walker said her ancestors were happy that she was practicing with an aspiration for freedom. I said my ancestors are telling me to get up from there. What was I doing sitting around doing nothing in the middle of the day after all the education and taking care of other people and running for freedom and all of it? My teacher said that's you talking. Sit with how that feels. I did that. I do that.

Thay says of walking practice: The act of making a step is an act of freedom; an act of liberation. You liberate yourself, you liberate your ancestors. It's an act of revolution.

I walk for mine. Because, in this land, my people could rarely walk slowly and empty-handed and sometimes had to run. Some of them also got high.

I teach and sometimes my lesson may arrive later out of a fog, because I'm asking that we do a hard thing. Denial feels like the only way to survive. Because it feels that facing my grief and anger will kill me. And there's no way to know it won't except to do it. And to do that I must see it And then take a breath. Pause.

For instance, I taught at a detention center and after meditation and discussion about how thoughts and feelings are painful, impermanent, and not personal, a seventeen-year-old said: "I never knew I wasn't my anger."

That comprehension—however fleeting—is the first step to the huge freedom of not making a familiar self out of the thoughts and feelings and habits. It is particularly revealing as a Black Buddhist. In my neighborhood, I think young people especially and perhaps all of us to some degree believe that if we are not angry, they who have oppressed us have gotten away with it.

I am one of the faces of "People of Culture" Buddhists at this time in an increasing number of places. Because that is where the practice takes me. And not just my face, but I bring my whole self to the cushion. I believe we as Black Buddhists can provide a healing role for ourselves and for our sanghas and for our communities by showing up and learning and releasing.

But what am I releasing? I practice to release, not feed, my hunger, to give up the illusion of a momentary gratification, to recognize the "dumb" numbness of dependency.

But how? My practice teaches me to pause, notice what's going on. Literally, what comes and what inevitably goes on. I'm reminded that sensual pleasure is impermanent and unsatisfactory, and then the contentment wears off. When I come down from my high, I will be left with my suffering. And I will need to desire again.

The Dhammapada collection of Buddhist teachings says:

> If, by giving up a lesser happiness,
> One could experience greater happiness,
> A wise person would renounce the lesser
> To hold the greater.

—DHAMMAPADA 290

That is why we as Black people need to wake up from the ills of addiction. Practice is how we wake up.

I remember being in a rage about something going on in the nation and my grandmother whose father was enslaved in Kentucky as a boy asking me, "What did you expect?" I yelled, "Justice!" And she just walked out of the room shaking her head. My practice has shown me a middle way between futility and rage.

Maybe you are connecting with the obstacle in your own mind to the possibility of happiness. Or wanting to hold on to or get more of the "good stuff." Or maybe you are meeting a familiar aversion in this moment.

See it. Breathe.

Equanimity is what we wake up to. It's not indifference. It's the practice of a lot of things. Two that I love: (1) equanimity is an open-hearted practice; (2) equanimity is a practice that allows me to honor doubt and don't-know mind. To stay open to uncertainty. And know, at this moment, this is enough. I am enough.

That reminds me of the story of Prince Siddhartha who lived a life free of suffering in a gated community. Then, as a young man, one day went outside where he witnessed an old man, a sick man, a corpse, and a traveling holy man. These are called the heavenly messengers. The sight of the first three aroused in him a sense of commotion and urgency called *samvega* in Pali, the language spoken at that time (now 2,500 years ago). That shock of knowing would not allow him to be content in the habits of his life of denial. The fourth messenger offered a way to an authentic way to be in the world—*pasada* in the Pali. His path led him to freedom and he became a Buddha. Awake.

My path out of active addiction feels like that. And as a Black Buddhist, I also see that anger can be a heavenly messenger offering the upset that, if I don't deflect the energy to denial and habitual reaction (rather than a thoughtful response, or perhaps, no active response), I can find a way away to authenticity.

Before I became a teacher, I offered the Harlem Sit. Now I offer Harlem Insight, with a rotating group of teachers, and this invitation.

The Harlem Insight Sit includes a period of guided sitting meditation, a conversation about what the Buddha taught, and walking meditation (sometimes outside). It is also a place to talk about morality and wisdom—developing generosity, nonharming, equanimity, loving-kindness.

There is amazing clarity in stillness and the opportunity for a skillful response rather than a reaction, even to injustice. And there is the possibility of equanimity and of freedom.

ENCOURAGE OTHERS BY OVERCOMING YOUR OWN SUFFERING

by Venerable Dr. Pannavati Bhikkhuni, Theri

ONE OF MY FAVORITE SUTTAS from the Buddhist scriptures is the Majjhima Nikaya 128. It tells a story of quarrels and resentment to which the Buddha responds: "He abused me, he beat me, he robbed me, he insulted me. Those who harbor such thoughts, in them hatred will never be appeased. He abused me, he beat me, he robbed me, he insulted me. In those who do not harbor such thoughts hatred will cease. Hatred is never overcome by hatred, but by nonhatred. This is a universal law." This is where we have to start. What will we do with this truth? How will we respond to it?

Our obstacles are very great. It is going to take a worthy opponent with a radical approach to overcome them. So long we have had the strategy. It was offered more than 2,500 years ago. Five hundred years later, that same message was echoed by another sage. It's about time we really tried it. We know what hasn't worked. Why not try it, now? Pacifists are not passive. Their actions are subtle but have transformative powers that have saved countless numbers of living beings.

The Buddha never tried to change society by protesting, picketing, staging sit-ins, and so forth. So, when I'm talking to practitioners, I don't either. Instead, I say, "You change." I am always pointing them back to their own thoughts, speech, and actions—regardless of what others do.

I marvel at how scared, anxiety-ridden, and plagued by feelings of insufficiency and guilt the long-term practitioners who attend my retreats and talks are. So, I offer them what I have—the dharma—and the courage and compassion to live it. The mindfulness movement has certainly gone wide. But, now it is time to go deep. That's the best way to show gratitude to the pioneering teachers and carry their work forward.

As a people, Black Americans continue to still struggle to overcome obstacles, threats, and lack. We have had to develop a sense of our own worth to survive a Western "caste" system. We are well acquainted with suffering and the stamina it takes to surmount and overcome adversity. So, I think two of the most important inspirations the Black community can offer to a growing Buddhist movement in the West are courage and compassion.

I remember when I was first asked to speak at different sanghas. I was invited to speak to the POC groups. I'd say, "I'm not a Black dharma teacher, I'm a dharma teacher. Call me back when you want me to speak to your whole group." And, they did!

Of course, I caught a lot of flack from younger Black Buddhist leaders because I wasn't a proponent of affinity groups from the start. I just think we all need to stay together and work at overcoming our discomfort with one another. That's not so easy to accomplish when we separate. Many centers that started this now permanently have a bunch of separate groups they call one sangha! I don't really call this progress. I think the dharma calls us to a higher resolution and unity.

But, that requires a strong and clear dharmic message around the cultivation of virtue, compassion for others, and practices of respecting others. Or, how else will we survive as a species? It also takes a commitment to holding our views without being attached to them and a kind of respect for oneself that can be maintained in the face of rejection.

To me, all this is what fierce compassion is. When we have the capacity to see the underlying ignorance, tendencies, and fears that cause people to act as they do, and we really care, we can hold a space with them, and if necessary, for them. But, if we are riddled with doubts about our worth, angry, resentful, and unaccomplished, we will not be of much use in proving the dharmic message of transformation as possible.

I remember speaking to a group of ninety-nine People of Color—one of the very few POC talks I've given. There was one white person who showed up for the talk and they wanted me to ask him to leave. I was told they didn't feel comfortable—didn't feel safe—with that one person there. I was dumbfounded! I asked them who put such a notion in their heads that one white person (they didn't even know) was that threatening? I did not ask him to leave. I gave an excellent talk that night on dharma that transcended racial disparity. They benefited and so did he. Anything I can say to one person, I can say to any person. It is not words as much as the spirit of harmlessness they ride upon.

When we walk into a room, we should come in loving and accepting ourselves. Don't you know our worth is not dependent on others loving us? Come with the love offering and the notion that wrapped up in that gift is the courage and compassion to deliver it *in person.*

The truth is, everybody is not going to love you or accept you. You have to have enough love and acceptance for yourself. And, when you keep building on just that, acceptance overflows and spills onto those who deserve it and those who don't. In other words, you can look on all people with the same equanimity, helping or instructing some when you can; accepting others when you can't.

When you don't have self-acceptance, resentment flourishes that leads to hatred and all manner of unrighteous conduct. Being a woman in this black skin for seventy years has taught me that! This is not about just race, but about all kinds of differences and biases. There is temptation to aversion everywhere! But, this is precisely what the dharma addresses and ensures victory over if we have the patience and courage to learn it, practice it, and perfect it.

What I know is true, is that we impart what is in us. So, there is this constant exchange of energies in the world. What is my contribution to it all? That's the question I ask myself again and again.

If we look at our country, we have to admit that things are much better on the surface as the centuries have passed. But, the perspectives that defined the emerging nation have not changed much from the 1600s. Some laws and rules have made things better, but scratch just beneath the surface and all the poisons and defilements are still there.

I see it in India and Thailand, too, as I work with inequities of outlawed "untouchability" and sanctioned patriarchy. I see it here in our society in regards to race, social injustice, income and opportunity disparity, immigration, and too many other issues. I also see it even within the small American bhikkhuni sangha of which I am a part, gatekeepers including and excluding sisters based upon narrow and debatable interpretations of "correct" procedures. Yes, when virtue is lost, we need to create laws. But, we should also recognize their insufficiency to change hearts. After all, laws are for the lawless.

So, what can change us from the inside? I believe that's the work of the sages—those who have cried out from their own bowels, "Give me a clean heart and renew an upright spirit within me . . . then will I teach transgressors the way"—and have then done the work. A certificate does not a sage make! So, we should be careful about overinflation of capability and eagerness to establish a "brand."

One cannot hold this station if they are not both ready *and* able to surrender all—fame, status, wealth—for the excellency of upholding the truth. It takes a superior vision beyond the ordinary worldly view, courage, and compassion. It also takes surrendering an attachment to the pains one has become acquainted with. That's the difficult part. We cannot play the victim. That will always presume a power over us. But, when we can honestly surrender our indignation and offense, we begin to open a possibility for true change in lineage, where people of all "colors" become sons and daughters of the Buddhas.

I believe in people's ability to change. I believe we all possess the Buddha-nature. We just need help discovering it. But, first, in our own minds we must move beyond the dichotomy of separation. While useful in speech for discussion, it becomes limiting for action and transformation.

Prologue: The above essay was written six months ago. Today, as I reflect on four days of civil unrest, increasing brutality in twenty-five states and more than 100 cities due to the public snuffing out of life of yet another Black man in police custody, I ask, Is my dharma still working? The act was brazen; people witnessed it in real time over the internet. There is little end in

sight as each act of aggression precipitates another by the opposing force. Now is not the time for essays, it is the time to put into
practice what I know. How do I "feel" about what I "see"? I feel
like fighting. One man's terrorist is another's freedom fighter.
One man's hero (to the victor belongs the spoils) is another man's
thug. What do I do? Recalling the principles hidden within my
heart, I urgently turn inward and whisper, "Open my heart—I
want to see." From this space duality dissolves and I can hold
the pain and know my position. When a building is no longer
fit for habitation, one craftsman tears it down, another assem-
bles new materials, and the third one rebuilds. I allow the right
craftsmen to do their work . . . and I know my role. This clarity
brings peace to the moment. The dharma finds me, and suffering
is no big deal.

THE WEB DANCER
DarkNight, Zamani, Dip

by Sojourner Wright

Dear Dancer: I feel like Blackness has another, ANOTHER definition altogether. Will you help me find it?

In neopagan traditions there is a triple goddess archetype that includes three different goddesses representing the phases of a woman's life: the Maiden, Mother, and Crone. The Maiden represents youth, innocence, and vitality. The Mother is the phase of life when the woman creates through giving either biological birth or birth to herself and the world. The Crone phase represents the wisdom that comes with being near the end of life. She represents death and the reality of change. The belief is that these three phases exist all at once, in all women.

After understanding that the seeds of this concept were questionably* conceived by a white man, Robert Graves, who was a mid-twentieth-century poet and mythographer, and later expanded upon by Starhawk, a white woman theorist of neopaganism and ecofeminism, in her book *The Spiral Dance* released in 1979, I became curious about African-centered beliefs around the feminine. In *The Invention of Women: Making an African Sense of Western Gender Discourses*, Oyeronke Oyewumi dissects the implementation of male and female sexes, and man and woman identities, as Western colonial constructs. In the Yoruba traditions that Oyewumi talks about, the entire culture thrived without the patriarchal hierarchy that exists in today's gender binary. Rather, skill and lineage were *centered* in the *distinguishment* of place in society. When the British first colonized Yorubaland, they did not consider Black people men or women. This worked to maintain the hierarchy of whiteness over Black folks.

The names Mother, Maiden, and Crone hold the misogynistic weight of a Westernized view of gender, being that the man innately has power over the woman. Maiden implies *ownability* as it traditionally means a young, unmarried girl. Mother resigns the body to the utility of reproduction. And Crone conjures a grumpy, ugly old woman.

How can these phases be renamed as gateways for an expansive reimagining and embodiment of the feminine to emerge as a celebration of blood memory and personal power? I conducted intergenerational interviews of Black women and femmes as a part of a collective excavation for a performance piece called

---

*Robert Graves's biographer and nephew, Richard Perceval Graves, documents Robert Graves's peer Laura Riding as reading *The White Goddess,* from which the Triple Goddess archetype emerged, and proclaiming, "Where once I reigned, now a whorish abomination has sprung to life, a Frankenstein pieced together from the shards of my life and thoughts."

"Femme Body," about the phases of life in queer Black woman and femme-identified bodies. My elders cringed at the term "Crone," catalyzing the curiosity for a new name. Zahra Baker, a Black queer Chicago storyteller on the scene for more than thirty years, and my performance collaborator who is just turning the corner into these wise elder years, recommended "Zamani" to me as a replacement for Crone. The renaming/claiming began.

Dear Dancer: What's in the change of life?

Zamani means: past, before, formerly, or long ago in Swahili. Dip took the place of Maiden. Dip is inspired by a song from my early '90s childhood, "Da' Dip," by Freak Nasty, and juking, a dance also from the '90s that I remember gave us preteens permission to get as close to sex as we dared with our swirling hormones. DarkNight takes the place of Mother. The *creatrix* actively rides the phases of the moon creating and weaving the world, and owning the sensual power that is hidden away till the dark hours of night.

Western views of being a woman and of feminine energy exist in a constructed biological binary. Gender is not biological. The Maiden, Mother, and Crone phases, as they are generally practiced as the Triple Goddess, are trans and nonbinary exclusive.

I hold a queer-*centered* ritual and meditation space for femmes of color called "Stillness." This is a space for trans, QPOC, *womxn,* cis women, and gender-nonconforming femmes of color. Stillness is a circle where I guide folx to create their own ritual and spiritual practices using tools of intuition, dreams, movement, dancing, singing, creativity, and emotional intelligence. All of these tools are cultivated personally within each practitioner, and the engagement of biology is left to the experience of each person's relationship with their own body. It has been my job to dissect and translate all things created from a mindset of "women-born women"* into an inclusive understanding of feminine embodiment.

The Stillness target audience has evolved as I have evolved in my understanding of my own queerness beyond sexuality, and as I connect deeper to my chosen queer family. Stillness used to be a space for "Women of Color." Then a space for "Women and Femmes of Color," now a space for "Femmes of Color." The name journey of Stillness began when I invited someone I perceived to fall into my demographic as "woman" to attend. They told me they would not come because they identified as a "nonbinary femme," not a woman, and did not feel the space would be for them. This conversation sent me into a dismantling of the term "woman," and into making the space femme-centered. Soon after, I had another conversation with a friend of mine who is a trans man. He asked me if he would be allowed to attend because he identified as femme. Again, a paradigm shift that has, in all honesty, never ended.

Dear Dancer: *Whenever I ask myself what I really want, the answer I get is, "I want to be with the earth/god/divine/trust. I want to surrender to you."*

As I practice meditation, ritual, and performance in order to share this space with others, I ask myself again and again, what is this feminine wisdom when there are male-identified folks who also align with the moon? When there are women I know who feel like they hold the role of the "man" in their marriage? Is it really only contained to the wisdom that emerges when one bleeds with the moon, gives birth, and breastfeeds? These are powerful elements of existing in a body that reproduces that

---

*"Woman-born woman" is a phrase that came out of second-wave feminism. It is meant to exclude trans women from spaces. It reduces gender to biology and says that if a person was not born with a vagina they are not a real woman.

are taboo and *invisibilized* by white supremacist patriarchy. The experiences of a body that reproduces must be *centered* as marginalized but not *essentialized* at the expense of other marginalized experiences. There is also space for women and non-binary folks who will never give birth. There is space for people who identify as men to breastfeed. There is space for everyone to understand the cycles of nature and become softly beautiful whenever they want to.

The Triple Goddess, renamed through my Black femme body, the "Web Dancer," is archetypal energy that represents who we were before we had to fight for the constructed identity of woman. The Web Dancer weaves their inheritance of blood memories around and through an awareness of birth, life, and death. They align with the seasons. They receive the keys to liberation in the rising and the setting of the sun. We Dancers learn as we find ourselves repeating habits of destruction, that our breath reaches back to the darkness of a slave ship, and we love ourselves. We open the possibility for a timeless existence. We can feel Zamani in our five-year-old bodies. In our forty-year-old bodies we can hold on to our play and innocence of the child. Our creatrix selves, DarkNight, masterfully navigate the world as they also access their wise elder and find earthy desire in the physical and energetic womb. Orgasms unfold for our future.

This experience of three Dancers in one body is underneath our societal ideals of if we are cis or trans, male or female, non-conforming, or other. I don't mean underneath as in less than. I mean when we trust our heart and gut intelligence, and move through the world from the body, the truth that rests underneath the chaos and the busyness of our socially constructed minds, *we find liberation* in the possibility of becoming, relating to, healing, and dancing with all of our-selves. In relationship to socially constructed masculine and feminine definitions that exist in a binary and deem masculine as linear, logical, and void of feeling and intuition, everything that is opposite to or other than this framing of the masculine is placed in the category of feminine. Within the binary then, this *spiralic* and embodied existence is a feminine one. However, anyone can exist in this experience of feminine. Anyone can welcome in the Web Dancer: Dip, Dark-Night, and Zamani if you can feel how to. Within the binary, the feminine is a toolkit for a sensual, nonlinear, and *interdimensional* existence. Beyond the binary? Maybe. Like the spectrum of gender, there is a spectrum of phases that arise from the Blackness that exists when everyone closes their eyes to remember a stillness from before they were ever even in a body.

Dear Zamani: When I see you, you are in a field of tall grass and wildflowers. You are standing, and in love with your feet in the moist soil. The earth is your home and you are a master of listening to the winds. I am DarkNight right now and I am afraid that you have no one around you. That you are lonely. I will surrender and let my lovers catch me.

Dear Dip: I love you. I love you so so much. You be hurt with that big heart. Sad that your power is strong and it does not get you adorations, teenage lovers, acceptance from the pretty ones, or understanding. Those days spiders spooked you, child. One day, you will see yourself in eight leggeds. The others, they won't ever know nothin' bout that.

Just letting you know that we can play play play as long and loud and messy and big as we want to.

Your Guardian Zamani, standing barefoot in the field.

Dear DarkNight:

> *I am here*
> *I am prosperous*
> *Right now, right now?*
> *The earth is my witness*

Everything is warm and sensual
I can feel the truth in magic.
I practice.
I am touched with love and alchemize again and again.
I am seen in my cycles of feelings.
It is beautiful
My hands make and make
I breathe in my own creations, weaving Grandma's love of
Black people into my own heart before I even know it.

I love you, Grandma Maxine. We are free when we're
together.
I'm gonna get that yellow dress and dance in it with you.

FOR ALL BEINGS

by Zenju Earthlyn Manuel

May all beings be cared for and loved,
Be listened to, understood, and acknowledged despite different views,
Be accepted for who they are in this moment
Be allowed to live without fear of having their lives taken away or their bodies violated
May all beings
Be well in its broadest sense,
Be fed
Be clothed
Be treated as if their life is precious
Be held in the eyes of each other as family
May all beings
Be appreciated
Feel welcomed anywhere on the planet

Be freed from acts of hatred and desperation including war,
    poverty, slavery, and street crimes
Live upon the planet, housed and protected from harm
Be given what is needed to live, fully without scarcity
Enjoy life, living without fear of one another,
Be able to speak freely in a voice and mind of
    undeniable love
May all beings
Receive and share the gifts of life,
Be given time to rest, be still, and experience silence
May all beings
Be awake

INDEX

Afrikan Wisdom

African/Afrikan mindfulness
(continued)
how Ubuntu mindfulness should
be used to liberate BIPOC in
the Diaspora, 233–235
lack of information on, 217–218
and leadership of elders, 235
and links to world traditions, 225
movement mindfulness, 221
as (perhaps) source of all
mindfulness traditions, 225
wisdom passed from generation to
generation, 228
African/Afrikan Wisdom
traditions, 173–182
African/Afrikan origins of
spiritual practices, 6–7, 17, 225
commonalities among, 174
female genital power in, 178–179
four questions asked by
healers, 272
gender of deities, 179
goddesses in, 15, 175–176, 179,
266
as grounded in the earthy and
embodied, 178–179
honoring of diverse genders
in, 179
and links to world traditions, 225
masks in, 178
music and dance in, 175–176
and nonduality, 46
rituals in, 178
African/Afrikan Yoga. *See* Kemetic
Yoga
Afri-Can Food Basket, 122
Africanity, concept of, xvi, 128
Africans, The: A Triple Heritage
(Mazrui), 92
afterlife, Mama Yaa on, 130
Against the Stream Buddhist
Meditation Society, 208
Agozino, Biko
biography, 340
on why Jesus turned water into
wine, 263–270
Ahimsa, 145–146
ethos of, 153
Ahmadiyya movement, 94
Ahosi, 177

Aisvarika, 17
Aiye, 220
Akan, 131
Akhenaten, worshipped one
God, 92
Akram, Al-Hajj Wali, 94–95
alafia, 220
Alcoholics Anonymous, 144
alcoholism, 269
in Africa/Afrika, 263–269
Alexander, Noliwe, 1
Ali, Noble Drew, 94
alienation, feelings of, 44–45
Allione, Tsultrim, 118
ally, in Vajrayana Buddhism, 119
Almamate, 87–88
Almamy, 88–89
Amanirenas, 176–177
Ambedkar, Babasaheb, 20
Amen-Ta, 249
America. *See also individual topics*
related to
human rights in, 95, 128,
160–163, 186
slavery in, 93–94
America's Racial Karma: An Invitation
to Heal (Ward), xiv
Amma, 299
Amodeo, Laurie
biography, 338
interview with JoAnna
Hardy, 205–214
Ananda, Venerable, 194
Anatsui, El, combatting alcoholism,
264
ancestors. *See also* Ancestralization
establishing relationship
with, 259–261
remembering, 144
in search of Hypolites, 285–294
work done by, 260–261
Ancestralization, 129–130, 257–261
ancestral ritual, 260–261
and correction of
patterns, 259–261
"Ancestralization" (Marriott), xvi
Ancestry.com, 291
Ancient Egyptian Buddha, The
(Ashby), 14
Anacalypsis (Higgins), 18

vital, 251
Vodoun/Vodun, 83, 177n†

W

waking, 301
Walker, Alice, 1, 311
Walker, James, 169
walking practice, 311
walking Qur'an, 88–89
Ward, Larry, xvi
    *America's Racial Karma: An
        Invitation to Heal*, xiv
    biography, 336–337
    homage to Martin Luther
        King, Jr., 157–164
warrior cultures
    invoking energy of your ancestral
        warriors, 56
    and Sadhana of Awakened
        Melanin, 55
    Universal Lineage of
        Warriorship, 56
warriors
    calling of warriors in Sadhana of
        Awakened Melanin, 58–59
    Universal Lineage of
        Warriorship, 59
    warrior's way in Africa/
        Afrika, 221
Way of Tenderness, The (Manuel), xiv
Web Dancer, 325–326
"Western Enlightenment," 2–3
"What do humans really need and
    long for?" 203
"When Will We Sing Again?" 271–281
white supremacy, 7, 166, 241, 280,
    293, 325
    Black Liberation theology
        and, 83
    parenting and, 29, 37
    a world of, 136
Whitney Slave Plantation, 292
"Why Buddhism for Black America
    Now?" (Johnson), 188
wilderness, finding salvation in, 85
williams, angel Kyodo, 1, 112
    being black, xiv
Williams, Delores, 85
Williams, Monier, 17

Willis, Jan, 1, 112
    biography, xvii
    "Buddhism and Race: An African
        American Baptist-Buddhist
        Perspective," xiv
    on historical context of *Afrikan
        Wisdom*, xiii–xvii
    "Yes, We're Buddhists Too," xiv
Wilson, Bill, 144
wine, two kinds of, 267
wisdom. *See also* African/Afrikan
        Wisdom
    all-accomplishing, 116
    in Buddhist practice, 191
    folktale about origin of, 264–265
    need for, 199
    passed from generation to
        generation, 228
wisdoms, five, 116
Woden, 20
Wolof man, initiation of, 222–223
Woman, Native, Other (Minh-ha), 242
women/womxn
    expectation to adhere to dominant
        norms, 241
    meaning of term "women," 240
    and racism, transphobia, and
        transmisogyny, 140
    woman-born woman, 324n*
    womxn in African/Diasporic
        liberation struggles, 176–178
Women's War (Igboland), 266
worth, personal, 317
worthiness, seeing one's own, 195
Wright, Sojourner
    biography, 342
    on DarkNight, Zamani, and Dip,
        321–327

X

X, Malcolm. *See* Malcolm X
Xola, 122

Y

Yaa, Mama. *See* Mama Yaa
"Yes, We're Buddhists Too" (Willis),
    xiv
Yoga
    as Black/African tradition, xvi

purpose of, 251
and union, 247
YogaSkills Method, 250–253
ten components of, 251–253
Yoruba Gelede masquerade, 178
Yoruba Temple (Harlem), 175,
175n*
Yoruba tradition
on alcoholism, 266
and mindfulness, 219–220

Z

zakāt, 96
Zamani, defined, 323
zawadi, 124–125
Zen Buddhism. *See also* Buddhism;
mindfulness
Plum Village Community of
Engaged Buddhism, 23–24
Zindzi, 231

ACKNOWLEDGMENTS

FIRST, THANKS MUST GO TO all the contributors: thank you so much for helping to create an inspirational book for our generation and generations to come. Thank you to Keith Donnell, my developmental editor, for walking this journey with me and your excellent notes. Thank you to Tim McKee, who said "Yes" based on three chapters and no synopsis. And to the team at North Atlantic Books. Gratitude to Jan Willis for putting this book into context, and for her keen, talented eye. Thank you to Pamela Ayo Yetunde, Justin von Bujdoss, and Satyani McPherson for their support and generosity. Thank you to the ancestors roaming in Canada, the US, and the UK. We hear you loud and clear, and your wisdom is here, right on these pages. Thank you to my partner for always supporting me in my writing process. Thank you to the ocean for keeping me sane during these turbulent times.

CONTRIBUTOR
BIOGRAPHIES
(IN ORDER OF APPEARANCE)

Poet, author, and public speaker **Valerie Mason-John (Vimalasara)** is the award-winning author/editor of nine books. Their debut novel, *Borrowed Body,* won the 2006 Mind Book of the Year Award. They co-edited the award-winning anthology *The Great Black North: Contemporary African Canadian Poetry* and co-produced blackhalifax.com. They co-authored the award-winning book *Eight Step Recovery: Using the Buddha's Teachings to Overcome Addiction.* Their most recent book, published in 2020, *I Am Still Your Negro: An Homage to James Baldwin,* has won critical acclaim. They began writing as an international correspondent covering Aboriginal deaths in custody and land rights in Australia, and went on to edit the first anthology to document the lives of Black and Asian lesbians in Britain. Their box office plays *Sin Dykes* and *Brown Girl in the Ring,* written in the 1990s, take a critical look at issues of systemic racism, issues that are still prevalent today. They are a senior teacher in the Triratna Buddhist Community and one of the leading African descent voices in the field of mindfulness for addiction. In 2005 they were awarded an honorary doctorate for their contribution to the African and Asian Diaspora. They live on the Sunshine Coast, British Columbia, and can be found online at valeriemason-john.com.

Shaka N. Khalphani was born December 19, 1956, in Chicago, Illinois. Raised on the South Side of Chicago, Khalphani attended Wentworth grade school in the early 1960s before moving to the

Bronx, New York, and attending P.S. 63. A few years later, they returned to Chicago and finished schooling at Guggenheim Elementary School and Francis Parker High.

Marisela B. Gomez is a mindfulness practitioner in the tradition of Thich Nhat Hanh's Order of Interbeing, a public health scholar activist, and a preventive/alternative medicine physician. Of Afro-Latina ancestry, she lives in Baltimore and is involved in social justice activism and community building/research. She is the author of *Race, Class, Power, and Organizing in East Baltimore* and other popular and scholarly publications. Her blog, www.mariselabgomez.com, explores the intersection of wisdom justice and mindfulness. Her TED Talk is on healing racism through waking up.

Allyson Pimentel, EdD, is a psychologist and longtime Vipassana meditation practitioner and teacher who works at the intersection of mindfulness, mental health, and social justice. She teaches at UCLA, USC, and InsightLA, where she also serves on the board of directors.

Anouk Aimée Shambrook, PhD, integrates the latest in neuroscience with trauma resilience, meditation, the Aware Ego Process, and embodied nonduality. Her executive coaching as well as equity training blends traditions to promote healing and system change.

Justin F. Miles (Shiwa Chuwo), MA, LCPC-S, LGAD-S, is a Baltimore, Maryland–based psychotherapist, hip-hop practitioner, and philosopher. Miles is also a Buddhist teacher in the Shambhala Buddhist tradition.

Andrea Murray-Lichtman's interests include liberation for the oppressed, spirituality, wellness, racial justice, and critical pedagogy. Andrea believes that faith includes action, and like the faith of her ancestors, empowers and inspires personal and collective transformation. She is invested in this work on behalf of Black, brown, and other marginalized communities.

Ashton Murray's interests include diversity, equity, and belonging within the academy and beyond. Ashton is intrigued with how different groups of people practice meaning-making individually and collectively, and how that process creates social cohesion or exclusion.

Nisa Muhammad is an educator, researcher, and activist. She's also a Muslim chaplain known for spreading the joys and challenges of being Black and Muslim on college campuses across the United States.

Elisha Precilla was born in Hackney, London, in 1991 to an English-Nigerian mother and a Trinidadian father and works as a teaching assistant in an inner-city primary school. They are an avid plant-based cook and advocate of natural foods.

Karla Jackson-Brewer, MS, has been a Vajrayana practitioner and a student of Lama Tsultrim Allione for thirty-two years. She is a Tara Mandala Authorized Teacher who has been practicing Chöd for thirty one years. In October 2012 she received the Chöd Empowerment from His Holiness the 17th Gyalwang Karmapa, Ogyen Trinley Dorje.

Dr. Afua Cooper is professor of Black History at Dalhousie University and Halifax Poet Laureate, 2018–2020. She is the author of *The Hanging of Angélique: The Untold Story of Canadian Slavery and the Burning of Old Montreal* (HarperCollins and the University of Georgia Press). She is Poet Laureate: Halifax Regional Municipality and immediate past president of the Black Canadian Studies Association.

Cicely Belle Blain is a Black/mixed, queer femme from London, UK, now living on the lands of the Musqueam, Squamish, and Tsleil-Waututh people. Their ancestry is a mix of Gambian (Wolof), Jamaican, and English. Cicely Belle harnesses their passion for justice, liberation, and meaningful change via transformative education, always with laughter, and fearlessly in the face of systemic oppression. They are noted for co-founding Black Lives Matter Vancouver and subsequently being listed as one of Vancouver's fifty most powerful people, BCBusiness's 30 Under 30, and one of CBC's 150 Black women and nonbinary people making change across Canada. They are now the CEO of Cicely Blain Consulting, a social-justice-informed diversity and inclusion consulting company with clients across North America, Europe, Asia, and Africa. Cicely Belle is author of *Burning Sugar* (Arsenal Pulp Press, 2020).

Rev. Seiho Mudo Morris | 清峰 (Clear Peak) | is an ordained Rinzai Zen Buddhist monk, having trained and practiced in the Zen tradition for nearly three decades, as well as receiving formal training and empowerments in Tibetan Nyingma and Sakya lineages in various teachings and practices over the past three years. He provides workshops and immersion practices related to cultural/racial bias, racism and otherism, harmonizing the Four Noble Truths, the Eightfold Path, and a specifically revised expression of Twelve-Step principles, in an effort to help support and advance a path of change related to racism. He's been in long-term recovery for the last thirty-three years, with regards to addictive disease. He's a former addictions counselor, program director, and facility administrator, and is currently on the administrative team of an addictions treatment center in the state of Maryland.

Larry Ward, PhD, is the author of *America's Racial Karma*. The assassination of Dr. Martin Luther King Jr. was the catalyst that sparked the young Ward's journey into a life of planetary peace-making. Ward joined the staff of the Ecumenical Institute—Institute of Cultural Affairs in 1969, and received his Christian ordination in 1972. He lived and worked for the next twenty-five years in more than twenty countries, specializing in organizational change and local community renewal. He currently serves as advisor to the Executive Mind Leadership Institute at the Peter F. Drucker School of Management, in Claremont, California. Ward's introduction to Buddhist practice began in Calcutta, India, in 1977, but it was when he met Zen Master Thich Nhat Hanh in 1991 that the practice became truly central to his life. He is ordained as a dharma teacher in Thich Nhat Hanh's Plum Village tradition and has accompanied Thich Nhat Hanh on peace-building missions internationally, as well as throughout the United States.

George Elliott Clarke, the 4th Poet Laureate of Toronto (2012–2015) and the 7th Canadian Parliamentary Poet Laureate (2016–2017), was born in Windsor, Nova Scotia, in 1960. Clarke is a pioneering scholar of African Canadian literature, with two major tomes to his credit: *Odysseys Home: Mapping African-Canadian Literature* (2002) and *Directions Home: Approaches to African-Canadian Literature* (2012). He holds eight honorary doctorates, plus appointments to the Order of Nova Scotia and the Order of Canada at the rank of Officer. His recognitions include the Pierre Elliott Trudeau Fellowship Prize, the Governor General's Award for Poetry, the National Magazine Gold Award for Poetry, the Premiul Poesis (Romania), the Dartmouth Book Award for Fiction, the Eric Hoffer Book Award for Poetry (US), and the Dr. Martin Luther King Jr. Achievement Award.

Arisika Razak, MPH, professor emerita and former chair of the Women's Spirituality Program at the California Institute of Integral Studies, is a core teacher at the East Bay Meditation Center in Oakland, California, and a graduate of Spirit Rock's Dedicated Practitioners Program. Her teachings incorporate diverse spiritual traditions, multicultural feminisms, and contemporary diversity theory. For more than twenty years, Arisika served as an inner-city midwife, providing birthing care to women from more than seventy countries. She has facilitated spiritual, healing, and empowerment workshops for more than thirty years, and performed nationally and internationally as a spiritual dancer.

Arisika is a regular contributor to books and journals, and presents at numerous conferences on the subjects of womanism, diversity, women's health and healing, and embodied spiritual traditions. Her film credits include *Fire Eyes* (the first full-length feature film by an African woman on female genital cutting) and *Who Lives, Who Dies* (on health care for the indigent).

Alex Kakuyo is a Buddhist teacher and breathwork facilitator. A former Marine, he served in Iraq and Afghanistan before finding the dharma through a series of happy accidents. Alex is the author of *Perfectly Ordinary: Buddhist Teachings for Everyday Life*.

Audrey Charlton has her PhD in Anthropology from Columbia University. She lives in Houston and has been working with prisoners for the past six years. She is a Soto Zen practitioner; prior to retirement, she was an organizational consultant in New York City.

Amaragita Pearse has been in love with meditation for the last thirty-three years. Her favorite conversations with people are those that open up possibility. As a mother of two children and a twenty-year ordained member of the Triratna Buddhist Order, she draws on her experience to lead retreats for mothers, intergenerational retreats, and meditation courses. Day to day, Amaragita is a trainer and facilitator and teaches coaching and communication skills. She is also currently the chair of Buddhafield—a charity committed to land-based Buddhist practices and ecological renewal.

Laurie Amodeo is a first-generation Haitian and co-founder of the BIPOC Meditation Collective. She has been a practitioner of Buddhism for more than fifteen years, studying in Zen, Shambhala, and Vajrayana traditions. She facilitates practices as a meditation guide and Yoga teacher. In her creative practice, Laurie is a vocalist, songwriter, dancer, and student of Sogetsu Ikebana.

Olusola Adebiyi, a.k.a. Sola Story, has been described as a "captivating African performance Storyteller." He grew up in a Yoruba (people of what is now called Nigeria) household and hails from a lineage of orators, priests, and hunters. Founder and director of Narrative Mindfulness Ltd., he has inspired children, young people, and adults in Africa, the US, and the UK through his Awakening Creative Genius Programme, helping them develop self-belief, emotional intelligence, and creative confidence through the power of arts blended with storytelling. He is the author of *Nyinka's Daughter,* published in 2016, and is in the midst of publishing more.

Elizabeth Nyirambonigaba Mpyisi is a bilingual human rights lawyer, barrister, and international diplomat who served the United Nations in conflict zones for more than twenty-five years. Her strong sense of social/racial justice drew her to the world of mindfulness, Black Lives Matter, and Buddhism. She runs a charity for Black, Asian, and Minority Ethnic (BAME) mindfulness practitioners, Mindfulbame.network, and she volunteers as diversity and inclusion advisor for the UK Houses of Parliament. Based in the UK with two daughters, Elizabeth is a trustee of the Desmond Tutu Foundation, working on youth/police dialogue.

Rima Vesely-Flad, PhD, is an associate professor of Religion and Social Justice and the director of Peace and Justice Studies at Warren Wilson College. She is currently writing *Black Buddhists and the Black Radical Tradition: The Practice of Stillness in the Movement for Liberation* (NYU Press, 2021).

Yirser Ra Hotep (Elvrid Lawrence) is a master instructor of Yoga and the creator of the YogaSkills Method. He is the most senior instructor of Kemetic Yoga in the United States with more than forty-five years of experience practicing and teaching. Yirser was involved with the original research and documentation of Kemetic Yoga (ancient Egyptian or African Yoga) in the

1970s. He has trained and certified more than 5,000 Kemetic Yoga instructors across the globe through his school, YogaSkills School of Kemetic Yoga, and conducts historical/cultural/spiritual tours of Egypt, Ethiopia, Ghana, South Africa, and other parts of the African Diaspora. Yirser holds master's degrees in Social Service Administration from the University of Chicago and in Inner City Studies from Northeastern Illinois University.

Cosmore Marriott is a psychotherapist who earned his MA in Transpersonal Counseling Psychology from Naropa University in Boulder, Colorado, in 2012. Since then he has worked as a mental health therapist and an addiction counselor in Washington, DC. Cosmore has also studied energy healing. He is a master Reiki practitioner and a Chios master teacher. He met Malidoma Somé in 2011 when he was introduced to African spirituality. He was then called to go through an initiation process in 2015 to become an elder in the Dagara tradition. Today he lives in Fort Lauderdale, Florida, where he is developing an energy healing modality to heal transgenerational issues and to help people tap into the vibration of their divine blueprint.

Biko Agozino was named among the "Top Influential Criminologists Today" by AcademicInfluence.com. He is a professor of Sociology and Africana Studies at Virginia Tech. He is the author of *Black Women and the Criminal Justice System* (Routledge, 2018) and of *Counter-Colonial Criminology* (Pluto Press, 2003).

Kabir Hypolite is an African American single father, spiritualist, historian, writer, poet, artist, attorney, public health advocate, gay activist, and humanitarian. He enjoys practicing Native American flute and West African djembe. Kabir lives in Oakland, California, with his eighteen-year-old son, Hanif.

Dr. g (Claudelle R. Glasgow) is a queer, West Indian hybrid writer and storyteller. Doc compels the reader to feel the inseparability of composer and audience through arresting imagery, daring questioning, bold answers, and abstract glimpses of the mundane. In addition, Dr. g has a private psychotherapy practice in Seattle and is a Buddhist teacher engaging the intersections of topics such as race, gender, identity, meditation, trauma, recovery, and somatic healing through group work, public speaking, teaching, and consultation/mentoring.

Thomas Davis IV is a Mindful Awareness practitioner who resides in Los Angeles, California. His orientation to the Mindful Awareness practice began at the East Bay Meditation Center in Oakland, California, where he was introduced to the Theravadan tradition of Vipassana in 2012. Thomas's spiritual engagement began in the Christian communities of the Northern California East Bay area, where he served as a community volunteer and lay minister for more than eighteen years. In 2017, Thomas graduated from the Spirit Rock Community Dharma Leaders Training Program, the Sati Center Buddhist Chaplaincy Training, and the UCLA Mindful Awareness Research Center's Mindfulness Facilitator Training. Thomas co-founded the Insight Richmond Meditation Group and currently teaches Mindfulness in marginalized communities of Los Angeles and leads a People of Color Mindfulness Community with InsightLA Meditation Center.

Angela Dews published *Still, in the City: Creating Peace of Mind in the Midst of Urban Chaos* in 2018 (Skyhorse Publishing). She teaches at Harlem Insight and New York Insight and is fictionalizing her experience in politics, government, and journalism in a series of novels set in Harlem, which is a complex character in each story.

Venerable Dr. Pannavati Bhikkhuni, Theri is co-founder and spiritual director of Heartwood Refuge in Hendersonville, North Carolina, a multi-lineage retreat center and intentional spiritual community; and co-abbot of Embracing Simplicity Hermitage, a twenty-first-century trans-lineage Buddhist order. Ordained in Theravada and Mahayana traditions, a published author, and a recipient of numerous humanitarian awards at home and abroad, she currently serves the Global Buddhist Bhikkhuni Association as a vice president for the United States.

Sojourner Wright, she/her, they/them, is a Chicago-based storyteller, performance artist, and ritual-space holder. Sojourner graduated from Naropa University in 2006 with a BFA in Interdisciplinary Performance. They have been facilitating a ritual and meditation space for femme and nonbinary People of Color since 2011.

Zenju Earthlyn Manuel, author and Zen Buddhist priest, is the author of *The Deepest Peace: Contemplations from a Season of Stillness; Sanctuary: A Meditation on Home, Homelessness, and Belonging;* and *The Way of Tenderness: Awakening through Race, Sexuality, and Gender.*

About North Atlantic Books

North Atlantic Books (NAB) is a 501(c)(3) nonprofit publisher committed to a bold exploration of the relationships between mind, body, spirit, culture, and nature. Founded in 1974, NAB aims to nurture a holistic view of the arts, sciences, humanities, and healing. To make a donation or to learn more about our books, authors, events, and newsletter, please visit www.northatlanticbooks.com.